LEGAL ASPECTS OF HEALTH CARE REIMBURSEMENT

Robert J. Buchanan, Ph.D.
Research Institute of Pharmaceutical Sciences
University of Mississippi

James D. Minor, J.D.
School of Law
University of Mississippi

AN ASPEN PUBLICATION®
Aspen Systems Corporation
1985
Rockville, Maryland
Royal Tunbridge Wells

Library of Congress Cataloging in Publication Data

Buchanan, Robert John
Legal aspects of health care reimbursement.

"An Aspen publication."
Includes index.
1. Medicare—Law and legislation. 2. Medicaid—Law and legislation. I. Minor, James D. II. Title.
KF3605.B82   1985   344.73'0226   84-21716
ISBN: 0-89443-568-X   347.304226

Publisher: John R. Marozsan
Associate Publisher: Jack W. Knowles, Jr.
Editor-in-Chief: Michael Brown
Executive Managing Editor: Margot G. Raphael
Managing Editor: M. Eileen Higgins
Editorial Services: Ruth Bloom
Printing and Manufacturing: Debbie Collins

Copyright © 1985 by Aspen Systems Corporation
All rights reserved.

Aspen Systems Corporation grants permission for photocopying for personal or internal use, or for the personal or internal use of specific clients registered with the Copyright Clearance Center (CCC). This consent is given on the condition that the copier pay a $1.00 fee plus $.12 per page for each photocopy through the CCC for photocopying beyond that permitted by the U.S. Copyright Law. The fee should be paid directly to the CCC, 21 Congress St., Salem, Massachusetts 01970.
0-89443-568-X/85 $1.00 + .12.

This consent does not extend to other kinds of copying, such as copying for general distribution, for advertising or promotional purposes, for creating new collective works, or for resale. For information, address Aspen Systems Corporation, 1600 Research Boulevard, Rockville, Maryland 20850.

Library of Congress Catalog Card Number: 84-21716
ISBN: 0-89443-568-X

Printed in the United States of America

1 2 3 4 5

In memory of

John Mark Johnecheck

(1962-1984)

*His contributions to this book included research assistance
and friendship*

Table of Contents

Acknowledgments ix

Chapter 1— Introduction: The Legal System 1

    Sources of Law 1
    Major Areas of the Law 3
    The Federal-State Dichotomy 4
    Medicare and Medicaid Laws 6
    Administrative and Court Procedures
        Affecting Medicare and Medicaid 11

PART I— THE MEDICARE PROGRAM 17

Chapter 2— Medicare: Inpatient Hospital Reimbursement 23

    The Acute Care Hospital 23
    Cost Containment 29
    Reimbursement Based on DRGs 31
    Capital-Related Costs 36
    Labor/Delivery Room Days 45
    Hill-Burton 49
    TEFRA 54
    Outlook 55

Chapter 3— Medicare: Long-Term Care 63

    Skilled Nursing Facility 63
    Medicare Reimbursement Law 67

	Capital-Related Costs	70
	Related Organization Principles	78
	Outlook	83

Chapter 4— Medicare: Hospice Care **87**

Hospice Coverage	87
Conditions of Participation	88
Reimbursement Legislation	90
Reimbursement Regulations	91
Outlook	96

Chapter 5— Medicare: End-Stage Renal Disease **101**

ESRD Medicare Program	101
Conditions of Participation	103
Reimbursement Legislation	107
Reimbursement Regulations	108
Outlook	113

Chapter 6— Fraud and Abuse in Medicare **123**

Statutes	123
Regulations	126
Cases	131
Outlook	133

PART II— THE MEDICAID PROGRAM **137**

Chapter 7— Medicaid: Inpatient Hospital Reimbursement **147**

Legislative History of Medicaid Reimbursement	147
Federal Regulations	148
State Reimbursement Policies	149
Reasonable and Adequate Litigation	153
Limits to Paid Care	159
State Reimbursement Methodologies	162
Outlook	179

Table of Contents vii

Chapter 8— **Medicaid: Long-Term Care Reimbursement** **185**

    The Skilled Nursing Facility 185
    The Intermediate Care Facility 186
    Medicaid Reimbursement Law 189
    Medicaid Reimbursement Policies 198
    Property Cost Containment 204
    Reimbursement Factors 212
    Family Responsibility and Long-Term Care 221
    Outlook 228

Chapter 9— **Abortion and Family Planning Services** **237**

    U.S. Supreme Court Cases 237
    Legislative Restrictions 240
    Regulations 242
    Litigation 243
    Sterilization 247
    Outlook 249

Chapter 10— **Fraud and Abuse in Medicaid** **253**

    Statutes 253
    Regulations 255
    Cases 263
    Outlook 269

Epilogue **273**

Table of Cases **279**

Index **283**

Acknowledgments

The authors would like to thank Mike Brown, Sandy Cannon, Ruth Bloom, and Gail Martin of Aspen Systems for their assistance in bringing this book to print.

In addition, the authors are particularly grateful to Professor Nancy Fuller of the Pharmacy Library, Dr. Tom Steele and Mr. Chet Bunnell of the Law Center Library, and Dr. Annie Mills of Government Documents at the University of Mississippi Library. They were indispensable not only in obtaining necessary reference material but also in helping us to use the resources of their libraries efficiently.

The authors especially want to thank the federal administrators of the Medicare program and the federal and state administrators of the Medicaid programs; they are too numerous to mention individually but without their patient assistance and cooperation completion of this project would have been impossible.

The support of this research by Dean Parham Williams of the School of Law, Dean Wallace Guess of the School of Pharmacy, and Dr. Thomas Sharpe, Associate Director of the Research Institute of Pharmaceutical Sciences at the University of Mississippi, was appreciated by the authors.

Ms. Robin Bynum must be thanked for her assistance in preparing the manuscript and for going the extra mile in these efforts.

The authors depended on the research assistance of John Mark Johnecheck and we are grateful for his efforts and enthusiasm that he brought to this project.

Finally, we want to thank our families for their support and for the sacrifices they made so we could complete this book. James Minor would especially like to thank Ardessa.

Chapter 1

Introduction: The Legal System

The law is the body of rules that are prescribed by the sovereign to regulate conduct or procedures. The word *law* may also be used to describe any one of these rules. Individual citizens must follow these rules or risk sanctions provided by the law. In the United States, these rules are set forth specifically by legislative enactments or indirectly by the legislature through an administrative body. Occasionally, these rules are derived from generally accepted principles that have developed over many years, having been applied and clarified by the court system.

The fundamental law of the United States and the states is embodied in their constitutions. A constitution is relatively brief and concise, but it lays the groundwork for an entire legal system. It typically defines the distribution of power and responsibility among an executive branch, a legislative branch, and a judicial branch. It sets forth the relation of these branches to one another and to the general citizenry. Any government action contrary to this fundamental law is said to be unconstitutional or invalid. This concept of unconstitutionality is generally applied to legislative enactments or administrative regulations that go beyond the powers granted by a constitution. Specific laws of day-to-day application are normally found in sources other than constitutions.

SOURCES OF LAW

The law can be found in a number of sources, including statutes, the common law, administrative regulations, and judicial construction. Enacted by legislative bodies, statutes are written laws that require, restrict, or allow some action or activity. The term *statute* is often used to connote the difference between the written and the unwritten law. Laws that are not written, even though they are valid, are not statutes. Generally, statutes are collected in volumes or "codes." Within these collections of written laws, various kinds of statutes are grouped together. One volume might contain only real estate laws; another, criminal laws; yet another, health-related laws.

The fact that the common law is not passed by a legislative body, but derives its authority from usage and custom over a long period of years distinguishes it from statutory law. The term *common law* is usually applied to the common law of England and is found in the opinions, judgments, and decrees of the English courts. Often, the common law is called the unwritten law, although it is written in the opinions and records of the courts. Unlike legislative enactments, the common law is not collected and logically structured in a single source. The common law is judge-made law; however, many state legislatures and the U.S. Congress have passed statutes based on the common law. Occasionally, in a much broader sense, the term *common law* is used to distinguish the English system of laws from the Roman system, the ecclesiastical laws, or other legal systems.

Because a legislature cannot pass all the laws needed in a particular area, it enacts fairly broad laws that can be applied to limited situations and circumstances by means of administrative regulation.[1] The relationship of statutes and administrative regulations is not unlike the relationship between constitutions and statutes. In each instance, the latter must be consistent with, and get its direction from, the former. Administrative regulations, then, are largely specific rules fashioned from broad rules provided by the legislature. This practice is defensible on the theory that the administrative body has greater expertise in its limited area than does the legislature. Additionally, it is impossible for a legislature to pass laws that cover every conceivable occurrence. The accountability to the electorate is maintained because the legislature sets up the broad outlines for regulations and, through legislative action, can change the regulations issued by the administrative body.

Under judicial review of statutes, the courts decide whether a statute is constitutional. This principle was established in the landmark case of *Marbury v. Madison*.[2] Today, however, it is occasionally said that courts make law. Actually, they interpret the law. Sometimes a statute or regulation is subject to two or more interpretations, or novel situations arise that apparently fall between two or more laws, requiring clarification by the courts. When the courts interpret the law, they explain the meaning of the constitution, statutes, or administrative regulations. Therefore, in order to know the law, it is necessary to look further than the printed text of the particular law and to discover the ways in which the courts have construed that statute.

In interpreting the nonstatutory or case law and statutory law, courts follow the rule of *stare decisis*, which mandates that courts follow earlier decisions on the same subject. Courts seldom overrule previous cases or precedents and may be expected to decide similar cases in the same manner as long as the written law is unchanged.

MAJOR AREAS OF THE LAW

The study of law normally begins with the study of several general areas of the law, such as property, contracts, torts, and criminal law. An additional area that covers all forms of the law is procedure. The first four areas are areas of substantive law; the latter is procedural law. Law is also occasionally referred to as public and private law.

Substance and Procedure

To the nonlawyer, substantive law is the law. It includes not only property, contracts, torts, and criminal law, but also numerous other areas, such as constitutional law and family law. Substantive law defines the law and states rights and duties.

Procedural law sets forth the method and machinery for deciding substantive law. In some respects, procedural law is as important as substantive law, since it can determine whether a litigant is successful. In this regard, a legal proceeding is similar to an athletic contest. The best team may lose in football, for example, if it commits numerous violations and is penalized excessively. The litigant in a court of law who fails to follow the proper procedures, such as filing certain papers by the date required or summoning certain witnesses to testify, may also lose, even though that party would have won had proper procedures been followed. Procedural flaws in the trial of cases are normally termed legal technicalities by people unfamiliar with the law. These legal technicalities are required to protect the public and to ensure the orderly functioning of the judicial process, however.

Public and Private Law

Public law is that branch of the law that is concerned with the relations between the government and the general citizenry. Criminal laws are classic examples of public law. Criminal laws apply to everyone, and offenses committed are deemed to be against the state or government as well as against the victims. Constitutional law and administrative law also fall within this general classification.

Private law is concerned with the relations between individuals. It generally involves contract actions, property actions, and tort cases. Even though private law regulates conduct between individuals or relatively small groups, however, everyone is subject to private law when conflicts arise.

THE FEDERAL-STATE DICHOTOMY

In the United States, there are two distinct, yet overlapping, court systems. The federal courts hear primarily cases involving conflicts arising under federal law and suits between citizens of different states. The state court systems most often affect the day-to-day activities of the citizenry. Traffic offenses, divorces, collection actions, and real property matters are virtually always handled by state courts.

Because of the supremacy clause of Article VI, Section 2, of the U.S. Constitution, both state and federal courts must follow valid federal laws, even when they conflict with state laws. In addition, cases may involve a number of issues, some arising from federal law and others from state law. Consequently, although the court systems are distinct, the same law may be applied in federal or state courts. Litigants who believe that federal law has been wrongly construed by state courts can seek review in the federal court system.

The Federal System

There are three judicial levels in the federal system: the district courts (i.e., the federal trial courts), the appellate courts, and the Supreme Court. There are also special limited jurisdiction courts.

There is a district court in every state; the number of judges on each depends on the volume of cases filed in that court. The district courts are general jurisdiction courts that hear all federal proceedings except a few heard by the limited jurisdiction courts and a very rare few heard initially by the Supreme Court. Under certain circumstances, when citizens of different states are parties to litigation, district courts often decide cases based on state law because of their diversity jurisdiction. Such cases may be heard in federal court even if there is no other federal issue.

The courts of appeals are divided into twelve circuits, one for the District of Columbia and eleven numbered circuits for the states. Cases from within these areas may be appealed to the court of appeals for that circuit. Like the district courts, the number of judges on the individual courts of appeal varies according to caseload; however, three judges normally represent the entire court in hearing an appeal. Occasionally, the entire court hears an appeal. When this is done, it is called an *en banc* hearing.

The true court of last resort is the U.S. Supreme Court. Although cases are said to reach the Court by appeal, or by petition for *certiorari* or certification, the Court actually decides which cases it wishes to hear. This is perhaps undesirable, but necessary, since there are thousands of cases each year and only nine judges to hear them. Many of these cases come through the federal system; for example, they may arise from trial in the district court and appeal to the court of appeals. Cases may also come to the Supreme Court through state court cases that involve federal questions, direct appeals from district courts, suits between states (which originate in the Supreme Court), and cases from other special courts of limited jurisdiction (Figure 1-1).

The Typical State System

Generally, states also have three levels of courts. First, there are trial courts, in which the facts are determined by a judge or a jury. Limited jurisdiction trial courts, such as traffic courts or small claims courts, deal with a very narrow area; these courts generally do not have juries, nor do the litigants necessarily have lawyers. At a higher level within this trial court level are the courts of general jurisdiction. Called district courts, circuit courts, superior courts, county courts, or some similar name, these courts handle a broad range of cases, from suits for damages and criminal trials to suits regarding contracts and appeals from the limited jurisdiction trial courts. These courts also may review actions of state agencies and commissions that are of a judicial nature.

Figure 1-1 Federal Court System

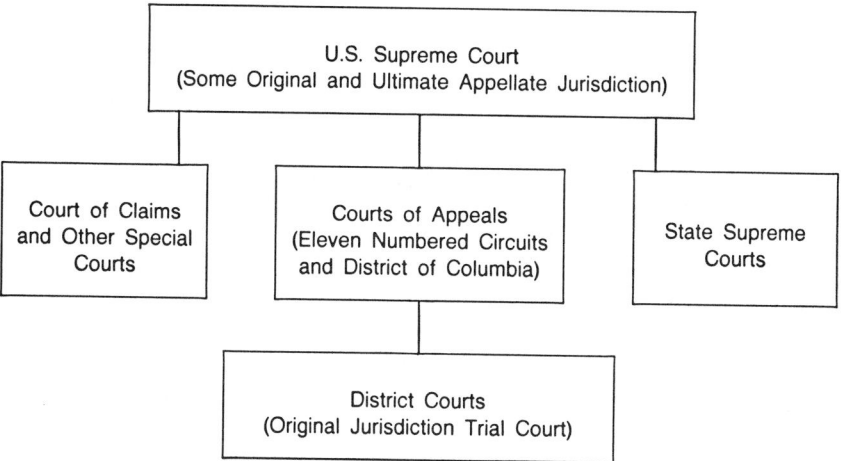

Most states have an intermediate appellate court that hears appeals from cases already decided by a lower court. General trial courts occasionally hear appeals from traffic or small claims courts, but their primary function is to conduct trials; consequently, they are not considered appellate courts in a general sense. If the intermediate appellate courts handle only civil cases, they are generally called courts of civil appeals; if they hear criminal cases, they are generally called courts of criminal appeals. If these courts handle all cases, they are generally called courts of appeals.

Courts of appeals help to limit the number of cases that come to the highest state court, the state supreme court. While a party normally has a right to appeal to an intermediate appellate court for review of a lower court decision, parties may not have a right to appeal to the supreme court for such a review. Rather, they may petition the highest court, which may or may not decide to review the case.

Figure 1-2 outlines the flow of cases through a typical state court system.

MEDICARE AND MEDICAID LAWS

Because of the complexity of Medicare and Medicaid laws, Congress cannot make adequate provisions for all situations. Therefore, the administrative agencies under the Department of Health and Human Services may promulgate regulations in regard to Medicare and Medicaid.

United States Code

The Medicare and Medicaid statutes passed by Congress may be found in Title 42 of the *United States Code* (*U.S.C.*). The code is reproduced commercially in two sets that can be found in most law libraries: the *United States Code Annotated* (West Publishing Company) and the *United States Code Service* (Lawyers Cooperative Publishing Company). The numbering system in both publications is the same. Any changes that Congress makes after the publication of the main volume are published annually in a form that can be placed in a pocket on the volume's back cover. When there have been a number of changes, they are published in a small paperback volume. Cases that have involved individual sections of the law are cited and briefly described after each section. These brief descriptions of cases are called annotations. Some laws of limited applicability are not reproduced in these volumes.

Figure 1-2 Typical State Court System

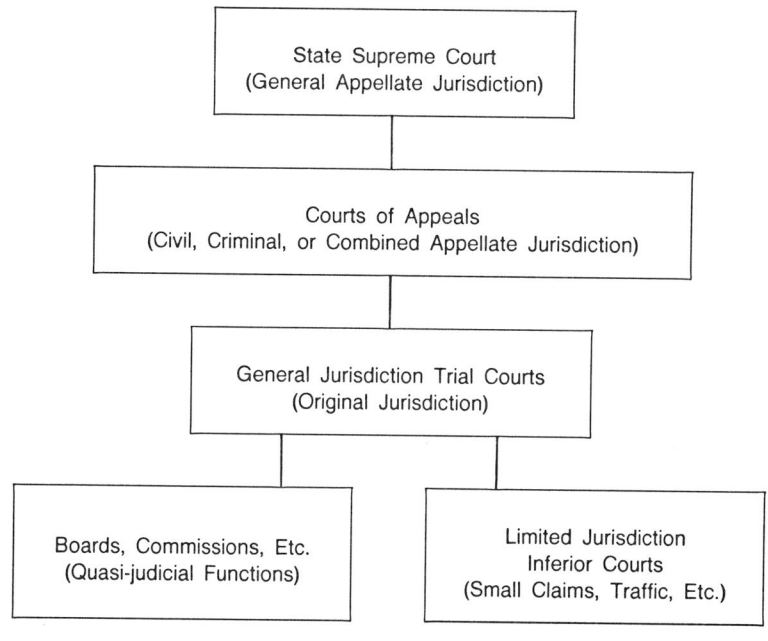

Federal Register

On a periodic basis, regulations are promulgated to implement laws. The vast number of regulations issued by government agencies and departments pursuant to authority granted by Congress or the president are published in one source so that they can be easily located. Proposed regulations are published initially in the *Federal Register*, and interested persons are allowed to respond. Consequently, health care professionals may have some input into the drafting of Medicare and Medicaid regulations.

Since the *Federal Register* contains all regulations in its hundreds of volumes, it is difficult to locate a specific regulation or regulations on a particular subject. Likewise, it is difficult to determine whether a known regulation has been changed. The regulations are indexed periodically, and yearly accumulations are provided, but in the interim, it is necessary to examine daily, monthly, or quarterly accumulations to determine if there have been changes or new regulations that affect a particular business. To remedy these and similar problems, the *Code of Federal Regulations (C.F.R.)* was devised.

Code of Federal Regulations

The *C.F.R.* is similar to the *U.S.C.* in that both codify laws or regulations under subject areas. The *C.F.R.* is revised annually and includes only regulations in effect at the time of publication. It is divided into fifty titles. Each title may include several paper-bound volumes. Title 42, which is of most interest to health care providers, is issued on October 1 of each year. Consequently, regulations found in the current Title 42 of the *C.F.R.* are effective as of the previous October 1.

The *C.F.R.* incorporates the most recent regulations from the *Federal Register* annually in quarterly installments. The pamphlets or cumulative volumes are issued on roughly the following schedule:

Titles 1 through 16: January 1
Titles 17 through 27: April 1
Titles 28 through 41: July 1
Titles 42 through 50: October 1

Therefore, each volume normally remains in the set for one year from its issuance.

Because certain regulations may have been issued approximately a year before they appear in the *C.F.R.*, a system for updating has been devised. Each month, a listing of "*Code of Federal Regulations* Sections Affected" is published. Every three months, an issue cumulates sections passed for the next set of regulations to be incorporated into the *C.F.R.* The December issue lists cumulatively the changes for Titles 1 through 16; the March issue, Titles 17 through 27; the June issue, Titles 28 through 41; and the September issue, Titles 42 through 50. Thus, with a complete *C.F.R.* and the "*Code of Federal Regulations* Sections Affected," it is possible to update regulations to the preceding month or to the last month for which a "*Code of Federal Regulations* Sections Affected" is available.

A particular *C.F.R.* section can be further updated by consulting the most recent issue of the *Federal Register*. In each volume is a table entitled "*CFR Parts Affected During [The Current Month]*." When a recent monthly list of "*Code of Federal Regulations* Sections Affected" is missing, the last *Federal Register* for that month may be consulted to determine whether changes have been made.

In order to find material when a section or part is unknown, the researcher should initially consult the *CFR Index and Finding Aids.* This volume is normally the first one in the *C.F.R.* set. A number of indexes appear in this volume, including a *C.F.R.* index, an alphabetical listing of agencies that appear in the *C.F.R.*, and a table of acts that were published in the *Federal Register.*

Reporters

In the United States, records of actual cases are not usually published for general use. Many appellate court decisions are explained in the opinions of these courts and are reproduced in the "reporters." These reporters are numbered in a series rather than by years.

The U.S. Supreme Court's opinions can be found in a number of sources; however, four sources predominate. The first is the *U.S. Reports,* cited in an abbreviated form as U.S. and considered an official reporter since it is published by the U.S. government. It is relatively easy to find a case in this reporter, because the volume and page number almost always follow immediately after a reference to the case. If the volume and page number are unknown, but the year is known, the index in the volume for that year may be consulted. The opinion of the Court is often accompanied by concurring opinions (opinions of judges who agree with the decision, but have different or additional reasons for their opinions) and dissenting opinions.

The other three predominant reporters are private commercial reporters: the *United States Supreme Court Reports* (Lawyers Cooperative Company, cited as L.Ed. or L.Ed.2d), *Supreme Court Reporter* (West Publishing Company, cited as S.Ct.), and *United States Law Week* (Bureau of National Affairs, cited as U.S.L.W.). *United States Law Week* is a loose-leaf service that disseminates opinions almost immediately and is the accepted source for finding recent cases quickly. The other two reporters also provide temporary issues that are published soon after decisions, but they are noted for their permanent editions that include references to other cases or comparisons of opinions in several cases. Generally, cases are cited by reference to the official reporter.

Because of the large volume of cases decided, opinions of lower federal courts, the circuit courts of appeals, and the district courts are published selectively. A number of the opinions of the circuit courts of appeals can be found in the *Federal Reporter* (West Publishing Company, cited as F. or F.2d). Several new volumes of this reporter appear each year.

The federal district courts occasionally generate written opinions on points of law. The reporter for these opinions is the *Federal Supplement* (West Publishing Company, cited as F. Supp.). Because the district courts are primarily trial courts, a very small portion of these cases require written opinions and only selected opinions are included in the *Federal Supplement*, which also adds several volumes each year.

Many states publish official reports of the decisions of their supreme courts or other appellate courts. The opinions of the courts of these states, as well as those of several other states that do not have official reporters, appear in one of a series of reporters published by West Publishing Company. The state reports are grouped into nine regional reporters (New York and California cases appear both in the regional reporters and in separate state reporters). Collectively, these reporters are referred to as the National Reporter System. These unofficial reports are no less accurate than official reports; the distinction is that they are published by a private company. Although all these reporters add several volumes yearly, each volume has an index of cases by state.

When the numbers become large, it is common for a reporter to start again at Volume I with a note that it is a second or third series. Many of the regional reporters are in a second series. Before the permanent bound volumes appear, temporary paperback volumes provide the text of recent opinions. When bound volumes are published these are discarded.

The National Reporter System includes a cross-reference system—the key number system—in which cases are classified according to the legal issues they present. These points of law are briefly summarized and placed in digests that are also published by West Publishing Company. The first volume of the digest that covers a particular state explains where similar cases can be found. The key number system basically consists of a subject category and a section number. For instance, cases concerning one of the narrow issues included in *Alabama Nursing Home Association v. Califano*[3] might be found in a digest under Social Security and Public Welfare, key number (or section number) 241.115.

Loose-leaf Services

A researcher seeking the latest developments in the law must be familiar not only with various court reporters and the *C.F.R.*, but also with state and federal codes, citators, annotations, and legal periodicals. Fortunately, in many specialized areas, commercial loose-leaf services provide pertinent law in a form that can be supplemented periodically.

The great value of loose-leaf services in the Medicare and Medicaid area springs from the constant barrage of administrative regulation. The loose-leaf format makes it possible to insert new regulations and to discard old ones. References to new court cases can also be inserted, since materials are placed under subject areas (or paragraphs). Page numbers are of secondary importance and are used more to file supplements than to find the applicable laws, regulations, or cases. Generally, loose-leaf services are used in areas involving regulations that are changed often and at irregular intervals.

Commerce Clearing House's four-volume *Medicare and Medicaid Guide* is a good example of a loose-leaf guide. Like other loose-leaf guides, it has a limited coverage; it provides information only about Medicare and Medicaid. It also includes references to applicable state and federal court opinions. Major topics are grouped together and marked by tabs of different colors. The major organizational tools in this loose-leaf guide are the topical indexes, the finding list, and the cumulative index. A detailed explanation of the use of such guides always appears near the front of the volume or in the first volume if the set contains multiple volumes.

Good loose-leaf services should be used whenever possible, since they are designed to provide one-stop access to all the law in a particular area. The services usually cover procedure, applicable law, regulations, and cases. Loose-leaf services are much more expensive than other law-related books, but they save a substantial amount of research time.

ADMINISTRATIVE AND COURT PROCEDURES AFFECTING MEDICARE AND MEDICAID

Regulations promulgated by the secretary of Health and Human Services or any other agency are merely implementations of the will of Congress and the president. To the extent that a regulation exceeds the statutory authority or restricts a right specifically granted by the statute, it is of no effect. Providers should have a general knowledge of the law and should not rely on manuals and regulations exclusively. When the regulations and similar communications do not comply with the law, providers and recipients should contest the interpretation. In addition, when appropriate, providers should comment on proposed rules and regulations published in the *Federal Register*.

Reviews and Appeals under Medicare

Under certain circumstances, providers of Medicare services may obtain reviews of issues regarding reimbursement. The statutory basis for such a review is set forth primarily in 42 *U.S.C.* §139500. The secretary of the Department of Health and Human Services has also promulgated regulations pursuant to the statutes at 42 *C.F.R.* §405, Subpart A.

A provider may obtain a review when

1. it is dissatisfied with the final determination of its fiscal intermediary or of the secretary as to the amount of reimbursement

2. it has not received a determination on a timely basis after filing a proper cost report
3. it has not received a final determination on a timely basis after submitting supplementary cost reports when the initial report did not comply with requirements

Additionally, the amount in controversy must be $10,000 or more, and the request for a hearing must be made within 180 days.[4] When there is a question common to a group of providers, there may be an appeal by the group.[5] In either instance, the provider has the right to legal counsel and to examine and cross-examine witnesses.[6]

Intermediaries perform a number of functions under the regulations. For purposes of the present discussion, intermediaries receive, disburse, and account for funds in making Medicare payments as discussed at 42 *C.F.R.* §421.100. The regulations detail the requirements that the intermediary must fulfill in its determinations at 42 *C.F.R.* §§405.1803-405.1833. Initially, a dissatisfied provider should request a hearing with the intermediary. These hearings are open to all parties and the Health Care Financing Administration (HCFA). Provisions are made for discovery of information, and evidence not admissible in a court of law may be considered. A record is made of these intermediary hearings. The intermediary hearing decision is final and binding upon the parties, unless, within three years, the HCFA notifies the intermediary that its determination or decision is inconsistent with the applicable law.

The statutes establish the Provider Reimbursement Review Board (PRRB) as a second stage of review. The PRRB is composed of five members appointed by the secretary. As with intermediary hearings, prehearing discovery is allowed in PRRB hearings, and evidence may be considered that is inadmissible in a judicial proceeding. Witnesses may be summoned, briefs may be submitted, and oral arguments may be made. A complete record is also made of the board hearing. Decisions of the intermediary may be affirmed, modified, or reversed. The PRRB may also make other revisions on matters covered by the cost report.[7] The final decision of the board must be supported by substantial evidence.

Decisions of the PRRB are final unless, within sixty days after the provider has been notified of the decision, the secretary reverses, affirms, or modifies the board's decision. Within sixty days of the date of a final decision of the board or of any reversal, affirmation, or modification by the secretary, providers have the right to initiate a civil action to obtain judicial review of the decision. This right of judicial review extends to any action of the fiscal intermediary that involves a question of law or regulation relevant to the matter in dispute. Providers may request that the board decide certain questions of law or regulation; if the board fails to perform this task or determines that it is without authority to decide the question, judicial review may also be obtained by instituting an action in an appropriate U.S. district court.[8]

Supposedly, certain findings of the PRRB are not subject to review. Provisions of the Administrative Procedure Act may allow some review even in these instances, however.[9] Furthermore, judicial review may be sought at any time upon adequate constitutional grounds.

Providers of emergency health care services, hospitals, independent laboratories, suppliers of portable x-ray services, ambulatory surgical centers, end-stage renal disease treatment facilities, and recipients of these services may have access to other appeal procedures under 42 *C.F.R.* §405, Subpart O. Initially, the secretary determines whether programs of these types are eligible and remain eligible. A party dissatisfied with the original determination may ask for reconsideration. By filing a written request, a party that remains dissatisfied after reconsideration may request a hearing.

Under this subpart of the regulations, an administrative law judge presides over these hearings. The hearings are open to the individuals involved and their representatives, as well as to the representatives of the institutions, agencies, or other entities concerned. Representatives of the secretary, technical advisors, and other persons necessary and proper in the judgment of the administrative law judge also attend. Evidence may be admitted liberally at such hearings, even if it would be inadmissible in court procedures, at the discretion of the administrative law judge. A complete record of the proceedings is made in all cases.[10]

Unless reviewed by the appeals council or revised in accordance with other provisions of Subpart O, the administrative law judge's decision is final.[11] When parties appeal to the appeals council of the Office of Hearings and Appeals, Social Security Administration, they are afforded reasonable opportunity to file briefs or written statements about the facts and the law. They also may appear and make oral or written statements about the facts and the law. In some instances, matters may be removed initially to the appeals council, but hearings must still be held as they would be held before an administrative law judge. Judicial review may be obtained after the appeals council has made a determination.[12]

Reviews and Appeals under Medicaid

In order for a state to deny, terminate, or fail to renew certification of a provider agreement for the Medicaid program, its plan must provide for appeals procedures that at a minimum meet the requirements of 42 *C.F.R.* §431, Subpart D. Except when a skilled nursing facility (SNF) is also subject to denial, termination, or nonrenewal for Medicare, the provisions of 42 C.F.R. §431.153 apply to the evidentiary hearing on termination. The Medicare procedures are listed in 42 C.F.R. §405, Subpart O. A final decision under the Medicare review is binding for Medicaid participation under the state plan.

Intermediate care facilities (ICFs) and SNFs whose provider agreement or certification has been denied, terminated, or not renewed must have an opportunity to request a full evidentiary hearing. When requested, a hearing must be given prior to the denial, termination, or nonrenewal, or within 120 days after that date. Hearings must include

(1) Timely written notice to the facility of the basis for the decision and disclosure of the evidence on which the decision is taken;
(2) An opportunity for the facility to appear before an impartial decision maker to refute the basis for the decision;
(3) An opportunity for the facility to be represented by counsel or another representative;
(4) An opportunity for the facility or its representatives to be heard in person, to call witnesses, and to present documentary evidence;
(5) An opportunity for the facility to cross-examine witnesses; and
(6) A written decision by the impartial decision maker, setting forth the evidence upon which the decision is based.[13]

In lieu of the full evidentiary hearing, the state must provide for informal reconsideration when an evidentiary hearing will be held after the effective date of denial, termination, or nonrenewal. This informal reconsideration must include

(1) Written notice to the facility of the denial, termination or nonrenewal and the findings upon which it was based;
(2) A reasonable opportunity for the facility to refute those findings in writing; and
(3) A written affirmation or reversal of the denial, termination, or nonrenewal.[14]

Although SNFs, ICFs, and hospitals may have a substantial interest in determinations regarding particular applicants or recipients, they are not necessarily parties to these proceedings. Provisions for fair hearings for applicants appear in 42 C.F.R. §431, Subpart E.

NOTES

1. *See, for example,* 42 U.S.C. §1302, which provides

    The Secretary of the Treasury, Secretary of Labor, and the Secretary of Health and Human Services, respectively, shall make and publish such rules and regulations, not inconsistent with this chapter [Social Security], as may be necessary to the efficient administration of the functions with which each is charged under this chapter.

2. 1 Cranch 137 (1803).
3. 433 F. Supp. 1325 (M.D. Ala. 1977).
4. 42 U.S.C. §139500(a).
5. *Id.*, (b).
6. *Id.*, (c).
7. *Id.*, (d).
8. *Id.*, (f).
9. 5 U.S.C. §706.
10. 42 C.F.R. §§405.1533-405.1549.
11. 42 C.F.R. §405.1572.
12. 42 C.F.R. §§405.1501(b) and (f).
13. 42 C.F.R. §431.153(c).
14. 42 C.F.R. §431.154.

Part I

The Medicare Program

The Medicare program, created by the Social Security Amendments of 1965 (P.L. 89-97), is a nationwide health insurance program for people aged sixty-five and over, for certain disabled persons, and for certain workers and their dependents who need kidney transplantation or dialysis. This health insurance is available to covered beneficiaries without regard to their incomes or wealth. Payroll taxes and premiums paid by beneficiaries are deposited in special trust funds that are used to pay for the medical care of individuals insured by the program. Medicare is a federal program with a uniform eligibility and benefit structure throughout the United States. It is composed of two parts, a Hospital Insurance Program (Part A) and the Supplementary Medical Insurance Program (Part B).

HOSPITAL INSURANCE PROGRAM (PART A)

The Hospital Insurance Program of Medicare is financed primarily through taxes on the earnings of employers, employees, and the self-employed; the 1984 rate was 1.3 percent on the first $37,800 of earnings. An individual can become eligible for hospital insurance coverage under Medicare (Part A) in several ways. The vast majority of Medicare beneficiaries are covered by Part A because they are at least sixty-five years old and are entitled to monthly Social Security, railroad retirement, or survivor benefits.[1] Individuals who are sixty-five years of age and older, but are not entitled to monthly Social Security or railroad retirement benefits can receive Part A coverage if they have paid Social Security payroll taxes for a certain number of quarters.[2] Individuals sixty-five years of age or older who cannot qualify for Part A coverage through the first two methods may enroll by paying a monthly premium, which during 1984 was $155.[3] Hospital insurance coverage is also available to those under sixty-five years of age if they have a disability that entitles them to monthly cash benefits under the Social Security or railroad retirement program and if they have received disability benefits for at least twenty-four months.[4] Finally, Medicare coverage is available to individuals with end-stage renal disease.[5]

Under Part A of the Medicare program, the beneficiary is covered for certain health services during each spell of illness or benefit period. A spell of illness or benefit period begins the first time a covered patient enters a hospital or skilled nursing facility (SNF) and ends after the beneficiary has not been an inpatient at either of these facilities for sixty consecutive days.[6] There is no limit to the number of benefit periods a beneficiary may have.

Part A of Medicare covers ninety days of inpatient hospital care per spell of illness.[7] It pays for the first sixty days of this care, except for an initial inpatient hospital deductible, which was $365 during 1984. For the sixty-first through the ninetieth day of inpatient hospital care per spell of illness, the patient is responsible for a co-insurance payment, equal to $89 per day during 1984. An additional "lifetime reserve" of sixty hospital days may be drawn upon if more than ninety days of inpatient hospital care are needed in the same spell of illness. The beneficiary is responsible for co-insurance payments for each reserve day; in 1984, these payments were $178 per reserve day.

The Hospital Insurance Program of Medicare also covers the care provided by SNFs if the beneficiary had been an inpatient at a hospital for at least 3 consecutive days and was admitted to the SNF within 30 days after this hospital discharge.[8] After the 20th day at the SNF, the Medicare beneficiary is responsible for co-insurance payments, equal to $44.50 per day during 1984.[9] Part A of the Medicare program also covers 210 days of hospice care, as well as kidney dialysis and transplantation.

SUPPLEMENTARY MEDICAL INSURANCE PROGRAM (PART B)

Individuals are eligible to enroll in the Supplementary Medical Insurance Program of Medicare if they are entitled to Part A coverage or are at least sixty-five years of age and are citizens of the United States. A legal resident, aged sixty-five, who has lived in the United States continuously for five years may also enroll.[10] The cost of this voluntary Medicare coverage was $14.60 per month during 1984. Federal regulations allow state governments the option of enrolling individuals receiving public assistance within their jurisdictions into Part B and paying their insurance premiums.[11] These public assistance recipients must meet the other eligibility conditions for Part B coverage, however.

Among the range of services covered under Part B of the Medicare program are

- physician services
- services and supplies related to a physician's care
- outpatient hospital services
- x-rays, laboratory, and other diagnostic tests
- physical therapy and speech pathology services
- emergency outpatient services
- prosthetic devices
- x-ray, radium, and radioactive therapies.[12]

There is a deductible of $75 of the cost of covered services delivered to a beneficiary during each year. In addition, Part B usually pays 80 percent of the reasonable charges of covered services, with the remaining 20 percent the responsibility of the beneficiary.

Table I-1 Medicare: Expenditures for Selected Services (Millions)

Year	Total Spending	Inpatient Hospital (%)*	Skilled Nursing Facility (%)	Hospice (%)	Renal Dialysis (%)
1985(E)[†]	$74,463	$48,085 (64.6)	$565 (0.8)	$210 (0.3)	$1,564 (2.1)
1984(E)[†]	$64,693	$41,845 (64.7)	$546 (0.8)	$130 (0.2)	$1,474 (2.3)
1983	$56,054	$36,525 (65.2)	$520 (0.9)	—[‡]	$1,459 (2.6)
1982	$52,200	$36,300 (69.5)	$465 (0.9)	—	$1,301 (2.5)
1981	$44,752	$31,400 (70.2)	$404 (0.9)	—	$1,108 (2.5)
1980	$36,828	$26,000 (70.6)	$365 (1.0)	—	$922 (2.5)
1979	$30,333	$21,200 (69.9)	$358 (1.2)	—	$757 (2.5)
1978	$25,932	$18,400 (71.0)	$352 (1.4)	—	$605 (2.3)

*The percentage in parentheses following each expenditure amount is the percent of total Medicare expenditures.
[†]E indicates estimated.
[‡]Medicare coverage began in Fiscal Year 1984.

Note: Data for all services for 1983, 1984, and 1985, and data for all years for skilled nursing facility, hospice, and renal dialysis were obtained from a survey of the Department of Health and Human Services, Health Care Financing Administration, Office of Management and Budget. All other data were obtained from "National Health Expenditures," *Health Care Financing Review* 3 (September 1981):44; 4 (September 1982):27; and 5 (Fall 1983):13.

TOTAL MEDICARE SPENDING

Inpatient hospital care absorbs the largest share of Medicare expenditures (Table I-1), with an estimated 65¢ of every $1 to be spent for this type of care during 1985. Although it is estimated that payments for care provided by SNFs, for hospice care, and for renal dialysis will reach $2.3 billion in 1985, they will make up less than 4 percent of total Medicare spending. Medicare payments for hospice care are projected to increase 61.5 percent between 1984 and 1985 (Table I-2). The growth rate in Medicare expenditures for hospice care is important, because coverage of this health care service is scheduled to expire on September 30, 1986, unless extended by Congress. Medicare expenditures for renal dialysis rose rapidly during the late 1970s, but these annual increases moderated after Congress passed cost containment legislation for dialysis services in 1978 and 1981 (Table I-2). Medicare payment levels for inpatient hospital care have risen rapidly in the past, and the question waiting to be answered is, Will the use of diagnosis-related groups moderate these cost increases?

Table I-2 Medicare: Annual Percentage Cost Increases

Year	Total Spending (%)	Inpatient Hospital (%)	Skilled Nursing Facility (%)	Hospice (%)	Renal Dialysis (%)
1985–1984	15.1	14.9	3.5	61.5	6.1
1984–1983	15.4	14.6	5.0	—	1.0
1983–1982	7.4	1.0	11.8	—	12.1
1982–1981	16.6	15.6	15.1	—	17.4
1981–1980	21.5	20.8	10.7	—	20.2
1980–1979	21.4	22.6	2.0	—	21.8
1979–1978	17.0	15.2	1.7	—	25.1
Average Annual Increase	16.3	15.0	7.1	—	14.8

NOTES

1. 42 C.F.R. §408.10.
2. 42 C.F.R. §408.11.
3. 42 C.F.R. §408.20.
4. 42 C.F.R. §408.12.
5. 42 C.F.R. §408.13.
6. 42 C.F.R. §409.60.
7. 42 C.F.R. §409.61.
8. 42 C.F.R. §409.30.
9. 42 C.F.R. §409.85.
10. 42 C.F.R. §405.206.
11. 42 C.F.R. §405.217.
12. 42 C.F.R. §405.231.

Chapter 2

Medicare: Inpatient Hospital Reimbursement

The Medicare program will spend an estimated $48 billion for inpatient hospital services during 1985, with almost 25¢ of every $1 spent on hospital care coming from the Medicare program. Inpatient hospital care is the largest item in the Medicare budget and is expected to absorb an estimated 64.6 percent of all Medicare expenditures during 1985.[1] Since 1978, total Medicare spending for hospital care has been rising at an average rate of approximately 15 percent each year. Table 2-1 shows the average Medicare payment per day of covered care for each year since 1974, along with the annual increases in this per diem. Between 1974 and 1983, the Medicare program paid for hospital care on a retrospective, reasonable cost basis. In an effort to contain rising hospital expenditures, Congress mandated that a prospective payment system be developed and implemented.

THE ACUTE CARE HOSPITAL

Federal regulations require that hospitals participating in the Medicare program conform to all relevant state and local laws governing the licensure of hospitals and be approved by the state or local agency responsible for hospital licensure in compliance with these laws.[2] Federal regulations also specify certain conditions required of hospitals for participation in the Medicare programs.

Governing Body

Hospitals participating in Medicare programs must have a "governing body legally responsible for the conduct of the hospital as an institution."[3] In the absence of a formal governing body, hospital personnel responsible for "the conduct of the hospital" must carry out the functions of the governing

Table 2-1 Acute Care Hospitals: Medicare Reimbursements per Day of Covered Care

Calendar Year	Per Diem Reimbursement	Annual Increase (%)	Covered Days per Bill
1983	$305.20	10.0	9.2
1982	$277.44	16.1	9.4
1981	$238.88	17.0	9.6
1980	$204.25	12.6	9.7
1979	$181.33	12.3	9.8
1978	$161.41	11.9	9.9
1977	$144.27	13.8	10.1
1976	$126.77	16.6	10.3
1975	$108.75	21.0	10.4
1974	$ 89.85	—	10.7

Note: The total amount reimbursed per year for inpatient hospital care was divided by the total number of covered days per year to yield the per diem reimbursement per day of covered care.

Source: Department of Health and Human Services, Health Care Financing Administration, *Medicare Data, Current Utilization Tabulations*, Table No. AA3, August 26, 1983.

body. The governing body must have bylaws that state the basis on which its members are selected, their terms of office, and their duties. The bylaws must specify not only to whom the governing body delegates responsibilities for the operation and maintenance of the hospital, but also how these individuals are to be held accountable for the exercise of those delegated responsibilities. The governing body must have meetings at regular, stated intervals to monitor and evaluate the operations and needs of the hospital.

The governing body should appoint an executive committee and other committees as needed for the hospital's activities. It must establish formal lines of communication with the medical staff through a joint conference committee or other appropriate means. The governing body is responsible for selecting physicians for the medical staff and defining their medical privileges. A qualified hospital administrator, appointed by the governing body, serves as chief executive officer and is responsible for the management of the hospital. The administrator also serves as the link between the governing body and the hospital staff. The administrator establishes departments and formal mechanisms of accountability for delegated duties.

Medicare patients may be admitted to a hospital only at the recommendation of a physician. Federal regulations also require that a physician be on duty or on call "at all times and available within 15 to 20 minutes at the most." In addition, the governing body must ensure that the physical plant is equipped to deliver needed services for patients. The governing body must prepare an annual operating budget that includes all anticipated income and expenses, as well as a capital expenditure plan. The capital expenditure plan must identify the sources of financing and the objectives of each capital expenditure in excess of $100,000 for at least three years in the future.

Medical Staff

The hospital's medical staff, organized under the bylaws approved by the governing body, is responsible for the quality of all medical care delivered to patients.[4] The medical staff is also responsible for the ethical and professional behavior of its members. New appointments to the medical staff are made by the hospital's governing body with the advice of the current medical staff.

Federal regulations require the hospital staff to have officers, either elected or appointed, who are responsible for "the government" of the medical staff. There must be a chief of staff who, in consultation with the hospital administrator, has responsibility for the administration of medical matters. In hospitals with more than seventy-five beds, the staff should be divided into services or departments to promote efficiency. The medical staff should have meetings, with a frequency determined by the staff, to "review, analyze, and evaluate the clinical work of its members." If a staff member misses more than a specified percentage of these regular meetings during a year without just cause, the staff member is considered to have resigned.[5]

Nursing Department

Hospitals participating in Medicare programs must have a licensed, registered nurse on duty and professional nursing services available for patient care at all times.[6] There must be a well organized departmental structure of administrative authority, including a director of nursing, assistant directors for evening and night services, and supervisory personnel for each department or nursing unit. If licensed practical nurses or nursing aides are on duty during the evening and night tours of duty in wards with patients who do not require skilled nursing services, a registered nurse supervisor must make frequent rounds and must be available to give skilled care, should it become necessary. There must be a written job description identifying the responsibilities and duties of each category of nursing personnel.

Federal regulations require constant review and evaluation of the nursing care delivered to patients. In addition, nursing care procedures must be written and updated continually to include the latest developments. Nursing care plans for patients must also be written. A registered nurse should plan, supervise, and evaluate the delivery of nursing services to each patient. Only a licensed physician, a registered nurse, or other designated health professionals under the supervision of a registered nurse may administer medications.

Pharmacy Department

Federal regulations require that a hospital have either a pharmacy directed by a registered pharmacist or "a drug room" administered according to accepted professional principles.[7] The pharmacist directing the hospital pharmacy must have a specialized knowledge of a hospital pharmacy's functions and is responsible for developing, supervising, and coordinating all its activities. If the hospital does not have a staff pharmacist, a consulting pharmacist must be responsible for the control and distribution of medications; the hospital's drug room serves only as a medication storage and distribution center. Records must be kept of the transactions of the pharmacy or drug room, and these records must be "correlated" when indicated with other hospital records.

Dietary Department

In order to participate in the Medicare program, a hospital must have an organized dietary department administered by qualified personnel.[8] The hospital may contract with an outside food management company to deliver dietary services, provided that the company has a therapeutic dietician working with the hospital and the company meets the standards required by the federal regulations controlling a hospital dietary department.

The hospital's dietary department must be under the supervision of a qualified dietician who is responsible for food production, service, and the education of the staff. If possible, the dietician should be a full-time employee, but the dietician may be either a part-time employee or a consultant in small hospitals. The facilities of the dietary department must be sufficient to meet the general dietary needs of the hospital, as well as to prepare special diets.

Laboratory Department

A hospital participating in the Medicare program must have a laboratory department equipped to perform laboratory services needed for patient care.[9] Regardless of hospital size, the laboratory must be capable of performing basic laboratory services for routine examinations. In addition, the hospital must be able to perform "adequate laboratory examinations, including chemistry, microbiology, hematology, serology, and clinical microscopy," either in its own laboratory or with an outside laboratory. The outside laboratory must be either part of a Medicare-approved hospital or a Medicare-approved independent laboratory. Laboratory services must be provided twenty-four hours a day, seven days a week. The services of the laboratory must be supervised by a physician trained in clinical laboratory services or a laboratory specialist qualified by a doctoral degree.

The laboratory must have facilities for obtaining, storing, and transfusing blood and blood products.[10] The hospital must have either a minimum blood supply to meet emergencies, be able to obtain blood quickly from outside blood banks, or have a donor list and the equipment necessary to obtain blood from them. When outside blood banks are used, there must be an agreement "governing the procurement, transfer, and availability of blood which is reviewed and approved by the medical staff, administration and governing body." Samples of each unit of blood used at the hospital must be retained for further testing by a review committee of the medical staff if there should be a patient reaction.

Radiology Department

Medicare regulations governing participation require that a hospital have diagnostic x-ray facilities available.[11] These radiological services must be provided in the hospital or by "an adjacent clinic or medical facility that is readily accessible to the hospital patients, physicians, and personnel." The hospital must have a qualified radiologist to supervise the department and to interpret the x-rays; the radiologist may be employed on a full-time, part-time, or consultant basis. A technologist must be on duty or on call at all times.

Other Departments

Medicare regulations do not require a hospital to have departments of surgery, anesthesiology, dentistry, or rehabilitation,[12] nor do they require a hospital to have an outpatient department.[13] A hospital is not required to have an organized emergency service or department, but it should have established procedures for dealing with an occasional emergency case.[14] If these services are provided, however, the hospital must have "effective policies and procedures relating to the staff, the functions of the service, ... and adequate facilities in order to assure the health and safety of the patients."

Utilization Review Plan

For participation in the Medicare program, a hospital must have a plan to review the services provided to inpatients receiving Medicare benefits.[15] The review plan must analyze the medical need for admission, stays of extended duration, and the professional services provided to the patients. The objectives of the review are to promote the provision of high-quality care and to ensure the effective and efficient use of the hospital's facilities and services. Federal regulations state that, if the secretary of the Department of Health and Human Services (HHS) determines that a state Medicaid program has developed utilization review procedures "superior" to those required by the federal regulations, the state's procedures may be substituted.[16]

Medical Records Department

In order to qualify for participation in the Medicare program, a hospital must have a medical records department that maintains records for every patient admitted to the hospital.[17] The records must contain sufficient information to justify the diagnosis and treatment, as well as to explain the end results. The records must be signed by a licensed physician. Only authorized hospital personnel have access to these records. The written consent of the patient is required for release of information contained in that patient's file.

Physical Environment

Federal regulations state that, before a hospital may participate in the Medicare program, its buildings must be "constructed, arranged, and maintained" to protect the safety of the patient, to provide facilities for diagnosis and treatment, and to deliver special hospital services to meet the needs of the community.[18] The hospital must have facilities to isolate patients, particularly those with communicable diseases.

The buildings must pass the inspections of appropriate state and local authorities. In the absence of state and local requirements, private rooms must have at least 100 square feet of floor space per bed, and multiple patient rooms must have at least 80 square feet per bed. The buildings must have emergency gas, water, and electricity supplies. The hospital must meet applicable provisions of the *Life Safety Code* of the National Fire Protection Association. The Health Care Financing Administration (HCFA) may waive certain provisions of the code if the rigid application would result in an unreasonable hardship on the hospital. The waiver, however, may not adversely affect the health and safety of the patients.

The hospital must have an infection committee, composed of members of the medical, nursing, and administrative staffs, which has the responsibility for investigating, controlling, and preventing infections within the hospital.[19] The committee must establish written infection control measures and develop techniques for discovering infections in the hospital.

As a condition for participation in the Medicare program, the hospital must have a medical library.[20] The library should be located in, or adjacent to, the hospital so that it is available at all times to the medical and nursing staffs.

COST CONTAINMENT

The seed for the new Medicare payment system based on diagnosis-related groups (DRGs) was contained in Section 223 of the Social Security Amendments of 1972 (P.L. 92-603). Section 223 amended the Social Security Act to authorize the secretary of what was then the Department of Health, Education, and Welfare (HEW) to set prospective limits to the "direct or indirect overall costs or to costs incurred for specific items or services" delivered by Medicare providers.[21] In addition, the ceilings could be "based on estimates of the costs necessary in the efficient delivery of needed health services."[22]

Beginning in 1974, the regulations implementing these limits on routine inpatient operating costs were published annually in the *Code of Federal Regulations.* Factors considered in setting limits were the type of provider (e.g., hospitals, skilled nursing facilities, home health agencies), the type of service, the geographical location of the provider, the size of the institution, and the mix of services delivered or the mix of patients treated. Estimates of necessary costs were based on cost reports or other data indicating current costs. Adjusted historical cost data were also used to estimate cost limits for an applicable period.

The Tax Equity and Fiscal Responsibility Act of 1982 (TEFRA, P.L. 97-248) further amended the Social Security Act with new provisions intended to slow the increase in hospital costs and improve the fiscal condition of the Medicare program. Section 101 of the act expanded the existing Section 223 authority to limit per diem routine inpatient operating costs to include authority to limit, on a per case basis, the operating costs of ancillary services (e.g., laboratory services) and the operating costs of special care (e.g., coronary care). The statute required that these cost limits be adjusted for differences in case mixes among hospitals.

In addition TEFRA established a new, separate, three-year control on hospital cost increases. This provision required the HCFA to "establish a ceiling target level for the allowable rate of increase of hospitals' inpatient operating costs per case." The HCFA was directed to provide incentive payments for hospitals that kept their costs below the target and penalties for hospitals that incurred costs above the target. A hospital with costs below its target would receive its costs plus the lesser of 5 percent of the target amount or 50 percent of the difference between its actual costs and the target. A hospital with costs above its target amount would receive the target amount plus 25 percent of its cost excess during the first two years and none of the excess cost in the third year. However, this payment level could not exceed the new cost limits set under Section 223. The statute provided that this three-year cost containment effort would end sooner than October 1, 1985, if a new prospective payment system were implemented for the Medicare program.

Section 101 of TEFRA required the secretary of HHS "to develop in consultation with the Senate Finance Committee and House Ways and Means Committee, Medicare prospective reimbursement proposals for hospitals, skilled nursing facilities and to the extent feasible other providers" by December 31, 1982. This legislative mandate led to the development of the DRG proposal, a form of prospective reimbursement, which was submitted to Congress in December 1982. Title VI of the 1983 Social Security Amendments (P.L. 98-21) required that, effective October 1, 1983, the Medicare program begin to reimburse inpatient hospital care with a prospective payment per discharge established for each of 467 DRGs. The legislative history of P.L. 98-21 reveals that Congress

> intended to improve the Medicare program's ability to act as a prudent purchaser of services.... More important, it is intended to reform the financial incentives hospitals face, promoting efficiency in the provision of services by rewarding cost/effective hospital practices. In contrast, the cost-based reimbursement arrangements under which Medicare has operated in the past lack incentives for efficiency.[23]

Diagnostic and therapeutic services provided by hospitals on an outpatient basis are covered under Part B of the Medicare program.[24] Hospitals are reimbursed for these outpatient services at the lesser of the reasonable cost of the services provided or the customary charges of the provider.[25] Payments to comprehensive outpatient rehabilitation facilities are based on the reasonable cost of services. According to the *Provider Reimbursement Manual*, Part B inpatient ancillary and outpatient services are paid retrospectively on a reasonable cost basis, and payments for these services are not included in the new DRG system.

REIMBURSEMENT BASED ON DRGs

The prospective payment method used in Medicare reimbursement is based on a classification system in which patients are divided into groups that are "clinically coherent and homogeneous with respect to resource use."[26] The basic system was developed at Yale University by researchers who used 1.4 million patient records from a nationally representative sample of 332 hospitals to develop the 467 DRGs.[27] The researchers based the DRGs on variables that describe the patient's clinical condition, such as principal diagnosis, secondary diagnosis, surgical procedures, age, sex, and discharge status.

Congress directed the secretary of HHS to calculate a price (or weight) for each DRG in relation to the average Medicare case. As an example, the House Ways and Means Committee stated that a craniotomy may be 3.5 times as expensive as the average case; thus, the weight of the craniotomy DRG would be 3.5. The actual weight factor developed for the DRGs of a craniotomy for trauma in someone older than seventeen is 3.2829.[28] The secretary is required by Congress to adjust the DRG classification and the weight factors for Fiscal Year 1986. The DRGs should be recalibrated whenever necessary, but no less than once every four years, to reflect changes in treatment patterns, technology, and other factors that affect the relative use of hospital resources.

Regional Adjustments

Congress wanted the prospective payment rates for each of the DRGs to be set separately for each of the nine census divisions of the nation to allow for regional cost differences and to ease the burdens of transition.[29] Within each census division, separate rates also apply to hospitals in rural and urban areas.[30] The regional adjustments apply only to the first three years that the DRG method is in effect; after October 1, 1986, prospective payment rates are to be determined on a national basis.

Transition Period

To ease the fiscal problems facing health care providers in changing from a cost-based retrospective reimbursement mechanism to a prospective reimbursement mechanism, the DRG system will be phased in over a three-year period.[31] During the first year, 25 percent of each hospital's reimbursement payment will be based on regional DRG rates, and 75 percent of the payment will be based on the hospital's cost base.[32] During the second year, 50 percent of each hospital's payment will be based on a combination of the regional and national DRG rates, and 50 percent of the payment will be based on the hospital's cost base. During this second year, 75 percent of that portion of each hospital's reimbursement payment based on DRG rates will be based on the regional DRG rate, and 25 percent on the national DRG rate. In the third year, 75 percent of each hospital's payment will be based on a combination of the regional and national DRG rates (50 percent regional and 50 percent national), and 25 percent of the payment will be based on each hospital's cost base. In the fourth year and thereafter, reimbursement payments will be based completely on national DRG rates.

During the phase-in period, that portion of the hospital's payment based on its own cost base will be subject to the rate-of-increase limits established by TEFRA. The hospital reimbursement penalties and bonuses created by TEFRA do not apply to the cost-based portion, however.

Fiscal 1984 DRG Payment Levels

The process for determining DRG rates for Fiscal Year 1984 is explained in both the legislative history of the 1983 Amendments to the Social Security Act and in regulations developed by the HCFA.[33] Calculation of the DRG rate begins with the determination of the allowable operating costs for each hospital for the most recent cost reporting period for which data are available. These data are adjusted for Fiscal Year 1983 by using the estimated industry-wide actual increase in hospital costs. The data are further updated for Fiscal Year 1984 by using the increase in the hospital market basket index plus one percentage point. These inflation-adjusted cost data are then standardized by excluding estimates of indirect medical education costs and adjusting for wage and case mix variations.

The secretary of HHS classifies all the hospitals in each of the nine census regions as urban or rural. Urban hospitals are defined as those within a standard metropolitan statistical area (SMSA), and rural hospitals are defined as those outside an SMSA. Next, by using the standardized costs for each hospital, urban and rural average costs are computed for each of the nine regions. Each of these eighteen standardized average amounts is then reduced to account for payments that will subsequently be made for atypical cases. Finally, these amounts are reduced to achieve "budget neutrality," which is an adjustment to ensure that the amounts paid at the DRG rate in 1984 equal the amount that would have been paid under TEFRA.

Separate urban and rural rates for all the DRGs in each census region are calculated by multiplying the appropriate urban or rural average standardized costs by the appropriate weight factor for each DRG. The product of this multiplication yields the prospective payment rate for each DRG, which is then further adjusted to account for differences between area hospital wages and average hospital wages at the national level. These standardized DRG payment rates for Fiscal Year 1984 are presented in Table 2-2.

Recognizing that the severity of illness or other complications makes the treatment of some cases within each DRG extraordinarily costly compared with the treatment of other cases in the same DRG and that the standard DRG rate would not adequately compensate a provider for treating these atypical cases, Congress directed the secretary to provide outlier payments. A case is classified as an outlier if it requires a hospitalization that exceeds the mean length of stay by some fixed number of days or by a certain number of

Table 2-2 Standardized DRG Payment Rates, Fiscal Year 1984

Region	Urban Labor Related	Urban Non-Labor Related	Rural Labor Related	Rural Non-Labor Related
1. New England	$2,332.56	$635.51	$1,994.31	$482.14
2. Middle Atlantic	$2,096.87	$628.04	$1,984.97	$488.97
3. South Atlantic	$2,183.42	$581.98	$1,796.04	$406.30
4. East North Central	$2,330.77	$677.44	$1,950.90	$455.12
5. East South Central	$1,982.32	$517.99	$1,811.73	$380.17
6. West North Central	$2,273.55	$602.65	$1,820.63	$390.59
7. West South Central	$2,137.03	$570.02	$1,754.37	$378.77
8. Mountain	$2,099.73	$605.05	$1,818.61	$425.10
9. Pacific	$2,210.17	$708.49	$1,900.63	$495.70
National*	$2,206.22	$631.69	$1,847.42	$416.58

*The 1984 DRG prospective reimbursement method does not include national rates, but only regional rates. The national rates are included only as a point of interest.

Note: Regional rates are taken from 49 Fed. Reg. 330 (January 3, 1984), Table 1; national rates, from 48 Fed. Reg. 39,763 (September 1, 1983).

standard deviations, whichever is less.[34] The additional payments for outlier cases are determined by the secretary of HHS and approximate the marginal cost of care beyond the outlier cutoff criteria.[35] Congress directed the secretary "to provide additional payments for outlier cases amounting to not less than 5 percent and not more than 6 percent of total projected or estimated DRG related payments."

For Fiscal Year 1985, the process of calculating the DRG prospective payment rates will be similar to that used in Fiscal Year 1984. The standardized payment amounts are to be increased to reflect the increase in the hospital market basket index plus one percentage point. For Fiscal Year 1986 and beyond, a Prospective Payment Assessment Commission will recommend to the secretary the percentage by which the payment rates should be increased. The commission, appointed by the director of the Congressional Office of Technology Assessment, is directed by Congress to consider changes in the hospital market basket index, in hospital productivity, in technological and scientific advances, in quality of care, and in the utilization of costly methods of care when making its rate of increase recommendations. Hospitals will also receive additional payments to cover other costs.

Exemptions and Exceptions

The DRG payment method was developed to reimburse acute care hospitals. Therefore, psychiatric, long-term care (average length of inpatient stay exceeding twenty-five days), and pediatric rehabilitation hospitals were exempted by Congress from the new prospective rate system.[36] For these hospitals, cost limits under Section 223 of the 1972 Social Security Amendments do not apply for cost reporting periods after September 1983; however, the TEFRA rate of increase limits, including the penalty and bonus provisions, do apply to these DRG-exempt hospitals.

Congress directed the secretary of HHS "to provide for exceptions and adjustments to take into account the special circumstances faced by sole community providers."[37] A sole community hospital is a facility that, because of its isolated location, weather or travel conditions, or absence of other hospitals, is the sole source of inpatient services "reasonably available."[38] Congress decided that these sole community hospitals would be reimbursed for cost reporting periods beginning on or after October 1, 1983, and for all subsequent periods, by means of the DRG method used in the first year for all other covered hospitals. Thus, 25 percent of the reimbursement payment to sole community hospitals will always be based on the regional DRG rates, and 75 percent of the payment will be based on each hospital's own costs. Furthermore, for cost reporting periods after September 1983 and before

October 1986, a sole community hospital that, owing to circumstances beyond its control, experiences a decline of 5 percent or more in its total number of inpatient cases since the prior reporting period will be fully reimbursed for its fixed costs and the reasonable cost of maintaining core staff and services.

Concerned that the DRG method may not adequately reimburse public hospitals and hospitals that serve disproportionately large numbers of low-income patients and Part A Medicare beneficiaries who are more severely ill than is the average patient, Congress directed the secretary to provide exceptions and adjustments that reflect the special needs of these hospitals. Similarly, the secretary is to make exceptions and adjustments for regional and national referral centers, including large hospitals in rural areas, hospitals involved extensively in cancer treatment and research, and hospitals "experiencing special problems because of their location in a particular census division." In addition, Congress authorized the secretary to adjust the DRG rates "to take into account the unique circumstances of hospitals located in Alaska and Hawaii." Congress exempted from the DRG method all hospitals located outside the fifty states and the District of Columbia.

Medical Education Expenses

The direct and indirect costs associated with medical education will continue to be paid on a reasonable cost basis.[39] Congress explicitly stated that providers are to be reimbursed for direct medical education expenses, such as the salaries of residents and interns in approved education programs, on a reasonable cost basis.[40] With respect to the indirect costs of medical education, Congress wanted to provide payments that are equal to twice the teaching adjustment applied under the Section 223 cost limits on reimbursement. The Section 223 limits allow a teaching adjustment factor of 6.06 percent; the new DRG legislation allows twice that as an adjustment for indirect teaching costs.[41] Congress recognized that an adjustment for indirect medical education costs was necessary because of a number of factors that may increase costs in teaching institutions, such as additional tests and procedures ordered by residents as part of the learning process and the severity of illness of patients who require the specialized services and treatment programs provided by teaching hospitals.

Administrative Judicial Review

Prior to the passage of the DRG legislation, federal law permitted a provider to request that the Provider Reimbursement Review Board (PRRB) review a fiscal intermediary's decision regarding items on the provider cost report. A provider was also allowed to appeal these PRRB decisions in federal court. If the dispute involved a question of law or a regulation that the PRRB had no authority to review, the provider could take the appeal directly to federal court.[42]

In the DRG legislation, Congress provided the same procedures for administrative and judicial review of payments, but made some important exceptions. Judicial and administrative review of the level of the prospective payment, the establishment of the DRG classification system, the method for classifying patients within such groups, or the appropriate weight of such groups is *not* permitted "because of the complexity of such action and the necessity of maintaining a workable system." The legislative history reveals that Congress intended that "the prospective payment will no longer have any relationship to a hospital's actual costs."[43] Therefore, "a hospital would not be permitted to argue that the level of the payment which it receives under the [DRG] system is inadequate to cover its costs." Errors of human judgment in coding an individual patient's case are reviewable, however. Also reviewable, for example, is a decision determining sole community hospital status.

CAPITAL-RELATED COSTS

For cost reporting periods prior to October 1, 1986, Congress directed the secretary of HHS to continue to reimburse providers for capital costs on a reasonable cost basis. After October 1, 1986, however, providers are to be reimbursed for capital expenses on the basis of a prospective method. Congress directed the secretary to "complete, within 18 months, a thorough review of the methods by which capital, including return on equity, can be incorporated into the prospective payment system."[44] Based on these studies, Congress expects to develop legislation to deal with capital-related issues on a prospective basis before October 1, 1986. The method of reimbursement for capital-related costs could be incorporated into the DRG system, or it could be entirely separate.

Return on Equity

For the period during which capital costs are to be paid on a reasonable cost basis, Congress expressly stated that the secretary should define capital to include a return on equity. In its original version of the DRG legislation, however, the House of Representatives proposed that the reimbursement of a return on equity be phased out over a three-year period. During the first year of the transition into the DRG system, the House proposed reimbursing hospitals for 75 percent of the return-on-equity payment they would receive under the reasonable cost system, 50 percent the second year, 25 percent the third year, and no payment the fourth year. The House noted that a return-on-equity payment was originally intended as an incentive to attract investment in the delivery of health care, but this incentive "is no longer necessary."[45]

The proposal of the House of Representatives regarding return on equity was not enacted into law. Congress as a whole not only provided that hospitals be fully reimbursed for return on equity in the three-year transition period, but also included return on equity in capital expenses when these costs are incorporated into a prospective rate after October 1, 1986. Congress did, however, reduce the percentage rate used by the Medicare program to reimburse hospitals for return on equity. Effective after April 20, 1983 (the date of enactment), the rate of return on equity was reduced from 1½ times the rate of interest paid on the debt issued by the Hospital Insurance Trust Fund to a rate equal to that interest rate. This reduction applied to hospitals, not to skilled nursing facilities.

In its version of the DRG legislation, the House of Representatives warned providers that, in any future treatment of capital expenses in a prospective system, the treatment of capital costs of new projects may differ from the treatment of capital costs of old projects or projects initiated before March 1, 1983. The Senate version included a milder warning to providers. In the Senate version, hospitals "may or may not" be reimbursed for new capital projects on a basis other than reasonable cost. Also, the date for defining "new" projects would be the date that capital costs are paid on a prospective basis, not March 1, 1983, as in the House version. The Congress as a whole maintained that "no assurances can be given that under a new system of paying for capital, projects obligated after the date of enactment of this legislation will continue to be paid on a reasonable cost basis."[46]

Depreciation

In February 1984, the PRRB issued a decision that prohibited High Point Memorial Hospital from changing the method it used to depreciate a 1971 addition to the hospital from a composite to a component lives method on its cost report for September 30, 1977.[47] During the construction of the $5 million addition, the hospital had employed three different controllers. Because of this turnover, High Point was unable to explain why the composite method of depreciation had been selected rather than the component method that the provider asserted it had used to depreciate the cost of previous additions to its physical plant. High Point contended before the PRRB that the disarray in the controller's office resulted in the selection of the composite method, which caused a material error in the method of calculating the depreciation costs of the 1971 addition.

There are significant differences between these two methods of calculating depreciation expenses. The composite method groups all the components of the 1971 addition into a single account for depreciation over a fifty-year estimated useful life. In contrast, the component method separates assets in order to depreciate them over estimated lives that more closely reflect their individual useful lives. Since the useful life of some of the components is shorter than fifty years, High Point Memorial Hospital could have claimed more depreciation expenses for Medicare reimbursement in prior years with the component method. Because the difference in the amount of Medicare reimbursement between the two methods was significant, the hospital sought relief from the PRRB when the intermediary denied its claim to recognize costs retroactively under the component method.

The PRRB agreed with the intermediary that the change to the component method was a change in the estimated useful life of the 1971 addition. The board noted that, according to Accounting Principle Board Opinion No. 20, a change in the addition's estimated useful life does not warrant a restatement of amounts reported in financial statements of prior periods. The PRRB further agreed with the intermediary that the useful lives of the assets in question can be reduced to justified levels only prospectively. The board also found that High Point had failed to establish that it had a prior policy of using the component method. In addition, the PRRB found the original useful life estimate was "not so unreasonable that it could only be viewed as an error." Therefore, the change from a composite to a component depreciation method could not be considered a correction of a material error. Citing 42 *C.F.R.* §405.415(b)(7)(iii), the board determined that the provider may use the component method of depreciation for the 1971 addition beginning with the fiscal year ending September 30, 1978. However, because the provider did not request a change for Fiscal Year 1977 "in a timely manner," the component method could not be used for that year. The PRRB ordered the intermediary to compute depreciation through Fiscal Year 1977 by means of the composite method. This PRRB decision was affirmed by the HCFA deputy administrator on April 3, 1984.[48]

In February 1984, the PRRB announced another decision relating to the useful life of a hospital addition.[49] In 1980, Finley Hospital added a service unit to its 1973 structure; the addition did not prolong the useful life of the existing structure. Because the addition would have no useful life beyond that of the 1973 hospital building, Finley Hospital wanted to depreciate the addition over the remaining thirty-three years of the 1973 building's forty-year useful life. The provider referred to 42 *C.F.R.* §405.415(b)(7), which states that the estimated useful life of a depreciable asset is its normal operating or service life to the provider. Also, citing Section 108.2 of the *Provider Manual (HIM 15)*, Finley Hospital contended that the cost of an improvement that increases the productivity of an asset must be capitalized and written off over the remaining useful life of the asset as modified by the improvement. The intermediary responded that the 1980 addition must be assigned a useful life of its own because of its "materiality or magnitude." In determining materiality or magnitude, the intermediary considered the cost of the acquisition, the useful square footage added to the existing facility, and the nature of the asset acquired.

The PRRB affirmed this decision, concluding that the intermediary correctly applied the principles of the *Provider Manual*, Section 104.17 when it calculated the useful life of the 1980 addition as forty years. Dismissing the provider's argument that the addition was not a free-standing facility and, hence, should have a useful life equal to the remaining years of the 1973 structure, the board ruled "that under Medicare principles one must look to the inherent useful life of assets and their usefulness as a productive facility under the Medicare program, and not to some potential future event, which may or may not occur." The board also noted that Finley Hospital agreed that the generally accepted physical life of steel and concrete-reinforced buildings similar to the addition is forty years.

In *American Medicorp, Inc. v. Schweiker*,[50] the U.S. Court of Appeals upheld the secretary's refusal to allow a provider to use accelerated depreciation for purposes of Medicare reimbursement. The dispute involved American Medicorp's (AMI) acquisition of a number of hospitals in December 1969. Federal regulations permit the use of accelerated depreciation for Medicare reimbursement if the provider participated in the Medicare program and acquired the depreciable assets before August 1, 1970, or entered into a valid contract to acquire them before February 5, 1970.[51]

The government argued that AMI was not a participating provider until after March 31, 1971, the closing date of the sale agreement, and was not entitled to accelerated depreciation under either provision of the regulations. The court observed that the acquired hospitals had continued to file their cost reports as participating providers up through March 31, 1971. The court stated: "We acknowledge that AMI had acquired a provider by the relevant time, but we cannot say that AMI itself was a participating provider." The court affirmed the secretary's decision that AMI was not entitled to accelerated depreciation.

Acquisition and Revaluation of Assets

The return on equity capital following the acquisition of one provider by another and the revaluation of assets for purposes of calculating depreciation expenses are controversial issues in Medicare reimbursement. For example, Pacific Coast Medical Enterprises (PCME) calculated its reimbursement claims for depreciation and return on invested capital on the basis of its costs in acquiring a hospital in 1969, rather than on the basis of the original costs of the assets to the acquired hospital. The secretary denied PCME's reimbursement claim based on her interpretation and application of Medicare regulations. This action reversed the PRRB which had allowed PCME's use of the stepped-up value of the acquired assets. The secretary viewed PCME's acquisition of the hospital as a two-step transaction. First, PCME acquired 100 percent of the stock of the hospital on May 21, 1969. Second, on February 25, 1970, nine months later, PCME liquidated the acquired hospital as a corporation and distributed the assets to PCME. The secretary characterized the transaction as two independent events that must be evaluated separately under Medicare regulations. The secretary argued that PCME's acquisition of the hospital through a 100 percent stock purchase was simply a change in the acquired hospital's stockholders. The secretary emphasized the legal distinction between a corporation and its shareholders—shareholders do not own a corporation's assets. The secretary concluded that, since there was no change in ownership of the assets of the hospital as a result of the stock purchase, no revaluation of the assets could be allowed at that time.

Nine months later, when PCME dissolved the corporation that owned the acquired hospital's assets and distributed the assets to itself (the second event), the secretary recognized a change in asset ownership. The secretary concluded that this transaction was between related organizations, however, and Medicare regulations prohibit the revaluation of assets when ownership changes between related parties.[52] This interpretation and application of federal regulations by the secretary prohibited PCME from using the price it paid for the stock of the acquired hospital as its cost basis for Medicare reimbursement. The secretary's decision not only reduced PCME's Medicare reimbursement for depreciation and return on equity by $147,124 for Fiscal Year 1973, but also affected reimbursement in future years.

The U.S. Court of Appeals in *Pacific Coast Medical Enterprises v. Harris* reasoned that deciding if the PCME transaction was a single acquisition or multiple transaction "nearly determines our consideration of the secretary's decision."[53] The court stated that the secretary did not

> present any reason why the transaction should be viewed as two separate events.... When an agency proposes to define a transaction in a way which deviates from the common understanding, and which is not a definition foreseeably left to the Secretary's discretion

to establish, we must require some basis before we can say that such a decision is not arbitrary and irrational.[54]

The appellate court noted that a 100 percent stock purchase and subsequent dissolution are not unique to health care providers participating in Medicare, but rather are ordinary business transactions. The common understanding of such transactions is contrary to the secretary's interpretation. The court observed that PCME's approach is an accepted method for purchasing assets according to generally accepted accounting principles. PCME's acquisition was approved by the IRS, the Securities Exchange Commission (SEC), and California's Commissioner of Corporations as a purchase of assets. Finally, the court found that the secretary's decision denied to PCME the reimbursement of reasonable costs and return on equity, which violates congressional intent. The court concluded:

> [W]e must reject the secretary's attempt to restrict PCME's revaluation of assets by an interpretation of the Medicare regulations the Secretary has invoked. When the PCME transaction is properly viewed as a single acquisition of assets, the regulations invoked by the Secretary do not bear the application in this context. We find his [her] construction and application to be arbitrary and erroneous, and must set aside his [her] interpretations.[55]

In *American Medicorp, Inc. v. Schweiker*,[56] the court of appeals cited the *Pacific Coast* decision when it ruled that AMI could revalue the assets of the acquired Doctor's Hospital based on the price paid for the stock. The appellate court for the Ninth Circuit ruled that AMI's intent was to acquire the assets of the hospital, and that a 100 percent stock purchase and subsequent dissolution of the purchased corporation is a common method of acquiring assets.

In *Homan & Crimen, Inc. v. Harris*,[57] the court of appeals ruled that a provider corporation that purchased 100 percent of the stock of another provider could not receive Medicare reimbursement for depreciation and a return on equity based on an increase of the cost basis of the assets. On January 1, 1972, Medenco, through its wholly owned subsidiary Southwestern General Hospital, purchased 100 percent of the stock of Homan & Crimen. The purchase price of $1 million in cash and notes was negotiated at arm's length and reflected the fair market value of the hospital and its assets. Homan & Crimen was never liquidated, and it continued to own the assets and to participate in the Medicare program under the same provider agreement.

The purchase price plus other costs associated with the acquisition exceeded the net book value of the acquired hospital by almost $830,000. When Homan & Crimen submitted its Medicare cost reports for Fiscal Years 1972 and 1973, it claimed the $830,000 as an increase in the cost basis of its assets, resulting in higher reimbursement claims for depreciation, interest, and return on equity. The Medicare intermediary disallowed the acceleration, and Homan & Crimen appealed to the PRRB. The PRRB reversed the intermediary and allowed the additional reimbursement, ruling that the purchase of 100 percent of Homan & Crimen stock and actual assumption of the hospital's management by Medenco constituted a purchase of an ongoing hospital operation.

The secretary reversed the PRRB, deciding that the stock acquisition transaction was not a change of ownership that would justify increasing the cost basis of the assets from the historical cost of the assets to Homan & Crimen. This decision was reviewed by the district court, which in turn reversed the secretary, ruling that the secretary's interpretation conflicted with the statutory requirement that costs related to the delivery of services to Medicare patients should not be borne by non-Medicare patients.[58]

This decision was appealed to the court of appeals, which reversed the district court and agreed with the secretary. The appellate court noted that the district court made

> a strong argument which might well command our attention were we making the agency decision or devising the agency regulations. The standard review, however, requires that the agency decision be upheld if it is reasonably consistent with the statute.... The secretary's position is reasonable in that it is grounded on long-established corporate principles.[59]

The appellate court agreed with the secretary's position that, under well-established principles of corporate law, the corporation, not the shareholders, is the owner of the corporate assets. The court concluded that "Homan & Crimen is thus the present owner of the assets in question. Its costs in acquiring the assets are the historical costs upon which depreciation reimbursement must be based." The court noted that, after Medenco purchased the stock of Homan & Crimen, "there was no corporate liquidation and therefore no two-step stock purchase and liquidation considered to be a purchase of assets by the Ninth Circuit" in the *Pacific Coast* case. The court of appeals affirmed the secretary's decision. The U.S. Supreme Court declined to review this ruling, thus allowing this decision by the Fifth Circuit Court to stand.[60]

In *Sun Towers, Inc. v. Heckler*,[61] the court of appeals referred to its decision in *Homan & Crimen* to uphold the secretary's refusal to include in a provider's Medicare reimbursement a return on equity capital invested in goodwill that had been purchased through 100 percent stock acquisitions of hospitals. During 1968 and 1969, Hospital Corporation of America (HCA) acquired 100 percent of the stock of nine hospital corporations. The purchase price included $21,983,554 for goodwill. None of these acquired hospitals was subsequently dissolved by or merged with HCA. Furthermore, none of the assets of the acquired hospitals was distributed to HCA. On the contrary, each hospital continued to operate as a separate corporate entity, and each continued to hold its own assets. HCA included the cost of the goodwill purchased with the nine hospitals in computing the value of its equity capital; this value was then used to compute its Medicare reimbursement claim for a return on equity. (Medicare regulations do not allow providers to include the cost of goodwill in equity capital for a facility acquired on or after August 1, 1970.)[62]

The secretary, citing Medicare regulations, refused to pay this claim. The secretary noted that equity capital is defined as "the provider's investment in plant, property, and equipment related to patient care" and net working capital maintained for the operation of patient care services.[63] The regulations also specify that the investment in facilities is to be computed on the basis of historical cost used for depreciation,[64] which is defined as the "cost incurred by the present owner in acquiring the asset."[65] The secretary, therefore, maintained that return on equity may be paid only on the provider's investment in plant, property, or equipment. In addition, because the hospital corporations acquired by HCA continued to own the hospital facilities and continued to serve as the providers, the secretary asserted that they, not HCA, were entitled to a return-on-equity reimbursement and that the return on equity should be based on the value of the original investments by the acquired hospitals, not the price HCA paid for the corporate stock. The court of appeals agreed with the secretary.

Return on Equity for Nonprofit Providers

The U.S. Court of Appeals for the Seventh Circuit ruled in 1983 that nonprofit providers are not entitled to Medicare reimbursement for a return on equity capital.[66] The sixty-eight plaintiff hospitals all made claims for reimbursement for a return on equity for a variety of fiscal years, which the intermediary denied. The providers then pursued an administrative appeal to the PRRB, which ruled that the hospitals were entitled to a return on equity.[67] The deputy administrator of HCFA, using power delegated by the secretary, reversed the board's decision.[68] The hospitals then filed suit in federal district court.[69]

The nonprofit hospitals argued before the district court that the deputy administrator of HCFA had no power to reverse the PRRB's decision; that deference should be given to the PRRB's decision; that a return on equity is a reasonable cost of providing care under the Medicare act; that the refusal to reimburse nonprofit providers for these costs violates the just compensation clause of the Fifth Amendment; and that nonprofit hospitals are denied equal protection, since proprietary hospitals are ensured a return on net assets.

The HCFA deputy administrator maintained that the return is a profit, not a cost, and Medicare reimburses providers only for their reasonable costs in providing care to Medicare patients, including a proportionate share of the cost of capital investment related to patient care. If a return on equity were to be paid, the HCFA deputy administrator argued, "Medicare would be paying an amount in excess of its share of reasonable cost. This excess would be used to satisfy the burden of non-Medicare patients."[70] The HCFA deputy administrator concluded that a return on equity is not an out-of-pocket expense and not the type of cost contemplated by Congress when it passed the Medicare act.

The court district noted that Medicare regulations permit a "reasonable return on equity capital invested and used in the provision of patient care" to be paid to proprietary providers.[71] Since profit-seeking providers generally do not receive public assistance in financing capital expenditures and must rely on private investors who expect to earn a return, "[a] return on investment... is needed to avoid withdrawal of capital and to attract additional capital needed for expansion."[72] For this reason, the district court concluded that the secretary made no provision in the regulations for a return on investment made by nonprofit hospitals.

The district court ruled that the regulations, the legislative history, and case law supported the secretary's position. The district court, referring to the legislative history, declared, "It is clear that not only did Congress not consider a return on equity when it passed the Medicare Act, it specifically viewed this item during the 1966 Hearings as an expense which did not fall within" the act. The court concluded that the secretary did not misinterpret the Medicare act and that the regulations do not conflict with the statutory scheme.

The district court ruled that the statutory and regulatory scheme denying Medicare reimbursement of a return on equity to nonprofit hospitals did not violate the Constitution. The court of appeals affirmed this district court ruling. In 1984, the Supreme Court refused to review the appellate court's ruling, letting stand the decision that nonprofit hospitals are not entitled to Medicare reimbursement for a return on equity.

LABOR/DELIVERY ROOM DAYS

Surprisingly, one of the most controversial issues confronting Medicare reimbursement for hospital care involves the accounting method used for the costs and the patient days in labor/delivery room areas. The debate focuses not on the delivery of maternity care to Medicare patients, but on the method for apportioning the costs of routine care services between Medicare and other patients. The crux of the legal dispute is the method used by HHS to compute the average per diem cost for general routine inpatient care for Medicare reimbursement. Section 2345 of the HCFA *Provider Reimbursement Manual*, Part I, requires that patients who are in the labor/delivery room at the census-taking hour be counted as inpatients receiving routine care for that day when the average per diem cost of general routine care is calculated, even if these patients have not yet received routine care. This average per diem cost is equal to the annual cost of routine services divided by the total number of inpatient days. The hospitals argue that including labor/delivery room patients in the denominator, but excluding labor/delivery room costs from the numerator distorts the average per diem cost Medicare pays for routine care downward. The hospitals further contend that, since a portion of their Medicare payments is calculated by multiplying the average per diem cost for routine care by the number of Medicare patient days, the hospitals are not receiving proper reimbursement from the Medicare program.

Many hospitals have refused to follow Section 2345 and do not include labor/delivery room inpatient days in the number of total routine inpatient days they report to the Medicare intermediaries. When the intermediaries adjust these reports to include labor/delivery room days, the hospitals can appeal this action to the PRRB. For example, the Flushing Hospital and Medical Center appealed to the PRRB the decision of its financial intermediary to include labor/delivery room days in the computation of Flushing's average per diem cost for routine inpatient services. The PRRB determined that the hospital was correct and that labor/delivery room days did not have to be included in the calculations.[73]

Consistently, the PRRB has upheld the provider's exclusion of these labor/delivery room days, emphasizing that Section 2345 distorts the calculation of the per diem amount for routine services by mismatching costs and statistics.[74] The PRRB has also consistently found that the implementation of Section 2345 shifts some costs relating to the Medicare program to patients not covered under Medicare, in violation of Medicare law and regulations.[75]

Except for a few decisions involving 1975 cost reporting periods (prior to the implementation of Section 2345 on September 1, 1976), the HCFA deputy administrator has reversed every PRRB decision excluding labor/

delivery room days from the average per diem cost computation.[76] The deputy administrator argues that patients in the labor/delivery room area have traditionally been regarded as inpatients receiving ancillary services.[77] In addition, according to the deputy administrator, if labor room days are excluded from the computation, Medicare would incur a disproportionate share of the standby costs of reserving beds for maternity patients. Also according to the deputy administrator, the PRRB's conclusion that Section 2345 mismatches costs and statistics fails to consider that part of the cost of maternity care is the continuous availability of routine care that can be provided to the maternity patient if needed. With the HCFA deputy administrator always reversing the PRRB on the implementation of Section 2345, providers often seek judicial review of this HHS policy.

Cases Affirming Section 2345

In *Saint Mary of Nazareth Hospital Center et al. v. Schweiker* (later reversed on appeal),[78] the federal district court affirmed the deputy administrator's decision to include labor/delivery room days in the average cost computation. Deferring to the expertise of the agency, the court concluded that there is a rational basis for Section 2345 and that these regulations could easily and reasonably be understood to require including labor/delivery room days in the calculation of the average per diem cost of routine services. Noting that a lack of historical uniformity in the treatment of this aspect of Medicare reimbursement by both the agency and the hospitals illustrates that "the issue is not so one-sided," the court found an absence of agency irrationality. The district court concluded that Section 2345 is reasonably consistent with the controlling regulations. Citing this *Saint Mary* decision, another district court in April 1983 upheld the secretary's decision to include labor/delivery room days in the per diem cost calculations for routine care.[79]

In *Beth Israel Hospital v. Heckler*,[80] another district court upheld the implementation of Section 2345. (This decision was later reversed on appeal.) The court stated that the interpretation of a statute by the agency charged with its implementation "must be given considerable respect" and that the secretary's decision may be reversed only if it is arbitrary, capricious, an abuse of discretion, or not in accordance with law. This court ruled that Section 2345 was neither arbitrary nor capricious because, by the hospital's own figures, about half of its maternity patients receive routine services within twenty-four hours of their admission to the labor/delivery area. Furthermore, the court observed that the statute did not require the secretary to determine "the precise number of women receiving routine care on any given day." Therefore, the court ruled that the cost accounting methodology required by Section 2345 is not contrary to law.

Cases Reversing Section 2345

Baylor University Medical Center and Harris Hospital both sought judicial review in federal district court of the deputy administrator's reversal of the PRRB's decision to exclude labor/delivery room patient days from the average per diem cost computation.[81] The court ruled that the application of Section 2345 is not reasonable and is inconsistent with the Medicare act because it "results in subsidization of Medicare patients by non-Medicare patients. Such cross-subsidization, as noted by the PRRB, is barred by numerous Medicare regulations. See, e.g., 42 *C.F.R.* §405.452(e)(1)."

The court reasoned that Section 2345 failed to meet the reasonableness test because "to reasonably compute 'average costs per day,' one must match the total cost with the days in which those costs were incurred" and providers may not include the costs of their labor/delivery room areas in their total cost of routine services computations for Medicare reimbursement. Therefore, the court concluded, it was unreasonable for the secretary to assert that labor/delivery services are not routine for purposes of cost reporting, but are routine for purposes of counting days of care. The court held that the

> Secretary's positions are obviously inconsistent.... The Secretary's inconsistent treatment of labor/delivery services weakens the persuasive force of Section 2345.... Section 2345 is not reasonable and ... is not reasonably consistent with the underlying statute.... A review of the complete record shows that the Secretary's final decisions in these cases are arbitrary, capricious, and unsupported by substantial evidence.[82]

Relying on the *Baylor* decision, the federal district court in *Tarrant County Hospital District v. Schweiker*[83] found that Section 2345 "is unreasonable and is not reasonably consistent with the underlying statute." In another case involving Baylor University Medical Center and the same issues for a later fiscal year, the court relied on its earlier *Baylor* decision to rule that a hospital is not required to include labor/delivery room days in the calculation of the average per diem cost for routine inpatient services.[84]

The Court of Appeals for the District of Columbia reversed the district court ruling that had upheld the implementation of Section 2345 in *Saint Mary of Nazareth Hospital Center et al. v. Schweiker; Mount Zion Hospital and Medical Center v. Schweiker;* and *Washington Township Hospital District v. Schweiker.*[85] This appellate court ruled that

> the secretary must act rationally and within the constraints of the underlying law. We find on the record presented to us that he has

not done so. It is irrational to apportion to labor/maternity patients costs which they have not incurred without either including the costs that they have incurred or demonstrating that the distortion is balanced by some other aspect of the accounting process. Because labor/delivery area costs are not included in the calculation of the average routine cost per diem and because there is no evidence that this imbalance is made up elsewhere, non-Medicare payors are forced to bear some of the costs of the Medicare program. This is a concrete violation of the constraints placed on the Secretary's discretion in promulgating regulations[86]

under the Medicare statute.

The court of appeals noted that reversing the implementation of Section 2345 could have a substantial impact on the Medicare program. (The hospitals in this case alone claimed more than $1 million in lost reimbursement for one year because of Section 2345.) Hence, the case was remanded for the limited purpose of permitting the PRRB to take evidence on the question of whether the number of Medicare patients found nationally in other ancillary areas at the census hour is high enough to offset the dilution of Medicare reimbursement caused by Section 2345. If not, or if the secretary does not contest the issue, "the Secretary is directed to exclude labor/delivery room patients, who have not previously that day received routine services, from the inpatient count used to derive the average cost per diem for general routine services."

Subsequent to this ruling, the appellate courts for the Ninth Circuit and for the Fifth Circuit cited the *Saint Mary of Nazareth* decision in ruling that labor/delivery room days may be excluded from the average per diem computations. The Court of Appeals for the Ninth Circuit remanded its case, if necessary, for a recalculation of the relevant payments in accordance with the ruling in *Saint Mary of Nazareth*.[87] The Court of Appeals for the Fifth Circuit emphasized that the reversal of Section 2345 applies to

this case only and should not be construed to invalidate the practice of including labor and delivery room patients in the inpatient census in all situations. Hospital practices vary, and the secretary is free to produce evidence showing that the artificially low reimbursement alleged to result

from Section 2345 is offset by other accounting factors, including those recognized in the *Saint Mary of Nazareth* decision.[88] In addition, district courts have reversed the application of Section 2345 in *Johnson County*

Memorial Hospital et al. v. Heckler[89] and *Central DuPage Hospital et al. v. Schweiker.*[90]

As a result of the appellate court decision in *Saint Mary of Nazareth*, Beth Israel Hospital moved to have the district court reconsider its earlier decision.[91] In this second *Beth Israel* decision, the court declined to follow the appellate court's analysis in *Saint Mary of Nazareth* for two reasons. First, the hospitals in *Saint Mary of Nazareth* challenged Section 2345 only as it applied to women admitted directly to the labor/delivery area without receiving routine care. In its suit, Beth Israel Hospital challenged Section 2345 as it applied to all women in the labor/delivery area at the census hour. The district court reasoned that, if it struck down Section 2345 as Beth Israel Hospital requested, pregnant women receiving routine care prior to delivery would be excluded from the census. Second, the district court ruled that, although Section 2345 "is at best a system of rough averaging, it is not... arbitrary or irrational, nor does it shift impermissibly the cost of treating Medicare patients to non-Medicare patients." The district court denied the motion to reconsider.

The Court of Appeals for the First Circuit reversed the district court decision in *Beth Israel*, citing the appellate court ruling in *Saint Mary of Nazareth*.[92] Judge Bownes, writing the opinion for the First Circuit, stated, "We agree with the Ninth Circuit that this labor/delivery room census issue has been correctly answered by Judge McGowan in *St. Mary*. Accordingly, we adopt that opinion here." The case was remanded consistent with the remand order in the *Saint Mary of Nazareth* decision.

Following the remand orders issued by the Court of Appeals in *Saint Mary of Nazareth*, the secretary admitted that she cannot document that the use of ancillary services by Medicare patients compensates hospitals for the reduction of Medicare payments resulting from the inclusion of labor/delivery room patients in the calculation of average per diem costs for routine inpatient care.[93] Therefore, the district court ordered that labor/delivery room patient days must be excluded from the midnight census which was used to calculate Medicare reimbursement for the cost of routine inpatient care.

HILL-BURTON

The Hill-Burton Act[94] was passed in 1946 to help remedy the shortage and inadequacy of hospital beds in the United States. The act authorizes federal grants, loan guarantees, and interest subsidies to public or other nonprofit community hospitals for construction and modernization. In order to receive Hill-Burton funds, the hospitals are required to make two assurances. First, they must provide a reasonable amount of free services to the poor. The secretary of HHS promulgated regulations specifying that this free care obligation can be met by providing either free service worth an amount equal to 10 percent of the federal aid given, free service worth an amount equal to 3 percent of operating costs, or free service to all indigents who appear at the hospital in need of care (the open door policy).[95] Second, hospitals that receive Hill-Burton funds must provide a service available to all community residents, although the secretary has not established quantitative compliance provisions. The central legal question in Medicare/Hill-Burton disputes has been whether the cost of providing the free medical care to the poor required by Hill-Burton is reimbursable as a Medicare cost.

Medicare Reimbursement Allowed

Presbyterian Hospital of Dallas received an interest subsidy of more than $225,000 for four loans through the Hill-Burton program during the cost reporting period that ended September 30, 1976. The hospital met its free care obligation through the open door policy, estimating that it had provided free care worth $178,871. The hospital sought Medicare reimbursement for the program's share of the costs of this free care, which the intermediary did not allow. The provider appealed this determination to the PRRB.[96] The board did not dispute the hospital's responsibility to provide free care under the Hill-Burton program, but agreed with the intermediary that the free care costs were not reimbursable under Medicare. In support of this decision, the PRRB cited federal regulations that exclude the costs of charity care from allowable Medicare costs.[97] In addition, the board noted that regulations prohibit the Medicare program from paying the costs of care provided to patients not covered by Medicare. This decision not to allow reimbursement became the final decision of the secretary when the secretary did not modify it within sixty days of issue.

Presbyterian Hospital sought judicial review of this decision in federal district court.[98] The court reviewed the administrative record and concluded that the Social Security Act and the implementing regulations support the decision not to reimburse those free care costs the plaintiff incurred while meeting the Hill-Burton requirements.

Presbyterian Hospital then appealed the decision of the district court to the U.S. Court of Appeals, Fifth Circuit.[99] The appellate court ruled that the provider was entitled to Medicare reimbursement for the costs of the free care required by Hill-Burton, reversing that part of the decision by the district court and the PRRB. The appeals court cited its own ruling in *Cook v. Ochsner Foundation Hospital*:[100]

> The service to indigent patients is a quid pro quo exacted in return for the benefaction received from the taxpayers. The free care obligation is legally enforceable, and vests a course of action in the indigent beneficiaries to sue for the free care. *Saine v. Hospital Authority of Hall County*, 502 F. 2d 1033, 1034-35 (5th Cir. 1974).

The court noted the PRRB's explanation that no party disputed the provider's obligation to provide free care under Hill-Burton or the value of the interest subsidy in allowing the hospital to provide improved care.

Reviewing the PRRB's ruling, the appellate court decided that the board correctly applied the principle that the hospital is entitled to reimbursement only for the reasonable cost of services provided to Medicare patients. The court determined, however, that this principle "does not bar reimbursement for Hill-Burton free care expenses, for the hospital is legally obligated to make such expenses and receives, in exchange for this obligation, a government subsidy which benefits all of the hospital's patients, including those covered by Medicare." Agreeing with the logic employed by the federal district court facing this issue in *Rapides General Hospital v. Mathews*,[101] the appellate court reasoned that, although direct benefits of the free care go to the poor, "it indirectly benefits Medicare patients by qualifying the hospital for federal interest subsidies on construction and modernization projects which are ultimately used by Medicare patients."

The court stated that both the statute[102] and the regulations[103] define reasonable and indirect costs. The Court of Appeals for the Fifth Circuit summarized:

> It is undisputed that the Hospital was legally obligated to make such expenses, and it is also undisputed that the expenses indirectly benefited Medicare patients by qualifying the Hospital for interest subsidies on construction and modernization projects. The fact that such expenses also benefited indigent persons who were not Medicare beneficiaries is irrelevant to the determinative issue: whether the expenses were a reasonable cost incurred in the provision of services to Medicare patients. We conclude, therefore, that the free care expenses incurred by the Hospital in connection with its obligations under the Hill-Burton Act were reasonable costs of providing care to Medicare patients and are consequently reimbursable.[104]

The court decided that, before the provider can receive payment for Medicare's share of the free care costs, it must be determined to what extent the hospital had already been reimbursed for these costs during the disputed fiscal year. The exact amount of the unreimbursed costs must be calculated. The case was remanded to the PRRB to make these cost calculations so that the Medicare program could reimburse the provider for its share of these unpaid free care costs.

Subsequently, a series of federal district court rulings reversed PRRB decisions to deny Medicare reimbursement for free care costs incurred in satisfying Hill-Burton obligations. In *Metropolitan Medical Center and Extended Care Facility v. Harris*,[105] the district court agreed with the court of appeals decision in *Presbyterian Hospital* "that the Hill-Burton free care obligation is reimbursable as an indirect cost under . . . the Medicare Act." In *St. James Hospital v. Harris*,[106] the district court ruled that Hill-Burton required the provision of free care to the poor and that it was not charity. Also agreeing with the appellate court in *Presbyterian Hospital*, this district court ruled that the costs of complying with Hill-Burton produced benefits available to patients outside the program as well as to Medicare patients. In *Johnson County Memorial Hospital et al. v. Schweiker*,[107] the district court cited the decisions in both *Presbyterian Hospital* and *Rapides General Hospital* in its ruling that a portion of Hill-Burton free care costs are reimbursable under Medicare. In *Iredell Memorial Hospital, Inc. v. Schweiker*,[108] another district court, again citing the decisions in *Presbyterian Hospital* and *Rapides General Hospital*, held that the free care costs incurred in meeting Hill-Burton obligations were indistinguishable under Medicare. All four of these district court rulings were later reversed on appeal.

Medicare Reimbursement Not Allowed

Harper-Grace Hospitals sought judicial review in federal district court of a series of administrative decisions that it was not entitled to Medicare reimbursement for a portion of the free care costs associated with Hill-Burton obligations. The plaintiff argued that (1) the costs of the free care required by Hill-Burton are really interest and, hence, a Medicare reimbursable cost; and (2) the cost of the free care obligation is also an indirect cost reimbursable by Medicare.

The district court affirmed the administrative decisions.[109] The court dismissed the plaintiff's interest argument by interpreting the federal regulations to indicate that the expenses incurred in the use of borrowed funds are allowable as Medicare expenses if they are paid to a lender. The court observed that

> the care provided to the poor is not a payment to the lender of borrowed funds, if indeed, the grant here in question . . . can correctly be considered borrowed funds. The free care is not paid to

the lender and hence cannot be reimbursed as interest expense.... The plaintiff's claim that the Hill-Burton free care constitutes interest is without merit.[110]

Addressing the hospital's contention that the free care is an indirect cost reimbursable under Medicare, the court cited the federal regulation that charity expenses are not allowable costs under Medicare.[111] The court also observed that the secretary quantified the free care obligation after the regulations disallowing charity expenses were developed. The court reasoned that, "had the Secretary wished any portion of the charitable services attributable to the Hill-Burton requirement to be reimbursable costs, the section disallowing charity services would have been amended to permit such a result."

The court disagreed with the plaintiff's argument that the free care costs are indirect costs to the Medicare program since the Hill-Burton program creates better care for all patients, including Medicare patients. Aware that it was disagreeing with the Fifth Circuit Court of Appeals in *Presbyterian Hospital*, the district court stated that the Medicare statute prevents the Medicare program from bearing costs associated with the provision of care to non-Medicare patients. The court further concluded that allowing Medicare payments for the free care costs would allow hospitals to "double dip." Hill-Burton imposed the free care obligations as a condition for reducing the expenses of modernization. Although Congress imposed free care costs on hospitals through Hill-Burton, the program also reduced capital costs incurred by the providers. The court concluded that Congress did not "intend for the Medicare program to absorb the cost of indigent care provided as required by Hill-Burton." This ruling was affirmed by the court of appeals.[112]

Subsequently, other federal district courts ruled that the free care costs were not Medicare reimbursable costs. In *Saint Mary of Nazareth Hospital Center v. HHS*, the district court referred to *Harper-Grace Hospitals* and ruled that

> it would be illogical to obligate hospitals to provide a certain amount of free care to indigents as compensation for receiving federal funds and then reimburse the hospital, again with federal funds, for the obligation incurred through the initial receipt of federal monies.[113]

In *Catholic Medical Center v. New Hampshire-Vermont Hospitalization Services, Inc.*, the district court ruled that the rule of law that emerged from the decisions in *Harper-Grace Hospitals* and *Saint Mary of Nazareth* was better reasoned than the rule of law that emerged from decisions allowing

Medicare payment for the free care costs.[114] The court of appeals affirmed the district court decision in *Catholic Medical Center*.[115]

U.S. appellate courts for various circuits have reversed district court rulings that allowed Medicare payments for the free care costs. In *Metropolitan Medical Center and Extended Care Facility v. Harris*,[116] in *Johnson County Hospital et al. v. Schweiker*,[117] and in *Iredell Memorial Hospital, Inc. v. Schweiker*,[118] for example, the appellate courts reversed the district court rulings. In a consolidated appeal, the court of appeals reversed the district court decision that allowed Medicare payments for free care costs in the *St. James* decision and affirmed the district court decision that denied Medicare reimbursement in the *Saint Mary of Nazareth* decision.[119]

TEFRA

As a result of the appellate decision in *Presbyterian Hospital*, the secretary sought clarifying legislation from Congress that would exclude Medicare reimbursement of Hill-Burton free care costs.[120] Section 106 of TEFRA makes clear that, from the date of its enactment, free care costs are not reimbursable under Medicare. Section 106 did not apply to costs already allowed by a "final court order affirmed by a United States Court of Appeals," however. Thus, the Medicare reimbursement of free care costs allowed by the court of appeals in *Presbyterian Hospital* was not affected.

After TEFRA had been passed, a district court was asked to review an administrative decision denying Medicare payment for free care costs in *John Muir Memorial Hospital, Inc. and Mt. Diablo Hospital District v. Davis*.[121] This court stated that it was "persuaded by the Fifth Circuit's logic in *Presbyterian* and inclined to find that Hill-Burton free care costs are reimbursable indirect costs," but that "Congress . . . signaled its disagreement with the *Presbyterian* decision" through TEFRA. The court therefore affirmed the administrative decision denying reimbursement. This district court ruling was affirmed by the court of appeals.[122]

The appellate courts in the *Saint Mary of Nazareth* and the *John Muir* decisions have upheld the constitutionality of the TEFRA ban on Hill-Burton free care costs. In a rehearing of *Harper-Grace Hospitals* before the court of appeals to challenge the constitutionality of TEFRA, the appellate court rejected the plaintiff's argument that the ban on Medicare reimbursement of free care costs violates the Fifth Amendment prohibition against "taking" property without just compensation.[123]

In late 1983, the U.S. Supreme Court refused to hear and, therefore, let stand three appellate court decisions that had denied these payments: *Saint Mary of Nazareth Hospital Center v. HHS* and *St. James Hospital v. Harris*,[124] *Johnson County Memorial Hospital et al. v. Schweiker*,[125] and *Iredell*

Memorial Hospital, Inc. v. Schweiker.[126] In addition, two of these cases, *Saint Mary of Nazareth* and *Johnson County*, upheld the constitutionality of the TEFRA ban. Therefore, all avenues of challenge to the legality of denying Medicare reimbursement for Hill-Burton free care costs appear to have ended.

OUTLOOK

An issue of future importance will be the prospective payment by Medicare of capital costs incurred in the provision of inpatient hospital care. Congress has directed the secretary of HHS to develop proposals for incorporating capital expenses into a prospective rate-setting system. Congress itself expects to develop legislation for this purpose by October 1, 1986, and has given the secretary the opportunity to do so before then. Reimbursing capital costs on a prospective basis may have an impact beyond Medicare reimbursement for inpatient hospital care. Often, Medicare reimbursement procedures serve as models for state Medicaid programs in setting payment rates for hospital and nursing home services.

In a related development, the General Accounting Office (GAO) has conducted a study of the changes in hospital costs resulting from the 1981 acquisition by HCA of Hospital Affiliates International (HAI).[127] On August 26, 1981, HCA purchased HAI's assets, consisting of 54 hospitals, 18 nursing homes, at least 10 medical office buildings, and 42 other corporate entities, such as hospital management companies. In return for these assets, HCA paid $425 million in cash (which HCA borrowed) and 5.39 million shares of HCA stock valued at $190 million. HCA also assumed $270 million of HAI's debt. HCA, in turn, sold the nursing homes to Beverly Enterprises, a company of which HCA owns 18 percent.

The GAO study focused on changes in depreciation expenses, interest expenses, and corporate level management expenses. According to this study, when an operating hospital is acquired, the new owner usually records the value of the acquired assets in its book at a higher amount than the previous owner did. This happens because the new owner usually pays more for the hospital than the depreciated book value. The depreciation expense to the new owner increases because of the higher asset value carried on the books, even though the acquired assets themselves have not been altered. Also, the purchaser often borrows funds to cover a large portion of the purchase price, resulting in higher interest expenses than the previous owner incurred. The GAO study noted that these increased capital costs may be offset to some extent by decreases in operating costs if the new owner can run the acquired hospital more efficiently than the previous owner did.

The GAO analysis indicated that overall interest costs allocated to the assets HCA acquired from HAI increased by approximately $62.5 million for the first year after the acquisition, because HCA had borrowed funds to finance the acquisition. In addition, depreciation costs allocated to the acquired assets increased by approximately $8.4 million per year, an increase of almost 90 percent, owing to the revaluation of the acquired assets by HCA. Based on data provided by HCA, the GAO estimated that the acquisition produced home office cost savings of about $15.7 million during the first year. The savings were attributed to an overall reduction in home office staffs and the allocation of home office expenses over a larger number of hospitals. In other words, the acquisition resulted in the more efficient use of home office resources. Thus, the acquisition of HAI's assets by HCA resulted in an increase in net costs of $55.2 million during the first year after the acquisition.

To determine the impact of the acquisition on reimbursement costs to the Medicare and Medicaid programs, the GAO analyzed the Medicare cost reports of two Tennessee hospitals suggested as examples by an HCA official. The GAO used Medicare reimbursement principles to allocate the changes in depreciation, interest, and home office cost centers. The GAO computed the cost increases at these two hospitals for the year after the acquisition on an overall cost, Medicare cost, and Medicaid cost basis. The overall cost increases resulting from changes in these three cost centers were approximately $1 million at one hospital and $300,000 at the other. The Medicare portion of these overall increases was $426,118 (an increase of $26.35 per patient day) at one hospital and $94,269 (an increase of $21.34 per patient day) at the other. The Medicaid portion of these overall cost increases was $38,655 (an increase of $30.51 per patient day) at one hospital and $23,015 (an increase of $27.30 per patient day) at the other.

Another Medicare reimbursable cost center that could increase as a result of the acquisition is return on equity. HCA used $190 million in its stock to purchase the assets of HAI. The GAO concluded that this $190 million in stock would qualify as equity capital under Medicare. The GAO did not include this return-on-equity cost center in its calculations, however, because it would have been necessary to review all provider cost reports for HAI and HCA.

The GAO study focused on the rapidly increasing values of the assets of health care providers associated with changes of ownership.[128] While reviewing the cost reports of the hospitals involved in the HAI acquisition, the GAO noticed that some of these facilities had changed ownership two or more times and that most asset values increased with each change of ownership. These increases raise the interest and depreciation expenses for which providers are reimbursed by the Medicare and Medicaid programs.

The GAO noted that the new Medicare prospective DRG system will not help to contain these capital costs, because capital costs are paid on a reasonable cost basis, at least until October 1, 1986. Congress may authorize Medicare reimbursement of capital costs on a prospective basis after this date if it can develop an acceptable method. The GAO study suggests that, as long as capital costs are paid on a reasonable cost basis, more hospital mergers are likely.

As a result of this GAO analysis, the Subcommittees on Health and Oversight of the House Ways and Means Committee held joint hearings on March 21, 1984 on the impact that mergers and acquisitions have on capital costs for which the Medicare and Medicaid programs reimburse providers. As a result of the hearings, "remedial interim legislation" will be introduced to limit capital cost reimbursement until these costs are included in a prospective payment system.[129] The proposed legislation would not allow the revaluation of assets when a change in ownership occurs and reimbursement for depreciation to a new owner would be based on the seller's depreciated book value and schedule of depreciation. Payments for interest expenses and a return on equity "would be based on the seller's original book value before depreciation." The Congressional Budget Office estimated that not allowing the revaluation of assets when a change of ownership occurs could result in savings to the Medicare and Medicaid programs of $830 million over five years.

In an update on the DRG payment system for Fiscal Year 1985, HCFA proposed increasing the prospective rates 5.6 percent.[130] HCFA noted that on the basis of the hospital market basket index plus one percentage point, the prospective rates would be increased 7.4 percent. In setting the increase at 5.6 percent, however, HCFA stated: "It should be emphasized that we have no discretion in this matter—the FY85 payment rates must be made budget neutral to what would have been paid under prior law." Section 1886 (e)(1) of the Social Security Act requires budget neutrality. Because of more accurate data collected since the DRG system was implemented, HCFA also announced a proposed reduction of 2.4 percent for Fiscal Year 1985 in each DRG weighting factor.[131] In addition, HCFA proposed reducing payments for outlier cases from the 6 percent of total payments used in Fiscal Year 1984 to 5 percent for Fiscal Year 1985.[132] HCFA reasoned "it is in the greater interest of hospitals ... to eliminate some of the reserve for outliers and include the corresponding amount in the standardized amounts thereby providing hospitals with somewhat larger Federal rates for typical cases." In the final regulations HCFA increased the target rate percentage by only 5.2 percent instead of the proposed 5.6 percent and reduced the DRG weighting factors by only 1.05 percent instead of the proposed 2.4 percent reduction.[133]

The 1983 amendments to the Social Security Act (P.L. 98-21) did not include the costs of physician services in the DRG reimbursement method. Physicians providing services to patients in hospitals are paid on the basis of reasonable charges,[134] typically defined as customary or prevailing charges for the type of care delivered.[135] Because physician fees are excluded from the DRG rate system, the cost containment incentives for the hospital often conflict with the incentives for the physician.

Most hospital costs result from the diagnosis and treatment decisions of physicians; some estimates of these physician-generated costs run as high as 75 to 80 percent of total hospital costs.[136] The DRG-based prospective rates provide incentives to hospitals to use diagnostic testing and treatment procedures efficiently and to shorten the lengths of patient stays. In contrast, there are at least three *dis*incentives for physicians to cooperate. First, extra treatment and diagnostic tests can be justified in terms of their benefits to the patient and the quality of care. Second, physicians can benefit financially by having patients in the hospital for longer stays. Third, extra tests and treatments and longer hospital stays may provide physicians with some protection from malpractice suits.[137] In the future, Congress or the secretary of HHS may address this conflict in physician and hospital incentives to improve the effectiveness of the DRG method in cost containment. One hospital administrator has remarked, "It's just unreasonable, irrational, and unstable to have a system [the DRGs] where the physician's incentive is in one direction and the hospital's incentive is in the other."[138]

If in the future the Medicare DRG mechanism or individual hospitals provide incentives to physicians to contain hospital costs, conflicts of interest could arise for physicians. Giving physicians incentives to improve the financial health of hospitals could erode the role of the physician "as first, and foremost, the agent of the patient."[139] As physician-oriented cost containment incentives are built into the DRG hospital reimbursement system—and they will come either through hospital or federal policies if the system is to be effective—the conflict between the need to reduce cost and the physician's primary obligation to the patient will become more intense.

NOTES

1. Department of Health and Human Services, Health Care Financing Administration, Division of the Budget, survey.
2. 42 C.F.R. §405.1020.
3. 42 C.F.R. §405.1021.
4. 42 C.F.R. §405.1023.
5. 42 C.F.R. §405.1023(p).
6. 42 C.F.R. §405.1024.
7. 42 C.F.R. §405.1027.

8. 42 C.F.R. §405.1025.
9. 42 C.F.R. §405.1028.
10. *Id.*
11. 42 C.F.R. §405.1029.
12. 42 C.F.R. §405.1031.
13. 42 C.F.R. §405.1032.
14. 42 C.F.R. §405.1033.
15. 42 C.F.R. §405.1035.
16. *Id.*, (k).
17. 42 C.F.R. §405.1026.
18. 42 C.F.R. §405.1022.
19. *Id.*, (e).
20. 42 C.F.R. §405.1030.
21. 47 Fed. Reg. 43,282 (September 30, 1982).
22. *Id.*
23. U.S. Congress. House. Committee on Ways and Means. *Social Security Amendments of 1983*. House Report 98-25, Part 1. 98th Cong., 1st sess., March 4, 1983, p. 132.
24. 42 C.F.R. §405.231.
25. 42 C.F.R. §405.455.
26. *See* note 23, *supra*, p. 133.
27. 47 Fed. Reg. 43,303 (September 30, 1982).
28. *See* 48 Fed. Reg. 39,876 (September 1, 1983), Table 5, for a listing of DRGs, their weight factors, the mean length of stay, and the outlier cutoffs.
29. 42 C.F.R. §405.473.
30. 48 Fed. Reg. 39,766 (September 1, 1983).
31. 42 C.F.R. §405.474.
32. 48 Fed. Reg. 39,775 (September 1, 1983).
33. *See* note 23, *supra*, pp. 133-135. *See also* 48 Fed. Reg. 39,763 (September 1, 1983) and 49 Fed. Reg. 251 (January 3, 1984).
34. U.S. Congress. *Conference Committee Report on Title VI of H.R. 1900: Prospective Payments for Medicare Inpatient Hospital Services.* House Report No. 98-47. 98th Cong., 1st sess., March 24, 1983, p. 189.
35. 42 C.F.R. §405.475.
36. *See* note 34, *supra*, p. 191.
37. U.S. Congress. Senate. Committee on Finance. *Medicare Payments for Inpatient Hospital Services on the Basis of Prospective Rates.* 98th Cong., 1st sess., March 11, 1983, p. 54.
38. 42 C.F.R. §405.476.
39. 42 C.F.R. §405.477.
40. *See* note 23, *supra*, pp. 140-141.
41. Commerce Clearing House. MEDICARE AND MEDICAID GUIDE, 4219.
42. *See* note 23, *supra*, pp. 142-143.
43. *Id.*, p. 143.
44. *See* note 34, p. 189.

45. *See* note 23, *supra*, pp. 139-140.
46. *See* note 34, *supra*, p. 190.
47. PRRB Hearing Decision No. 84-D44, February 7, 1984. High Point Memorial Hospital v. Blue Cross and Blue Shield Association/Blue Cross/Blue Shield of North Carolina. In MEDICARE AND MEDICAID GUIDE, 33,635.
48. HCFA Deputy Administrator Decision, April 3, 1984. High Point Mem. Hosp. v. Blue Cross and Blue Shield Ass'n/Blue Shield of North Carolina. In MEDICARE AND MEDICAID GUIDE, 33,902.
49. PRRB Hearing Decision No. 84-D37, February 6, 1984. Finley Hosp. v. Blue Cross and Blue Shield Ass'n/Blue Cross of Iowa. In MEDICARE AND MEDICAID GUIDE, 33,645.
50. 714 F.2d 68 (9th Cir. 1983).
51. 42 C.F.R. §405.415(a)(3)(ii)(B) and (D).
52. 42 C.F.R. §405.427(c)(2).
53. 633 F.2d 123 (9th Cir. 1980).
54. *Id.*
55. *Id.*
56. *See* note 50, *supra.*
57. 626 F.2d 1201 (5th Cir. 1980).
58. 42 U.S.C.A. §1395x(v)(1)(A).
59. *See* note 57, *supra.*
60. 101 S.Ct. 1506, 450 U.S. 975, 67 L.Ed.2d 809 (1981).
61. 725 F.2d 315 (5th Cir. 1984).
62. 42 C.F.R. §405.429(b)(2).
63. 42 C.F.R. §405.429(b)(1)(i).
64. 42 C.F.R. §405.429(b)(1)(ii).
65. 42 C.F.R. §405.415(b)(1).
66. St. Francis Hosp. Center et al. v. Heckler. U.S. Court of Appeals, Seventh Circuit, No. 82-2458, August 12, 1983. In MEDICARE AND MEDICAID GUIDE, 33,049.
67. PRRB Hearing Decision No. 79-D95, December 17, 1979. Indiana Hosp. Ass'n Group Appeal v. Blue Cross Ass'n/Mutual Hosp. Insurance, Inc. In MEDICARE AND MEDICAID GUIDE, 30,163.
68. HCFA Deputy Administrator Decision, February 15, 1980. Indiana Hosp. Ass'n Group Appeal No. 1 v. Blue Cross Ass'n/Mutual Hosp. Insurance, Inc. In MEDICARE AND MEDICAID GUIDE, 30,333.
69. Indiana Hospital Association, Inc. v. Schweiker, 544 F.Supp. 1167 (1982).
70. *See* note 68, *supra.*
71. 42 C.F.R. §405.429(a)(1)(i).
72. 42 C.F.R. §405.429(b)(1).
73. PRRB Hearing Decision No. 84-D82, March 5, 1984. Flushing Hospital and Medical Center v. Blue Cross and Blue Shield/Blue Cross/Blue Shield of Greater New York. In MEDICARE AND MEDICAID GUIDE, 33,943.
74. MEDICARE AND MEDICAID GUIDE, CCH Explanation, Labor/Delivery Room Days, 6894.
75. 42 C.F.R. §405.452(e)(1).

76. See note 74, *supra*.

77. HCFA Deputy Administrator Decision, March 7, 1984. Michigan Labor/Delivery Room Days Group Appeal v. Blue Cross and Blue Shield Ass'n/Blue Cross/Blue Shield of Michigan. In MEDICARE AND MEDICAID GUIDE, 33,925.

78. U.S. District Court, District of Columbia, Civil Action Nos. 80-3280, 81-0396, and 81-0994, November 9, 1981. In MEDICARE AND MEDICAID GUIDE, 31,594.

79. University of Tennessee v. HHS, 573 F. Supp. 795 (1983).

80. 572 F. Supp. 573 (1983), reversed on appeal, see note 92.

81. Baylor Univ. Med. Center and Harris Hosp.-Methodist v. Schweiker, 563 F. Supp. 1081 (1983).

82. See note 81, p. 1084.

83. U.S. District Court, Northern District of Texas, Fort Worth Division, Civil Action No. CA-4-80-413-E, May 13, 1983. In MEDICARE AND MEDICAID GUIDE, 32,971.

84. Baylor Univ. Med. Center v. Schweiker, 571 F. Supp. 374 (1983).

85. 718 F.2d 459 (D.C. 1983).

86. See note 85, p. 473.

87. International Philanthropic Hosp. Foundation v. Heckler, U.S. Court of Appeals, Ninth Circuit, No. 82-5847, January 31, 1984. In MEDICARE AND MEDICAID GUIDE, 33,587.

88. Baylor Univ. Med. Center v. Heckler; Harris Hospital-Methodist v. Heckler, U.S. Court of Appeals, Fifth Circuit, No. 83-1442, April 23, 1984. In MEDICARE AND MEDICAID GUIDE, 33,924.

89. 572 F. Supp. 1538 (1983).

90. U.S. District Court, Northern District of Illinois, Eastern Division, No. 82-C-0735, October 19, 1983. In MEDICARE AND MEDICAID GUIDE, 33,451.

91. Beth Israel Hosp. v. Heckler, U.S. District Court, District of Massachusetts, Civil Action No. 82-102-C, November 23, 1983. In MEDICARE AND MEDICAID GUIDE, 33,546.

92. Beth Israel Hosp. v. Heckler, U.S. Court of Appeals, First Circuit, No. 83-1884, May 18, 1984. In MEDICARE AND MEDICAID GUIDE, 33,963.

93. Saint Mary of Nazareth et al. v. Heckler; Mount Zion Hosp. and Medical Center v. Heckler; and Washington Township Hosp. District v. Heckler, Civil Action No. 80-3280; No. 81-0396; No. 81-0994, U.S. District Court, District of Columbia, June 29, 1984.

94. 42 U.S.C. §291 et seq.

95. 42 C.F.R. §53.111(d).

96. PRRB Hearing Decision No. 79-09, February 28, 1979. Presbyterian Hosp. of Dallas v. Blue Cross Ass'n/Group Hospital Service, Inc. In MEDICARE AND MEDICAID GUIDE, 29,653.

97. 42 C.F.R. §405.420(c).

98. Presbyterian Hosp. of Dallas v. Harris. U.S. District Court, N.D. of Texas, Civil Action No. Ca-3-79-0529-D, March 28, 1980. In MEDICARE AND MEDICAID GUIDE, 30,581.

99. 638 F.2d 1381 (5th Cir. 1981).

100. 559 F.2d 968, 972 (5th Cir. 1977).

101. 435 F. Supp. 384 (W.D. La. 1977).

102. 42 U.S.C. §1395x(v)(1)(A).

103. 42 C.F.R. §405.451(c)(3).

104. See note 99, p. 1387.

105. 524 F. Supp. 630 (1981).

106. 535 F. Supp. 751 (1981).
107. 527 F. Supp. 630 (1981).
108. U.S. District Court, Western District of North Carolina, No. ST-C-81-52, January 7, 1982. In MEDICARE AND MEDICAID GUIDE, 31,837.
109. Harper-Grace Hospitals v. Schweiker. U.S. District Court, Eastern District of Michigan, Southern Division, CA-80-72082, April 1, 1981. In MEDICARE AND MEDICAID GUIDE, 31,037.
110. *See* note 109, p.10,217.
111. 42 C.F.R. §405.420(g).
112. 691 F.2d 808 (6th Cir. 1982).
113. U.S. District Court, Northern District of Illinois, Eastern Division, No. 81-C-2750, January 14, 1982. In MEDICARE AND MEDICAID GUIDE, 31,821.
114. U.S. District Court, District of New Hampshire, Civil No. 81-637-D, August 20, 1982. In MEDICARE AND MEDICAID GUIDE, 32,333.
115. 707 F.2d 7 (1st Cir. 1983).
116. 639 F.2d 775 (8th Cir. 1982).
117. 698 F.2d 1347 (7th Cir. 1983).
118. 699 F.2d 196 (4th Cir. 1983).
119. 698 F.2d 1337 (7th Cir. 1983).
120. The Germantown Hospital and Medical Center et al. v. Heckler, U.S. District Court, Eastern District of Pennsylvania, Civil Action No. 82-5016, September 31, 1983. In MEDICARE AND MEDICAID GUIDE, 33,527.
121. 559 F. Supp. 1042 (1983).
122. 726 F.2d 1443 (9th Cir. 1984).
123. 708 F.2d 199 (6th Cir. 1983).
124. 698 F.2d 1337 (7th Cir. 1983).
125. 698 F.2d 1347 (7th Cir. 1983).
126. 699 F.2d 196 (4th Cir. 1983).
127. U.S. Congress, General Accounting Office, *Hospital Merger Increased Medicare and Medicaid Payments for Capital Costs*, GAO/HRD-84-10, December 22, 1983.
128. *Id.*, p. 16.
129. MEDICARE AND MEDICAID GUIDE, "Report Letter," No. 422, p. 10.
130. 49 Fed. Reg. 27,433 (July 3, 1984).
131. *Id.*, 27,442-27,444.
132. *Id.*, 27,441.
133. 49 Fed. Reg. 34,728 (August 31, 1984).
134. 42 C.F.R. §405.550.
135. 42 C.F.R. §405.502.
136. *Wall Street Journal*, February 6, 1984, p. 22.
137. *Id.*
138. *Wall Street Journal*, January 19, 1984. p. 31.
139. *Wall Street Journal*, February 6, 1984. p. 22.

Chapter 3

Medicare: Long-Term Care

Surprisingly, despite its role as the health insurance program for the elderly, the Medicare program is not the major government purchaser of long-term care in the United States. Only an estimated 1.5¢ of every dollar spent on nursing home care will come from the Medicare program during 1985. Of the estimated total Medicare expenditures of $74.5 billion during 1985, a relatively minor sum of $565 million will be spent for long-term care, or less than 1 percent.[1] At least two federal policies help to explain this low level of Medicare expenditures for nursing home care. First, Medicare reimburses a skilled nursing facility (SNF) for a maximum of 100 days of patient care in any one stay. Second, the Medicare program does not cover services provided at an intermediate care facility.

Paradoxically, the major public burden of paying for nursing home care falls on Medicaid—the health program for the poor. Medicare reimbursement policies are important, however, because they affect Medicaid reimbursement practices. Many states have adopted Medicare reimbursement methods to calculate the nursing home rates that their Medicaid programs pay. Furthermore, federal regulations prohibit state Medicaid programs from paying more for long-term care than they would pay if the amount were determined by means of the Medicare payment principles.

SKILLED NURSING FACILITY

The 1972 amendments to the Social Security Act created a single definition for an SNF for both the Medicare and the Medicaid programs. Effective July 1, 1973, an SNF certified to participate in one program became eligible to participate in the other.[2] The care given by an SNF is defined as services provided directly by or requiring the supervision of skilled nursing personnel, or skilled rehabilitation services, which the patient needs on a daily basis, and which as a practical matter can only be provided in a skilled nursing facility on an inpatient basis.[3]

At the SNF, the focus of medical care is on therapy and rehabilitation, control of prescribed medication, and continuous patient observation.

Health Services

Medicare regulations require an SNF to have a licensed physician as either a full-time or part-time medical director, depending on the needs of the patients and the facility.[4] The medical director not only ensures that patients receive adequate and appropriate medical care, but also monitors the health status of employees. A medical director may be responsible for health care services at a single facility or at multiple facilities through agreements with a group of physicians, a hospital medical staff, a medical society, or through similar arrangements. The secretary of the Department of Health and Human Services (HHS) may waive the medical director requirement if the SNF can document that the number of local physicians is inadequate to comply with the regulations "without seriously reducing the availability of physician services within the area."[5]

A patient is admitted to an SNF only at the recommendation of a physician and must remain under a physician's care.[6] A report that includes a description of the patient's current condition, diagnoses, and the attending physician's orders for immediate care must be made available to the SNF at the time of admission. Information about the patient's rehabilitation potential and a summary of prior treatment must be provided to the SNF within forty-eight hours of admission. The attending physician must see the patient at least once every thirty days to review the regimen of total care. Written procedures for obtaining a physician in case of an emergency must be placed at each nurse's station.

The SNF must provide services by licensed nurses at all times; the services of a registered nurse (RN) must be available at least during each day shift of duty.[7] The director of nursing, who must be an RN, is responsible for the administration, the coordination, and the supervision of the nursing services staff. A charge nurse, either an RN or a qualified licensed practical (vocational) nurse, is designated by the director of nursing to be responsible for the supervision of nursing functions at the SNF during each tour of duty.

Each SNF should have a transfer agreement with one or more Medicare-approved hospitals to provide prompt inpatient hospital care or other hospital services to the residents of the SNF when the attending physician determines that such care is medically appropriate.[8] The transfer agreement should also provide for the exchange of medical information necessary or useful to the care and treatment of the patient.

Medication Services

Under the Medicare regulations, an SNF must provide "appropriate methods and procedures" for dispensing prescription drugs and biologicals to its patients.[9] The SNF must have a qualified pharmacist to develop, coordinate, and supervise all pharmaceutical services. If not a full-time employee, the pharmacist must spend sufficient time at the SNF to meet these responsibilities. The pharmacist must also review "the drug regimen of each patient at least monthly" and report any irregularities to the medical director.

The SNF must have a pharmaceutical services committee, comprised of at least the pharmacist, the director of nursing, the administrator, and one physician. This committee develops written policies for "safe and effective drug therapy, distribution, control and use." The pharmacist must submit a quarterly written report to this committee, evaluating the performance of the SNF's pharmaceutical service and staff.

Rehabilitative Services

In addition to rehabilitative nursing services, the SNF must provide or arrange for rehabilitative services by qualified specialists "as needed by patients to improve and maintain functioning."[10] These rehabilitative services, such as physical therapy, speech and hearing therapy, and occupational therapy, are administered under a written plan of care developed by the attending physician in consultation with professional therapists and the nursing staff. Within two weeks of the start of the rehabilitative therapy, a progress report must be made to the attending physician. The physician and the appropriate therapists review the plan for rehabilitative therapy as needed, but they must review it at least every thirty days.

Laboratory and X-Ray Services

Laboratory, x-ray, and other diagnostic services must be readily available at an SNF.[11] If the SNF has its own laboratory and x-ray services, they must meet the requirements set for those services in hospitals. A hospital must have "a well organized, adequately supervised clinical laboratory with the necessary space, facilities, and equipment to perform those services commensurate with the hospital's needs for its patients"[12] and diagnostic x-ray facilities that "meet professionally approved standards for safety and personnel qualifications."[13] If the SNF does not provide these services itself, it must make arrangements to obtain laboratory and x-ray services from a physician's office, a participating hospital or SNF, an independent x-ray provider, or an independent laboratory approved to provide those services under Medicare. These services are provided only at the request of the attending physician, and signed, dated reports must be filed with the patient's medical records.

Dietetic Services

The SNF must have "a hygienic dietetic service that meets the daily nutritional needs of patients, ensures that special dietary needs are met, and provides palatable and attractive meals."[14] The dietetic service supervisor must be a full-time employee who, if not a qualified dietician, has regularly scheduled consultations with a qualified dietician. Menus should be planned to satisfy the nutritional needs of patients as stated in the orders of their physician. To the extent that the patients' medical conditions allow, menus should also meet the dietary allowances recommended by the Food and Nutrition Board of the National Research Council, National Academy of Sciences. A minimum of three meals or their equivalent must be served daily at regular hours, and not more than fourteen hours can elapse between the substantial evening meal and breakfast. If the patients' medical conditions permit, "bedtime nourishments" should be routinely provided.

Social Services and Patient Activities

The SNF must identify the medically related social and emotional needs of the patients.[15] These social and emotional needs can be met either by qualified SNF staff or by appropriate social agencies. In addition, the SNF must provide an activities program appropriate to each patient's needs and interests.[16] The objective of such a program is "to promote the physical, social, and mental well-being of the patients."

Physical Environment

Medicare regulations require the SNF to meet the applicable provisions of the National Fire Protection Association's *Life Safety Code*, published in 1981.[17] Specific provisions of the code may be waived if their rigid application would cause an SNF "unreasonable hardship," but only if the waiver would not adversely affect the health and safety of the patients. If state law requires the SNF to adhere to a fire and safety code that adequately protects the patients, the code may also be waived. The SNF must have an emergency power supply sufficient to light all exits, to maintain fire detection systems, and to maintain life support equipment. The SNF must be accessible and functional for patients, personnel, and members of the public who are physically handicapped.

Patient rooms should be designed and equipped not only to promote adequate patient care, but also to ensure the comfort and privacy of the patients. In most cases, patient rooms may have no more than four beds; in facilities that serve the mentally ill or mentally retarded, however, rooms may have as many as twelve beds. Single patient rooms should be at least 100 square feet in size, and rooms with more than one patient should have at least 80 square feet per bed. Room sizes may vary if the deviation from the regulations meets the needs of the patients and does not have an adverse impact on their health and safety. Each room should be "conveniently located near adequate toilet and bathing facilities." The SNF must also have an infection control committee, comprised of representative members of the professional staff, who are responsible for maintaining "a sanitary" environment and preventing "the development and transmission of infection."[18]

MEDICARE REIMBURSEMENT LAW

The Social Security statutes require the Medicare program to reimburse providers for the "reasonable cost" of services delivered to Medicare patients.[19] They also delegate to the secretary of HHS the power to "prescribe such regulations as may be necessary to carry out the administration of the insurance programs under this title [Medicare]."[20] To guide the secretary in developing regulations for reasonable cost reimbursement, the statutes direct the secretary to consider, "among other things," payment principles used by other national organizations and third party payers of health care. The secretary may determine costs on a per capita, per unit, per diem, or other basis.

The statutes further direct the secretary to reimburse both the direct and indirect costs of covered services that are efficiently provided to Medicare patients so that the cost of care provided to Medicare patients will not be borne by patients not covered by Medicare. Conversely, the Medicare payment should reflect only the direct and indirect costs of services provided to program beneficiaries and should not subsidize the care provided to patients not covered by Medicare. The statutes explicitly direct the secretary to include a return on net equity to proprietary SNFs. The rate of return "shall not exceed one and one-half times the average of the rates of interest . . . on obligations issued for purchase by the Federal Hospital Insurance Trust Fund."[21]

Reasonable Cost Regulations

Calculation of "fair and equitable reimbursement" rates for the care provided to Medicare beneficiaries is based on the "current costs of the individual provider, rather than costs of a past period or a fixed negotiated rate."[22] All proper expenses incurred in the provision of care are reimbursable. Reasonable cost reimbursement under Medicare, "with appropriate accounting support, will result in meeting actual costs of services to beneficiaries as such costs vary from institution to institution."

The regulations developed by the secretary of HHS also state the goals that have evolved for the system of reasonable cost reimbursement used by Medicare.[23] For example, payment should be "current" so that there is minimal delay between the provision of services and the receipt of payment. The reimbursement system should allow for retroactive adjustments to reflect cost increases incurred by providers. The allowable costs of services provided to Medicare and non-Medicare patients should be allocated according to the actual use of services. The payment system should be flexible to reflect "the great differences in the present state of development of record keeping." The reasonable cost principles should result in "equitable treatment" of both nonprofit and proprietary facilities. Finally, the need of providers "to keep pace with growing needs and to make improvements" should be recognized.

Limitations to Reasonable Cost Payments

Medicare payments to providers are subject to two limitations. First, the amount of the payment must be the reasonable cost of the services delivered or the customary charges of the provider for the same services, whichever is lower.[24] Second, there is a ceiling on Medicare reasonable cost reimbursement for skilled nursing care.[25]

In *Concourse Nursing Home v. Travellers Insurance Company*, the Provider Reimbursement Review Board (PRRB) used Medicare's prudent cost guidelines to rule on the reasonableness of the cost of drugs purchased for nursing home patients from two outside pharmacies.[26] The intermediary contended that the applications of the two tests, i.e., the "going price" and the maximum allowable cost, were consistent with the guidelines in the *Code of Federal Regulations*[27] and the *Provider Reimbursement Manual*,[28] both of which limited the cost of drugs and related medical supplies. The intermediary maintained that, since the drug costs for the disputed years exceeded those allowed under the guidelines and Concourse Nursing Home produced no evidence that the prices paid were reasonable, the adjustments were consistent with the Medicare provisions.

The provider argued that the regulations in the *Manual* apply only to provider-based pharmacies that purchase drugs wholesale, not to providers that obtain drugs from outside pharmacies. In addition, Concourse Nursing Home asserted that the outside pharmacies supplied not only drugs, but also consultation services. The provider maintained that the charges for these consultation services were included in the drug prices and should have been deducted before the reasonableness of the cost was determined. Finally, the provider maintained that the intermediary used outdated prices in determining reasonable cost, that the drug costs in question were consistent with guidelines used by the Medicaid program, and that other facilities have been reimbursed for similar costs without question.

The PRRB ruled that the intermediary's application of the reasonableness tests for drug costs incurred by the provider was indeed consistent with the regulations. The board also found that the imputed drug costs for the 1976 cost year were not incurred and, therefore, were not reimbursable by Medicare.

The Social Security Act[29] allows the Health Care Financing Administration (HCFA) to establish limits on the reasonable costs for which the Medicare program reimburses providers. The regulations state that the HCFA may calculate cost limits either on the basis of direct and indirect overall cost, or on the basis of costs of specific items, services, or groups of items or services. The HCFA also may set payment limits on a per admission, per diem, per visit, or other basis. "Reasonable provider costs may not exceed the costs estimated by HCFA to be necessary for the efficient delivery of needed health services."[30]

The method used to calculate the limits on Medicare payments to SNFs is announced in the *Federal Register*.[31] The limits actually apply only to the costs of routine inpatient services, which, according to the HCFA, average 80.4 percent of total Medicare payments to SNFs. Medicare's share of capital-related costs and the costs of ancillary services, which are 6.7 percent and 12.9 percent of payments, respectively, are fully reimbursable by the Medicare program and are not subject to this cost limitation.

In the calculation of the Medicare payment limit on per diem routine services, separate limits are calculated for labor costs and for nonlabor costs based on actual cost data for each freestanding SNF. Each freestanding SNF is placed into one of two groups depending on whether the SNF is located within a standard metropolitan statistical area (SMSA) or not. The labor component is then adjusted by an SMSA wage index to reflect different levels of labor costs in different geographical locations throughout the United States. The reported costs of the nonlabor component are adjusted for projected cost increases by applying the SNF market basket index. This index, developed by the HCFA, is based on the costs of goods and nonlabor services most commonly used by SNFs. The payment limit for each of these two cost components is set at 112 percent of their respective SMSA/nonSMSA group means.

CAPITAL-RELATED COSTS

As mentioned earlier, the Medicare program fully reimburses providers for the capital-related expenses they incur in the delivery of institutional skilled nursing care to Medicare patients. Federal regulations define these allowable expenses as

- net depreciation costs
- taxes on land or depreciable assets used for patient care
- lease and rental costs
- insurance payments for the coverage of depreciable assets
- the capital-related expenses of organizations that are associated or affiliated with the SNF and furnish supplies, services, or facilities to the SNF
- interest expenses on funds borrowed to purchase land and assets related to patient care
- return on equity capital for proprietary providers[32]

The costs of "betterments and improvements" that extend the useful life of an asset at least two years beyond its original useful life are also allowable capital-related expenses. In addition, providers must include in their capital-related expenses the costs of minor equipment if one-third of its net book value is depreciated each year.

Expenses that federal regulations exclude from capital-related costs are

- expenses incurred in the repair or maintenance of facilities or equipment
- any portion of rent or lease payments that covers repair or maintenance agreements
- any interest expense incurred in borrowing money to meet operating expenses
- general liability insurance or any other type of insurance that does not cover the replacement of depreciable assets or pay capital-related costs in case of business interruption
- taxes, unless the tax is assessed on the basis of some valuation of land or depreciable asset related to patient care
- the costs of minor equipment charged to expense rather than capitalized.

To the extent that these costs are allowable for Medicare reimbursement, they must be included with operating costs rather than capital-related expenses.

Depreciation

Federal regulations recognize the costs associated with the depreciation of buildings and equipment used in providing patient care as a Medicare reimbursable expense.[33] The depreciation charge is based on the historical cost of the assets, defined as the cost incurred by the present owner in acquiring them. For assets obtained after July 31, 1970, the historical cost cannot exceed the lower of (1) the current reproduction cost adjusted for straight-line depreciation over the life of the asset to the date of purchase, or (2) the fair market value of the asset at the time of purchase. The depreciation must be prorated over the useful life of the asset, which is the "normal operating or service life to the provider."

The provider may use the straight-line method of depreciation or, in certain situations, an accelerated method. With the straight-line method, the cost of the asset less its salvage value is determined. The result is then divided by the number of years of the asset's useful life. This method allocates equal amounts of depreciation costs to the provider's annual capital expenses for Medicare reimbursement over the useful life of the asset.

The Medicare program allows a provider to use the declining balance method or the sum-of-the-years' digits method as accelerated depreciation. With the declining balance method, the annual depreciation charge is computed by multiplying the undepreciated cost of the asset each year by a uniform rate, up to twice the straight-line rate, until the asset is fully depreciated. With the sum-of-the-years' digits method, the annual depreciation charge is calculated by multiplying the depreciable cost basis by a constantly decreasing fraction; the numerator of the fraction is the number of years remaining in the asset's useful life, and the denominator is the sum of all the years of the asset's useful life at the time of acquisition. With these accelerated methods, the provider is able to recover the costs of depreciation more quickly than with the straight-line method.

The accelerated methods can be used for Medicare reimbursement purposes when

1. the asset was depreciated for health insurance purposes by means of an accelerated method prior to August 1, 1970
2. the depreciable assets were acquired before August 1, 1970, but there was no depreciation method in effect, and the provider was a Medicare participant

3. construction of the depreciable asset was begun or a written contract was entered into prior to February 5, 1970, and the provider was participating in Medicare

A provider may use the declining balance method, regardless of the asset's acquisition date, if the provider's cash flow needs warrant the use of accelerated depreciation. Since depreciation is a noncash expense, increasing the depreciation charge by means of the declining balance method increases the provider's cash flow. The declining balance rate may not exceed 150 percent of the straight-line rate in this circumstance, however.

If a provider using an accelerated method of depreciation drops out of the Medicare program, or if the Medicare portion of a provider's allowable costs decreases, Medicare may have reimbursed the provider for substantially more depreciation costs than the program would have paid under the straight-line method of depreciation. In this case, regulations allow for the recovery of excess payments resulting from accelerated depreciation (i.e., the difference between the amount of depreciation costs calculated under the accelerated method and the amount calculated under the straight-line method). The excess depreciation reimbursement can be recovered either by reducing current payments to provider or, if the provider no longer participates in the Medicare program, by handling it as an overpayment.

In *Forest Hills Nursing Home, Inc. v. HHS*, the federal district court considered whether excess accelerated depreciation can be recovered when the provider's termination from Medicare participation is involuntary.[34] The nursing home had participated in the Medicare program from 1967 until July 31, 1976, when the secretary of HHS barred its further participation because of continued deficiencies in patient care. When a final determination of costs reimbursable to Forest Hills was made on July 22, 1977, the fiscal intermediary reduced the reimbursement payment by $57,318 to recover excess depreciation charges made in years back to 1967 through the use of accelerated depreciation. The action of the fiscal intermediary was affirmed by the PRRB. Forest Hills then appealed to the federal district court.

Originally, providers had been allowed to use accelerated depreciation when claiming Medicare reimbursement for the cost of capital assets used for covered services. On August 1, 1970, however, new regulations to eliminate the use of accelerated depreciation in the future and to recover excess depreciation payments resulting from the use of accelerated depreciation went into effect.[35] Forest Hills contended that (1) the depreciation recovery regulation could not be applied to recover depreciation payments made before the regulation's effective date and (2) the regulation could not be applied to recover depreciation payments made to a provider whose withdrawal from Medicare was involuntary.

In dismissing Forest Hill's argument that the secretary could not recover excess payments made before the effective date of the regulation (August 1, 1970), the court cited several rulings that upheld the retroactive application of the recovery rule.[36] There was no case law to guide the court in ruling on the validity of applying the recovery regulation to a facility that had been involuntarily terminated from Medicare participation, however. Noting that a court "should accord considerable respect to an agency's interpretation of its own regulations,"[37] the court ruled that the secretary's interpretation was "not precluded by the language of the regulation."[38] Finally, the court reasoned that the secretary's interpretation was consistent with the Medicare statute that forbids the subsidization of non-Medicare patients by Medicare patients.[39] "Failure to recapture would result in Medicare paying for asset depreciation that did not benefit Medicare patients."[40] The court affirmed the decision of the secretary.

In *Cambridge Nursing Home v. Blue Cross Association/Blue Cross/Blue Shield of Minnesota*, the acting administrator of the HCFA ruled that excess depreciation payments were to be recovered when a provider substantially decreases its Medicare utilization after using accelerated depreciation.[41] For reporting periods ending January 31, 1968 through January 31, 1977, Cambridge Nursing Home had claimed and was allowed accelerated depreciation as a Medicare cost equal to $49,348. Of this total, $12,350 was in excess of the cost that would have been claimed under straight-line depreciation. The provider's Medicare utilization percentage decreased from 36.3084 percent for the base period (January 31, 1972 through January 31, 1977) to 24.1157 percent for the period ending January 31, 1978, a drop of 33.58 percent. The number of days on which Cambridge Nursing Home cared for Medicare patients decreased from an average of 3,090 for the base period to 2,059 for the reporting period ending January 31, 1978, a drop of 33.37 percent. The *Provider Reimbursement Manual* requires recovery of excess depreciation payments when Medicare utilization and patient days in the reporting year decrease more than 25 percent from those in the base period.[42]

Observing this decline in Medicare utilization and following the instructions set out in the *Manual*, the fiscal intermediary recovered $12,350 in reimbursement attributable to the excess depreciation claimed for fiscal years ending January 31, 1968 through January 31, 1977. The provider appealed this action to the PRRB.[43] The board affirmed the intermediary's adjustment to recover excess payments for depreciation in reporting periods after August 1970, but reversed the decision in regard to reporting periods ending before August 1970. The acting HCFA administrator, on his own motion, reviewed this PRRB decision.

According to Cambridge Nursing Home, no recovery was necessary because the accelerated depreciation claimed was not substantially more than that which would have been allowed under the straight-line method. Cambridge also argued that, if recovery were necessary, it should be only for reporting periods on or after the effective date of the recovery regulations (i.e., August 1, 1970).

In reaching his decision, the acting HCFA administrator observed that, when accelerated depreciation is used, the highest depreciation allowance is realized in the early years that the asset is used. If the asset is held for its full useful life and the provider has a steady utilization rate by Medicare patients, the accelerated and straight-line methods result in the same total Medicare reimbursement for depreciation. If the Medicare utilization rate drops in later years, however, the use of the accelerated method in the early years of the asset's use grants the provider "more than its appropriate share of depreciation expenses from Medicare funds."[44] According to the acting administrator, this violates the reasonable cost concept, unless a recovery adjustment is made. The acting administrator also found that the retroactive recovery of excess depreciation payments was necessary because the statutes required that Medicare pay only its fair share of the costs and prohibited the use of Medicare funds to subsidize the care of non-Medicare patients. Therefore, he concluded that the 1970 recapture regulation "does not represent an abrupt departure from a well established practice. In fact, the 1970 Regulation sets forth what the law has required from the beginning."[45] The acting administrator also disagreed with Cambridge Nursing Home over the magnitude of the overpayment, deciding that the excess depreciation reimbursed with the accelerated method was "substantially more" than would have been paid with the straight-line method. The acting administrator observed that more than 25 percent of total depreciation reimbursed by Medicare to Cambridge Nursing Home was excess depreciation for the years in question.

The Medicare program reimburses providers for the depreciation of the assets that they are using at the time they enter the program, even if such assets have earlier been fully or partially depreciated on the providers' books.[46] As long as an asset is in use, the HCFA considers that its useful life has not ended. Consequently, for purposes of Medicare reimbursement, the asset can be depreciated under a revised estimate of the asset's useful life. For example, a provider is using a fifty-year-old building that has been fully depreciated on its books when the provider enters the Medicare program. It is agreed that the asset has a continued useful life of twenty years, or seventy years from the date of acquisition. The provider may claim depreciation over the next twenty years or a total depreciation of as much as twenty-sevenths of the asset's historical cost. Once an asset is fully depreciated by a provider for purposes of Medicare reimbursement, however, further depreciation is not allowed.

Interest Expenses

Medicare regulations allow the reimbursement of "necessary and proper interest" paid by the provider on both current and capital debt.[47] Medicare does not reimburse providers, however, for interest expenses resulting from judicial review in a federal court, overpayments to the provider, loans to repay overpayments, and loans not reasonably related to patient care.[48] Furthermore, only loans that meet the financial needs of the provider and do not result in "excess funds or investments" are considered necessary.

In *Estaugh Corporation v. Califano*, affirmed without opinion by a federal district court, the PRRB ruled that a portion of a provider's interest expense resulting from excess borrowing was not an allowable Medicare cost.[49] The residents paid an entrance fee to the provider for admission to a retirement village that included an SNF. These entrance fees covered a substantial portion of the cost of building the village, and the provider invested the amount of borrowed funds that was in excess of building costs in certificates of deposit. The PRRB ruled that the portion of the interest expense resulting from the excess borrowing was not allowable.

In another decision, the HCFA administrator ruled that the part of a bond issue that exceeded the cost of a construction project did not satisfy a financial need of the provider.[50] Because the interest expense of that excess portion of the bond issue was not considered necessary, the interest expense associated with that amount had to be offset by investment income.[51]

The purpose of the loan must be reasonably related to patient care.[52] For example, when a provider assumed the debts of a high school and a convent-nursing home as a consequence of a corporate reorganization,[53] the commissioner of Social Security ruled that the interest on these loans was not an allowable Medicare cost because the loans were not made to satisfy the financial needs of the provider, nor were they related to patient care.

Interest expenses for Medicare reimbursement must be reduced by any other interest income,[54] unless the interest income is generated through a separate fund of gifts and grants, funded depreciation, the provider's qualified pension plan, or judicial review by a federal court. In *Illinois Central Community Hospital v. Blue Cross Association/Health Care Service Corporation*, the PRRB ruled that interest earned on a remodeling and improvement fund must be offset against interest expenses.[55] The provider had issued bonds to establish the fund, which was held by a trustee and could be used only as set forth in the trust indenture. The provider argued that its interest expenses should not be reduced by the income earned by the fund because the money in the fund never came into the provider's hands and the provider exercised no discretion as to its use. The PRRB ruled, and the HCFA administrator later affirmed, that the income earned by the fund fell within the meaning of investment income as defined by the regulation and did not meet any of the exceptions outlined in this regulation.[56]

The proper rate of interest recognized by the Medicare regulations is the rate that a "prudent borrower" would pay "in the money market existing at the time the loan was made."[57] In addition, the loans should be made under the terms and conditions that a prudent borrower would accept in "arm's-length transactions with lending institutions."[58]

Interest paid on loans to the provider from the provider's donor-restricted fund of gifts or grants, from the funded depreciated account, or from the provider's qualified pension fund is an allowable Medicare expense; however, interest paid by the provider to partners, stockholders, or organizations related to the provider is not allowable. When interest on loans made to a provider by partners, stockholders, or related organizations is disallowed as a cost "solely because of the relationship factor, the principle of such loans shall be treated as invested funds in the computation of the provider's equity capital."[59] If owners use their own funds in a business, Medicare regulations also treat these funds as invested capital rather than borrowed funds.

In *Trustees of Indiana University v. Harris*, the PRRB affirmed the fiscal intermediary's decision to disallow reimbursement of the interest expenses incurred when the Indiana University Hospitals borrowed funds from Indiana University for working capital needs.[60] The board ruled that interest expenses associated with a loan between related organizations were not reimbursable under Medicare regulations. This decision was affirmed by the HCFA administrator. Claiming that the intermediary's adjustment to disallow the interest expenses paid by the provider to the trustees of the Indiana University was improper, the trustees of Indiana University then brought action in federal district court.[61]

The court relied on an earlier decision of the U.S. Court of Claims that involved the same parties and issues for different cost reporting periods.[62] In that decision, the court of claims had held that Medicare regulations did not prohibit Medicare reimbursement to Indiana University Hospitals for those portions of interest paid to Indiana University that were attributable to the delivery of Medicare services. The court of claims noted that the purpose of the regulations was "to protect the government against paying the cost of collusive loans with inflated interest rates."[63]

Relying on this reasoning, the district court ruled that "none of the evils" that the Medicare regulations were designed to prevent was present in the loan between the provider and Indiana University. The court pointed out that Indiana University could have received a greater return on its money by investing it elsewhere, because the interest on the disputed loans was six percent—consistently below the prime rate. Also, the district court noted that, under Indiana statutes, Indiana University Hospitals were allowed to borrow money for working capital only from Indiana University. The court concluded

> that the interest the Hospitals paid to the University, which was below the prime rate and was paid to the only source from which the Hospitals could borrow, was neither improper nor unnecessary. This interest was reasonable in all respects .... The court concludes that the plaintiff is entitled to reimbursement of these portions of interest the Indiana University Hospitals paid to Indiana University in 1973, 1974, 1975, and 1976 that are attributable to the provision of Medicare services.[64]

Return on Equity Capital

The Social Security Act explicitly directs the secretary of HHS to include a return on equity as a Medicare-reimbursable cost to proprietary providers of skilled nursing care.[65] The statute also mandates that this rate of return not exceed 1½ times the average of the rates of interest paid on debt obligations issued by the Federal Hospital Insurance Trust Fund (FHITF). Accordingly, Medicare regulations recognize "a reasonable return on equity capital" invested in the provision of patient care as a reimbursable cost to proprietary providers.[66] The regulations set the rate of return at the maximum level allowed by statue.

The regulations define equity capital as the proprietary provider's investment in plant, property, and equipment (net of depreciation) related to patient care. In addition, funds that a provider must deposit to lease plant, property, or equipment and net working capital that a provider needs for "necessary and proper" operation of patient care activities are considered part of equity capital. The excess of any acquisition cost over the historical cost or fair market value of an asset or facility purchased before August 1970 is included in equity capital if it is "reasonable." After the cumulative allowable return equals 100 percent of the original excess, however, the excess of the purchase price over the fair market value at the time of purchase is no longer included in equity capital. Such an excess in the acquisition cost of an asset or facility purchased after July 1970 is excluded from equity capital.

Owners invest capital in SNFs with the expectation of earning a profit; therefore, return on this investment is essential not only to avoid withdrawal of resources from the industry, but also to attract additional capital for expansion. The inspector general of HHS argued in a report, however, that the rate of return paid by Medicare to skilled care providers should be reduced from 150 percent of the average of the rates paid on debts issued by the FHITF to 100 percent.[67] Such a reduction has already been made in the Medicare rate of return on equity capital reimbursed to proprietary providers of hospital care. It remains to be seen whether the Medicare rate of return on equity paid to providers of skilled care will also be reduced from the maximum rate allowed by statute.

RELATED ORGANIZATION PRINCIPLES

Under Medicare reimbursement practices, organizations related to a provider through common ownership or control are treated as if they were part of the provider. The costs of services, facilities, or supplies furnished to a provider by a related organization are included in the provider's allowable costs for Medicare reimbursement, but only at the cost to the related organization.[68] Federal regulations further limit such costs to the price of comparable items that could be purchased elsewhere.[69]

In *American Hospital Management Corporation v. Harris*, the U.S. Court of Appeals for the Ninth Circuit upheld the validity of the related organization principle.[70] The court ruled that substantial deference must be given to the secretary's interpretation of the pertinent law and deferred to the secretary's judgment that "there is a significant likelihood that charges incurred by providers in their transactions" with related parties "will be artificially inflated because of the absence of bona fide arm's-length bargaining."[71] The court concluded that, since the related party regulation was a reasonable method to achieve the purpose intended by Congress, i.e., to prevent the reimbursement of excessive charges resulting from self-dealing, no "constitutional infirmity" was found.

The U.S. Court of Appeals for the Fourth Circuit also upheld the regulation in *Fairfax Hospital Association, Inc. v. Califano*.[72] This appellate court ruled that the regulation met a legitimate goal of guarding against the potential abuse between related suppliers and providers. The regulation was rationally related to that goal and was not arbitrary.

Common Ownership and Control

The *Provider Reimbursement Manual* provides tests of common ownership and control that are used to determine whether a provider is related to a supplying organization.[73] These two tests are different and are to be applied separately. The existence of an immediate family relationship creates an irrebuttable presumption of relatedness through control or attribution of ownership.

The common ownership rule to determine whether an individual or organization possesses significant ownership in provider and supplying organizations is made on "the facts and circumstances in each case."[74] In one example used in the *Manual*, a man owns a 60 percent interest in a provider and a 55 percent interest in a supplier. These organizations are related for purposes of Medicare reimbursement because the same man owns significant amounts of each. In another example, a man owns 20 percent of the shares of a corporate provider and a 50 percent interest in a supplying partnership. The man's wife owns 30 percent of the shares of the provider. Together, the couple owns 50 percent of the provider, and the husband owns 50 percent of the supplier; this makes the organizations related through common ownership for purposes of Medicare reimbursement.

As explained in the *Manual*, the term *control* includes any kind of control, even if it is not legally enforceable and no matter how it is exercised. "It is the reality of the control which is decisive, not its form or the mode of its exercise."[75] To determine if control exists, the facts and circumstances of each case must be reviewed. One example given in the *Manual* involves a physician who is the medical director of a provider in which he has no ownership interest. This physician is also president and owner of a supplier that furnishes therapeutic services primarily to the provider. Because it can be presumed that the physician has the power to influence both the provider and the supplier, the organizations are considered related by common control for purposes of Medicare reimbursement.

In another example in the *Manual*, a provider enters into a management contract with a management company. Under the terms of the contract, the management company replaces several of the provider's key employees with company employees and makes a substantial loan to the provider for working capital. In addition, the company owns and leases to the provider the building, fixed equipment, and land; the lease can be cancelled only by the company, and the company would assume all the assets and liabilities of the provider at the time of cancellation. Because the combination of all these factors gives the management company significant power over the provider's actions and policies, the company and the provider are considered related through control.

In a PRRB decision, a provider and a limited partnership that entered into a sale and lease-back agreement for land, building, and equipment were held to be related through common control.[76] The board made this determination because the partnership's limited partners were also physicians on the provider's medical staff. Furthermore, the partnership's general partner was the provider's administrator and president of the board of directors. By holding these positions, this one person had the power to influence both parties significantly.

In another PRRB decision, an SNF and a provider of physical therapy services were held to be related organizations because the provider was able directly or indirectly to control the affairs, contracts, and costs of the physical therapy services organizations.[77] The owners of the SNF had close relatives who owned 50 percent of the stock of the provider. Also, control was demonstrated through contractual relationships and terms.

Exceptions to the Related Organization Principle

There are a few exceptions to the related organization principle.[78] To qualify for the exception, the provider must clearly demonstrate to the intermediary that certain criteria have been met. The supplying organization must be a separate sole proprietorship, partnership, joint venture, association, or corporation; it cannot be merely an operating division of the provider. A substantial part of the supplying organization's business must be transacted with other unrelated parties in an open, competitive market. In addition, the services, facilities, or supplies furnished by the supplying organization should generally be obtained from outside sources and should not be basic elements of patient care that the provider itself would ordinarily furnish to patients. Finally, the charge to the provider should approximate the price for comparable services, facilities, and supplies in an open, competitive market. If all these conditions are met, the charges by the supplier to the related provider are allowable Medicare costs.

In a provider appeal decision, the hearing officer ruled that the costs of a pharmacy related to a provider by joint ownership had to be substituted for the charges claimed by the provider because the provider could not meet the burden of proof necessary to establish an exception to the related organization principle.[79] The hearing officer decided that, although the pharmacy was a bona fide separate organization, the provider failed to present convincing evidence that a substantial part of the pharmacy's business was with unrelated providers. The hearing officer noted that "without the provider's business, the pharmacy would not have survived."[80] The hearing officer also did not agree with the provider's assertion that there was an open, competitive market for the pharmacy's services. Finally, the provider could not document that the pharmacy's charges to the provider were the same as those to the general public.

Purchase of Facilities

If a facility is purchased from a related organization, the purchaser's basis for depreciation may not exceed the seller's basis under the Medicare program.[81] Even if a facility converts from proprietary to nonprofit status as a result of a purchase and the buyer and seller are related by common ownership or control, the purchaser's basis for depreciation may not exceed the seller's basis under the program less accumulated depreciation recognized under the program.

In *Goleta Valley Community Hospital v. Schweiker*,[82] the court of appeals upheld a PRRB decision that a provider and a partnership from which the provider had purchased the facility it was leasing were related by common control. The provider's board of trustees consisted entirely of seven individuals who owned approximately a 70 percent interest in the partnership. The court found no merit in the provider's contention that the related organization principle is contrary to the Medicare Act or to the U.S. Constitution. In addition, the court rejected the provider's argument that reimbursement of depreciation is governed by the depreciation regulations outlining regular depreciation procedures[83] rather than the special rule for claims between related parties.[84] For this reason, the court of appeals upheld both the denial of the interest expense attributable to the transaction and the decision to keep the depreciable basis of the assets to that used by the partnership.

In another case, a nursing home provider terminated a fifteen-year lease ten years before its expiration date in order to purchase the building, even though the terms of the purchase caused the provider's capital-related costs to double.[85] The owner of the provider was the brother of the owners of the corporation that had leased the facility and equipment to the provider and subsequently sold the same property to the provider. The HCFA deputy administrator concluded:

> It is unlikely that reasonably prudent businesspersons would voluntarily forego 10 years of a 15 year term under a favorable lease to purchase the leased property when such a purchase would effectively double their capital-related costs. However, when one considers that much of this increase in capital-related costs would be merely passed through to government health care programs, ... such a transaction does not appear unreasonable from the standpoint of the businesspersons. When, in addition, family members are on each side of the transaction, whether there was a bona fide business purpose would become questionable. The primary reason for such a transaction would appear to be for obtaining additional reimbursement from the government at no real loss or risk to either of the parties.[86]

The deputy administrator ruled that the provider was associated or affiliated with the corporation that had leased and then sold the facility and related equipment to the provider. Therefore, the transaction was between related parties. The costs of ownership of the facility and related equipment were allowable Medicare costs to the provider, but only at the level of the previous owner's costs. The amount claimed by the provider in excess of the previous owner's costs was an unnecessary cost and was not reimbursable with Medicare funds. Furthermore, because of the related organizations principle, the interest paid by the provider to the corporation that sold the property was not reimbursable.

Rental Expenses

A provider is permitted to lease a facility from a related organization, but the rent paid is not an allowable cost.[87] The provider is allowed, however, to include in its reimbursable costs the costs of owning the facility that it rents. Generally, these costs are depreciation, interest on the mortgage, real estate taxes, and other expenses attributable to the leased facility. "The effect is to treat the leased facility as though it were owned by the provider."[88] In addition, the owner's equity in the leased assets can be included in the equity capital of a proprietary provider.[89]

In *Fallston General Hospital v. Harris*, the federal district court upheld the secretary's decision that, because of interlocking ownership, the provider and the real estate partnership that leased the facility to the provider were related by common ownership and control.[90] The general partner in the limited partnership that operated the provider consisted of four individuals who owned 95 percent of the real estate partnership that leased the facility to the provider. The secretary decided that the cost of ownership to the real estate partnership should be substituted for the rental expense in the provider's Medicare costs because of the related organization principle. The court agreed that, through the interlocking ownership, the provider was in effect renting the facility from itself. The court also ruled that the secretary's decision need not be reversed because the general partner contracted with a management company to operate the provider and, therefore, exercised no control over the daily operations of the provider, nor because the rent paid was reasonable.

In another case, the PRRB ruled that a provider and the partnership that leased the land and facilities to the provider were related organizations because the organization that owned all the provider's stock was also the sole general partner in the lessor partnership.[91] The board ruled that the costs of ownership had to be substituted for the provider's rental payments in its Medicare costs because of the related organization principle. Furthermore, when the provider subsequently purchased the land and facilities from the partnership, it was not allowed to increase the cost basis of the assets.

OUTLOOK

The Tax Equity and Fiscal Responsibility Act (TEFRA) of 1982 directed the secretary of HHS to develop a prospective rate-setting method to establish Medicare payments for SNF services. The HCFA already uses a prospective system to calculate Medicare reimbursement rates for inpatient hospital services, kidney dialysis services, and hospice services. A major future development will be the application of the prospective payment system to Medicare reimbursement for services provided by SNFs.

When the new prospective rate method is developed, the HCFA may reduce the rate of return on equity for SNFs from 1½ times the average of the rates of interest paid on debt obligations issued by the FHITF to a rate of return equal to the average rates of interest paid on these debt issues, as it has already done for hospitals. On the other hand, with the adoption of a prospective rate mechanism, the return on equity may be eliminated as a Medicare-allowable cost in payments to SNFs; when the HCFA established Medicare prospective payments for kidney dialysis services, it eliminated return on equity as an allowable cost on the ground that a return on equity would weaken the efficiency incentives of the prospective methodology. The Social Security Act, however, directs the secretary of HHS to include a return on equity in Medicare payments for services delivered by SNFs. Congress, therefore, would have to amend the act before the HCFA could eliminate a return on equity in Medicare payments for SNF services.

As a result of a General Accounting Office study that showed a $55 million increase in capital costs, part of which was allocated to the Medicare and Medicaid programs, when the Hospital Corporation of America acquired Hospital Affiliates International, Inc. (see Outlook, Chapter 2), the Subcommittees on Health and Oversight of the House Ways and Means Committee began hearings on such mergers. These joint hearings could result in congressional action that changes the ways in which the Medicare and Medicaid programs value assets when there is a change in ownership. This, in turn, could affect Medicare and Medicaid reimbursement of a return on equity, as well as capital interest and depreciation expenses.

NOTES

1. U.S. Department of Health and Human Services, Health Care Financing Administration, Division of the Budget, survey by author and Research Institute of Pharmaceutical Sciences, January 1984.

2. MEDICARE AND MEDICAID GUIDE, 14,752.

3. HOUSE COMMITTEE ON INTERSTATE AND FOREIGN COMMERCE, BACKGROUND REPORT ON NURSING HOMES, 94th Cong., 1st Sess. 5 (1975).

4. 42 C.F.R. §405.1122.

5. 42 C.F.R. §405.1911.
6. 42 C.F.R. §405.1123.
7. 42 C.F.R. §405.1124.
8. 42 C.F.R. §405.1133.
9. 42 C.F.R. §405.1127.
10. 42 C.F.R. §405.1126.
11. 42 C.F.R. §405.1128.
12. 42 C.F.R. §405.1028.
13. 42 C.F.R. §405.1029.
14. 42 C.F.R. §405.1125.
15. 42 C.F.R. §405.1130.
16. 42 C.F.R. §405.1131.
17. 42 C.F.R. §405.1134.
18. 42 C.F.R. §405.1135.
19. 42 U.S.C. §1395x(v)(1)(A).
20. 42 U.S.C. §1395hh.
21. 42 U.S.C. §1395x(v)(1)(B).
22. 42 C.F.R. §405.402.
23. *Id.*
24. 42 C.F.R. §405.455.
25. 42 C.F.R. §405.460.
26. PRRB Hearing Decision No. 83-D152, September 27, 1983. In MEDICARE AND MEDICAID GUIDE, 33,596.
27. 42 C.F.R. §405.433.
28. PROVIDER REIMBURSEMENT MANUAL, HIM 15-1, §2119ff.
29. 42 U.S.C. §1861(v)(1)(A).
30. 42 C.F.R. §405.460.
31. 47 Fed. Reg. 42,894 (September 29, 1982).
32. 42 C.F.R. §405.414.
33. 42 C.F.R. §405.415.
34. U.S. District Court, District of Massachusetts, No. 80-2325-S, October 3, 1984. In MEDICARE AND MEDICAID GUIDE, 33,436.
35. 42 C.F.R. §405.415(d)(3).
36. Adams Nursing Home of Williamstown, Inc. v. Mathews, 548 F.2d 1077 (1st Cir. 1977); Fairfax Nursing Center, Inc. v. Califano, 590 F.2d 1297 (4th Cir. 1979); Summit Nursing Home, Inc. v. United States, 572 F.2d 737 (Ct. Cl. 1978); Springdale Convalescent Center v. Mathews, 545 F.2d 943 (5th Cir. 1977).
37. MEDICARE AND MEDICAID GUIDE, 33,436, p. 9231.
38. *Id.*
39. 42 U.S.C. §1395x(v)(1).
40. MEDICARE AND MEDICAID GUIDE, 33,436, p. 9231.
41. HCFA Acting Administrator Decision, June 17, 1980. In MEDICARE AND MEDICAID GUIDE, 30,552.

42. HIM-15, §136.4.
43. PRRB Hearing Decision No. 80-D21, April 21, 1980. In MEDICARE AND MEDICAID GUIDE, 30,492.
44. MEDICARE AND MEDICAID GUIDE, 30,552, p. 10,219.
45. *Id.*
46. 42 C.F.R. §405.417.
47. 42 C.F.R. §405.419.
48. 42 C.F.R. §405.419.
49. PRRB Hearing Decision No. 76-D36, June 10, 1977. In MEDICARE AND MEDICAID GUIDE, 4920.19.
50. HCFA Administrator Decision, April 13, 1979. In MEDICARE AND MEDICAID GUIDE, 29,702.
51. 42 C.F.R. §405.419(b)(2)(iii).
52. 42 C.F.R. §405.419(b)(2)(ii).
53. Commissioner of Social Security Decision, December 17, 1976. In MEDICARE AND MEDICAID GUIDE, 4920.80.
54. 42 C.F.R. §405.419(b)(2)(iii).
55. PRRB Hearing Decision No. 78-D46, June 26, 1978. In MEDICARE AND MEDICAID GUIDE, 29,218; *affirmed* by HCFA Administrator Decision, August 18, 1978, in MEDICARE AND MEDICAID GUIDE, 29,244.
56. 42 C.F.R. §405.419(b)(2)(iii).
57. 42 C.F.R. §405.419(b)(3).
58. 42 C.F.R. §405.419(c)(1).
59. 42 C.F.R. §405.429.
60. The Trustees of Indiana University (Indiana University Hospitals) v. Harris, U.S. District Court, Southern District of Indiana, Indianapolis Division, Nos. IP78-175-C, IP78-746-C, April 16, 1981. In MEDICARE AND MEDICAID GUIDE, 31,038.
61. *Id.*
62. Trustees of Indiana Univ. (Indiana Univ. Hospitals) v. United States, 618 F.2d 736 (Ct. Cl. 1980).
63. *Id.*, at 739.
64. *See supra*, note 60, at p. 10,233.
65. 42 U.S.C. 1395x(v)(1)(B).
66. 42 C.F.R. §405.429.
67. Office of the Inspector General, U.S. DEP'T OF HEALTH AND HUMAN SERVICES, MEDICARE PAYMENT OF RETURN ON EQUITY TO PROPRIETARY PROVIDERS, 8 (1983). Audit Control No. 09-32607.
68. PROVIDER REIMBURSEMENT MANUAL, Part I, §1000. In MEDICARE AND MEDICAID GUIDE, 5679.
69. 42 C.F.R. §405.427.
70. 638 F.2d 1208 (9th Cir. 1981).
71. *Id.*, at 1212.
72. 585 F.2d 602 (4th Cir. 1978).
73. Part I, §1004. In MEDICARE AND MEDICAID GUIDE, 5691.

74. Provider Reimbursement Manual, Part I, §1004.1. In Medicare and Medicaid Guide, 5694.
75. Part I, §1004.3. In Medicare and Medicaid Guide, 5700.
76. PRRB Hearing Decision No. 81-D91, September 22, 1981, Woodruff Gables Hosp. v. Blue Cross Ass'n/Blue Cross of Southern California. In Medicare and Medicaid Guide, 31,550.
77. PRRB Hearing Decision No. 80-D13, March 13, 1980, Waunakee Manor Health Care Center, Inc. v. Mutual of Omaha Ins. Co. In Medicare and Medicaid Guide, 30,460.
78. Provider Reimbursement Manual, Part I, §1010. In Medicare and Medicaid Guide, 5712.
79. Provider Appeal Decision, No. 00-78-13. In Medicare and Medicaid Guide, 29,161. *See also* Provider Appeal Decision, No. 00-77-25. In Medicare and Medicaid Guide, 28,463.
80. *Id.*, at 29,161 (p. 10,166).
81. Provider Reimbursement Manual, Part I, §1011.4. In Medicare and Medicaid Guide, 5719D. To calculate the seller's bases, see Provider Reimbursement Manual, §114. In Medicare and Medicaid Guide, 4745.
82. 647 F.2d 894 (9th Cir. 1981).
83. 42 C.F.R. §405.415.
84. 42 C.F.R. §405.427.
85. HCFA Deputy Administrator Decision, February 4, 1982, University Park Convalescent Center v. Aetna Life and Casualty Company. In Medicare and Medicaid Guide, 31,909.
86. *Id.*, at 9493.
87. Provider Reimbursement Manual, Part I, §1011.5. In Medicare and Medicaid Guide, 5719E.
88. *Id.*
89. Provider Reimbursement Manual, Part I, §1212. In Medicare and Medicaid Guide, 5794.
90. 481 F. Supp. 1066 (1979); *affirmed* in an unpublished order by the Fourth Circuit Court of Appeals, February 17, 1981.
91. PRRB Hearing Decision No. 81-D76, August 17, 1981, Medical Center of Tarzana v. Office of Direct Reimbursement, HCFA. In Medicare and Medicaid Guide, 31,488.

Chapter 4

Medicare: Hospice Care

The hospice concept is a program of care in which the focus of treatment for a terminally ill patient shifts from seeking a cure to making the patient's remaining days as comfortable and meaningful as possible. An interdisciplinary team provides medical, social, psychological, emotional, and spiritual services, combining the efforts of a broad spectrum of care-givers not only to relieve the pain of the patient, but also to assist the patient's family in coping with the stress of the patient's illness and impending death. The goal of hospice care is to help terminally ill patients remain primarily at home and continue life with minimal disruptions of normal activities.[1]

The Tax Equity and Fiscal Responsibility Act (TEFRA) of 1982 expanded the range of Medicare benefits by authorizing the coverage of hospice care for terminally ill beneficiaries.[2] Coverage began on November 1, 1983, and is scheduled to expire on September 30, 1986, unless Congress takes action to extend it. The legislative history indicates that Congress included this "sunset" provision because hospice care "is a relatively new concept" and "the experience of specific hospice programs is limited."[3]

HOSPICE COVERAGE

Hospice care benefits are available to a Medicare beneficiary who is certified as terminally ill;[4] Medicare regulations, as directed by Congress, define a terminal illness as one in which the life expectancy is six months or less.[5] A Medicare beneficiary who elects to receive hospice benefits waives all Medicare benefits except those for services provided by the attending physician. The Medicare program reimburses providers for two 90-day periods and one 30-day period of hospice care, for a total of 210 days during the patient's lifetime. The two 90-day periods cover care for the hospice patient's life expectancy of six months or less; the 30-day period covers additional care should the patient live beyond the six months. Federal regulations require the patient to use the two 90-day election periods of coverage before using the 30-day period. Congress directed the secretary of the Department of Health and Human Services (HHS) to make recommendations for changes in the length of the hospice benefit because "the average length of stay in hospice programs is significantly"[6] less than 210 days.

Within two days after care has begun in the first ninety-day period of hospice coverage, the hospice must obtain written certification of the patient's terminal illness in statements signed by the medical director of the hospice or the physician member of the hospice's interdisciplinary team and the patient's attending physician. Within two days of the beginning of a subsequent ninety-day or thirty-day period, the hospice must obtain a written certification signed by the hospice's medical director or the physician member of the interdisciplinary group.

An eligible Medicare beneficiary who chooses hospice care must file an election statement with a hospice.[7] A representative of the Medicare beneficiary who is authorized by state law to act on behalf of the patient may also file the election statement. This statement must include

1. the name of the hospice providing care
2. an acknowledgment by the patient or the patient's representative of the palliative rather than curative focus of hospice care
3. an acknowledgment that certain Medicare benefits are waived with the election of hospice care
4. the effective date of the election
5. the signature of the patient or the patient's representative[8]

The patient or the patient's representative may revoke the election of hospice care at any time.[9] In this event, the Medicare coverage of other services that was waived with the election of hospice care is resumed. Subsequently, the patient may elect to resume hospice care for any remaining eligibility periods. The Medicare beneficiary or the representative can change hospices while in an election period; this change is not considered a revocation of coverage.[10]

CONDITIONS OF PARTICIPATION

Administration

Federal regulations list the administrative criteria that a hospice program must meet in order to participate in the Medicare program.[11] It must have a governing body,[12] a medical director,[13] and professional management.[14] The hospice program must have a written plan of care for each patient[15] and a program to monitor the quality and appropriateness of the care provided.[16]

The legislative history shows Congress' concern that, once a beneficiary uses the 210 days of hospice care covered by Medicare, the hospice may discontinue or reduce the level of care provided.[17] In accordance with the authorizing statute, the implementing regulations prohibit a hospice from discontinuing or diminishing care provided to a Medicare patient because of the patient's inability to pay.[18]

Federal regulations require that the interdisciplinary team include at least a physician, a registered nurse, a social worker, and a pastoral or other counselor.[19] The hospice is also required to recruit, train, and use volunteers in administrative or patient care roles and must document the cost savings achieved through the use of volunteers.[20]

Core Services

"Substantially all" the core services must be provided directly by hospice employees,[21] although outside staff may be used to meet patient needs during peak patient loads or under extraordinary circumstances. The core services include nursing services,[22] medical-social services provided by a qualified social worker under the direction of a physician,[23] and physician services to keep the terminally ill patients comfortable and to meet their general medical needs.[24] Counseling for both the patients and their families, including dietary and spiritual counseling, is also considered a hospice core service.[25]

The regulations require the hospice to provide bereavement counseling for the family, but do not allow its reimbursement by Medicare.[26] Although the intent of Congress to include bereavement counseling for the family is clear in the legislative history, Congress explicitly stated "that reimbursement for such services, for other than the beneficiary [patient], was inappropriate under the Medicare program."[27]

Other Services

Additional services that must be provided either by the hospice itself or under arrangements with other providers include physical, occupational, and speech therapies;[28] home health and homemaker services;[29] medical supplies;[30] and short-term inpatient care.[31] A patient may need short-term inpatient care in order to control symptoms or to relieve the patient's family temporarily from the strain of caring for the patient. The inpatient care for symptom control can be provided by a qualified free-standing hospice, a hospital, or a skilled nursing facility (SNF). Inpatient respite care can be provided by one of these types of facilities or by a qualified intermediate care facility.

A freestanding hospice that provides inpatient care must

1. have nursing service available at all times
2. have a disaster preparedness plan
3. comply with all federal, state, and local laws, regulations, and codes pertaining to health and safety
4. comply with the National Fire Protection Association's Life Safety Code for fire protection
5. have patient areas designed for comfort and privacy of patients and their families
6. have patient rooms and baths that meet prescribed standards
7. have isolation areas
8. provide linen, meal, and pharmacist services that meet prescribed standards[32]

REIMBURSEMENT LEGISLATION

The TEFRA of 1982 directed that Medicare payments to a hospice organization should "be an amount equal to the costs which are reasonable and related to the cost of providing hospice care or which are based on such other tests of reasonableness as the Secretary may prescribe in regulations." The General Accounting Office (GAO), an arm of the Congress, concluded that a prospective rate-setting system for hospice care is consistent with the discretion granted to the secretary of HHS by Congress in the statute.[33] Furthermore, in the past, the secretary "has interpreted similar language used elsewhere in the Social Security Act to authorize prospective reimbursement" for renal dialysis under Medicare and for nursing home care under Medicaid.[34]

Also in the TEFRA, Congress expressed its desire to impose a cap on the total amount of reimbursement a hospice care provider could receive for Medicare patients. The first step in establishing this cap is to calculate the total amount of Medicare payments for conventional services provided to cancer patients in the last six months of their lives, based on data for the most recent twelve-month period available. A national average per capita expenditure is obtained by dividing this sum by the number of these Medicare patients. Under the TEFRA provision, this national average expenditure is adjusted to obtain a regional average per capita expenditure that reflects regional differences in the cost of providing health care. The total cap for each hospice provider is 40 percent of the regional average cost of providing conventional care, adjusted by the medical care category of the consumer price index (CPI), multiplied by the number of Medicare patients served. Congress intended this cap "to ensure that payments for hospice care would not exceed the amount that would have been spent by Medicare if the patient had been treated in a conventional setting."[35]

While Congress developed the TEFRA legislation, the Congressional Budget Office (CBO) examined the cost implications of Medicare reimbursement for hospice care. Using "recent" data from the Health Care Financing Administration (HCFA), the CBO estimated that Medicare payments for cancer treatment in the last six months of a Medicare patient's life would average more than $19,000 in 1983. Based on these CBO projections, Congress estimated a national cap for hospice care in excess of $7,000 per Medicare beneficiary.[36] When the HCFA made its own calculations for federal regulations, however, it developed a much lower cap of $4,200 for each Medicare patient.

The difference between the cap estimated by Congress, based on CBO projections, and the limit calculated by the HCFA can be attributed to two errors in the CBO projections.[37] First, the CBO projection of $19,000 as the average Medicare payment for cancer care was too high; there was a misunderstanding about what was the base amount and what was the cap amount. Second, the CBO used the rate of increase in Medicare program expenditures, rather than the CPI medical care component mandated in the legislation, as the inflation factor to adjust base year expenses.

Congress responded to this discrepancy by amending the Medicare provisions for hospice care reimbursement on August 29, 1983.[38] In this amendment, Congress established the cap at $6,500 per patient for the first year of the benefit, with the amount to be inflated annually by the percentage change in the medical care component of the CPI. When the original TEFRA legislation had been developed by Congress, the CBO estimated an average cost to Medicare of $5,010 per user of hospice services in 1983, based on the experiences of hospice demonstration projects.[39] This 1983 average Medicare cost for hospice care would have exceeded the $4,200 cap set by the HCFA, indicating the need for congressional action to raise the cap to $6,500. In addition, Congress eliminated in this amendment the regional adjustments of the cap that it had required in the original TEFRA legislation.

REIMBURSEMENT REGULATIONS

In creating the regulations to implement Medicare reimbursement of hospice care, the HCFA developed four prospective payment rates: (1) routine home care, (2) continuous home care, (3) inpatient respite care, and (4) general inpatient care.[40] When the HCFA announced its intention to reimburse hospice care on a prospective basis, it received a "substantial" number of comments objecting to this approach.[41] Some objected to basing the prospective rates on cost data from twenty-six demonstration hospices, contending that these hospices are not representative of the organizations that will provide hospice care to Medicare patients. The HCFA responded that cost data from the demonstration hospices and other Medicare programs provide "an adequate basis for development of a prospective payment system" and rates which are "adequate" to provide care meeting the needs of Medicare patients.

Others objected to the use of a prospective mechanism at all, asserting that Congress intended for hospice care payments to be cost-related. The HCFA responded that prospective rate setting is consistent with the broad authority that Congress delegated to the secretary to calculate payments for hospice care. In a further defense of its use of the prospective system for hospice care, the HCFA noted that it had established a prospective payment rate for renal dialysis under similar statutory language. Finally, HCFA cited a GAO letter noting that Congress did not "preclude" the use of prospective reimbursement for hospice care.[42]

It was suggested that the HCFA use a reasonable cost method of payment with retroactive adjustments during the initial years of the hospice benefit, thus developing an adequate cost data base that could be used to establish a prospective system in future years. The HCFA responded that the use of a reasonable cost retrospective method of payment "would encourage the proliferation of hospice costs without regard to effectiveness and efficiency. Moreover, the use of a cost reimbursement system would permit the early inefficiencies of this new benefit to become embedded in the rate structure."[43] The HCFA acknowledged that, while a more developed data base would be preferable, the data from the hospice demonstration are suitable.

On August 22, 1983, the HCFA published a proposed rule on hospice care that contained preliminary payment rates for the four classifications of hospice care.[44] These preliminary rates (Table 4-1) were based on data that the HCFA had obtained from the Medicare hospice demonstration projects. These cost data had not been finalized, however, for two reasons. First, since patient-based data are not entered into data files until three months after the patient has died, the cost data gathered to calculate the preliminary payment rates did not reflect the costs of all patients who received hospice care during that period. Second, the 1981 cost reports of the demonstration hospices had not yet been completely audited. The final payment rates (Table 4-1) are based on the 1982 cost reports of the demonstration hospices and on cost data from 3,889 Medicare patients who received hospice care between October 1, 1980, and April 1, 1983.

Table 4-1 Medicare: Per Diem Payment Rates for Hospice Care (1984)

	Preliminary Rates	Final Rates
Routine home care	$53.17	$46.25
Continuous home care		
Per day	$311.96	$358.67
Per hour	$13.00	$14.94
Inpatient respite care	$61.65	$55.33
General inpatient care	$271.00	$271.00

Source: Health Care Financing Administration, Department of Health and Human Services, 48 *Fed. Reg.* 56,008 (December 16, 1983).

Routine Home Care

Federal regulations define a routine home hospice care day as "a day on which an individual who has elected to receive hospice care is at home" and is not receiving the other three types of hospice care.[45] Based on 1982 cost data from the demonstration hospices, the HCFA identified three major cost centers for routine home care: the nursing center, the home health center, and the social service and therapy center.[46] The experiences of the Medicare patients in the demonstration hospices were used to determine the average use of these three centers per day. For example, the average cost of the nursing component was $65.30 per visit in 1982 dollars, with an average of 0.223 visits per day, yielding a cost per day of $14.56 in 1982 dollars. The home health component and the social service/therapy component yielded costs per day of $11.42 and $2.89, respectively, in 1982 dollars. The other cost components of the routine home care rate are

1. home respite ($1.31)
2. interdisciplinary group ($2.49)
3. drugs ($1.06)
4. supplies ($4.02)
5. equipment ($1.01)
6. outpatient hospital therapies ($2.68)

The total cost was $41.44 per day in 1982 dollars. To convert these amounts to 1984 dollars, the HCFA used a market basket index developed from the prices of goods and services purchased by home health agencies. In 1984, the final prospective hospice rate used by the Medicare program to reimburse a day of routine home care was $46.25.

Continuous Home Care

According to federal regulations, a continuous home hospice care day is "a day on which an individual who has elected to receive hospice care is not in an inpatient facility and receives hospice care consisting predominantly of nursing care on a continuous basis at home."[47] Home health services, homemaker services, or both may also be provided on a continuous basis with this type of care. Continuous home care is furnished only during a brief period of crisis, defined as a period when the patient needs continuous care to relieve or manage acute medical symptoms and to remain at home.

The hospice must provide a minimum of 8 hours of continuous home care in a day to receive the continuous home care rate.[48] The minimum per diem rate for continuous home care is calculated as eight hours at the hourly rate. Each additional hour or portion of an hour of this type of care is also paid at the hourly rate. The nursing component, at a cost per day of $302.40 in 1982 dollars, is the major cost center for continuous home care. The other cost components are

1. therapy (3.84)
2. drugs ($2.23)
3. supplies ($3.16)
4. equipment ($7.27)
5. interdisciplinary group ($2.49)

The total cost per day of continuous home care was $321.39 in 1982 dollars. Conversion to 1984 dollars with the home health care cost index yielded a cost per day of $358.67 or an hourly rate of $14.94 for continuous home care. The hospice payment on a continuous home care day varies according to the number of hours of continuous care services provided.

Inpatient Respite Care

Federal regulations define respite hospice care as "short-term inpatient care provided to the individual only when necessary to relieve the family members or other persons caring for the individual."[49] The Medicare program reimburses a provider for a maximum of five consecutive days of respite hospice care. Payment for the sixth consecutive day and any subsequent days of respite care is made at the routine home care rate.[50] The respite care rate is paid for the day of admission into inpatient care, but the appropriate home care rate is paid for the day of discharge. If the Medicare patient is discharged from respite care as deceased, however, the respite rate is paid for the final day.

The major cost center used in calculating the prospective per diem rate for respite care is the average per diem cost of routine care provided by an SNF in 1982 dollars ($44.85).[51] The HCFA selected the cost of skilled care as the basis for respite care reimbursement because an SNF provides the level of care that a hospice patient requires during respite care. To this per diem cost of skilled care, the HCFA added the daily cost of supplies, drugs, and the interdisciplinary group ($8.58), arriving at a total of $53.43 in 1982 dollars. These 1982 costs were updated to 1984 costs by means of a market basket index that measures the changes in the prices of goods and services purchased by SNFs, yielding a per diem rate of $58.24. Federal regulations permit hospices to charge Medicare patients 5 percent of the Medicare rate paid by the HCFA as co-insurance.[52] The Medicare cost of respite care calculated at a per diem rate of $58.24 is therefore reduced by 5 percent ($2.91) to reflect this co-payment. The prospective rate used by the Medicare program to pay for respite care during 1984 was $55.33.

General Inpatient Care

Federal regulations define general inpatient hospice care as care provided in an inpatient facility "for pain control or acute or chronic symptom management which cannot be managed in other settings."[53] The general inpatient care rate is paid for the day of admission into inpatient care, but the appropriate home care rate is paid for the day of discharge. If the patient dies during inpatient care, the inpatient rate is paid for the day of the patient's death. The total number of days of inpatient care (general plus respite) for which a hospice is reimbursed cannot exceed 20 percent of the total number of days of care that the hospice provides to its patients during a twelve-month period. For days in excess of this 20 percent limit, the hospice is reimbursed at the routine home care rate.

The HCFA used 1981 costs to calculate the preliminary Medicare rate for general inpatient hospice care.[54] The major cost centers were the daily operating costs of routine, hospital-based hospice care ($171) and the cost of ancillary services ($45). Adjustment of these total 1981 costs ($216) to 1984 levels yielded a per diem rate of $271 for general inpatient hospice care. When the HCFA recalculated these rates on the basis of 1982 cost data, however, it projected a lower per diem rate for 1984 of $255. The HCFA decided to use the higher $271 per diem rate, since the Medicare inpatient rate was based on the routine operating costs of a hospital-based hospice and hospices that are not hospital-based may have to arrange for inpatient care with hospitals at a higher rate than the cost of this care to hospitals.

Wage Adjustments

The federal regulations implementing Medicare reimbursement for hospice care permit adjustments in the payment rates for each of the four types of care to reflect geographical differences in labor costs.[55] The HCFA determined that 68.71 percent of the routine home care rate, 68.71 percent of the continuous home care rate, 61.26 percent of the inpatient respite care rate (the SNF cost component), and 80.77 percent of the general inpatient care rate are subject to adjustments to reflect geographical wage differences. The wage indexes used to adjust the hospice care rates are the same wage indexes used to adjust the Medicare diagnosis-related group prospective payment rates for inpatient hospital care.[56] In applying these wage indexes to hospice care rates, the HCFA decided not to apply an index lower than 0.8, even if a geographical area had wage costs below that level. The HCFA reasoned "that hospices will need to attract and retain sufficient skilled staff to provide the hospice benefit" and using a wage adjustment factor below 0.8 "will unduly jeopardize the availability of the benefit in these areas."[57]

OUTLOOK

Unless extended by Congress, Medicare reimbursement of hospice care will be available only until September 30, 1986. Therefore, the major uncertainty facing hospice programs in the future is the willingness of Congress to extend Medicare coverage. Also, Congress directed the secretary of HHS to make recommendations for changes in the hospice benefits. Since the average length of stay in hospice programs is shorter than the benefit period, the secretary may recommend a reduction in the number of covered days.

An issue of immediate importance to hospice organizations concerns the final level of the 1984 prospective rates that the Medicare program will use to pay for routine home hospice care. The HCFA reduced the payment rate for routine home care from the preliminary rate of $53.17 per day to the final rate of $46.25 per day. In December 1983, the National Hospice Organization was considering a challenge to this final rate in federal court.[58] By February 1984, however, the consensus of that organization's membership was to pursue legislative action in the Congress rather than to seek judicial action to increase the per diem rate for routine home care. At that time, the organization had no plans to challenge in court the decrease in the per diem rate for inpatient respite care.

Medicare reimbursement of hospice care is likely to be affected by the apparent reluctance of hospices to participate in the Medicare program. According to the National Association for Home Care, only 121 hospices had applied for Medicare certification by early 1984.[59] This reluctance to participate was attributed to the low Medicare payment rates and the prohibition against subcontracting for the delivery of core services. P.L. 98-369, signed by President Reagan on July 18, 1981, permits the secretary of HHS to waive the nursing care core services requirement for rural hospices in operation before January 1, 1983. Also, the law requires the secretary "to study the necessity and appropriateness of the 'core services' requirement, . . . and report the findings to Congress, prior to January 1, 1986." The HCFA announced that it had completed surveys of 150 hospices, with 34 more scheduled for survey and eight approved for participation. The HCFA added that 254 additional hospices responded to its query about applying for survey "and that only a small number . . . [of these 254 hospices] said that they did not want to be surveyed."[60] The HCFA had initially contacted approximately 1,500 hospices.

In a postscript on the cost-effectiveness of hospice care, the Hospice Council for Northern Ohio compared the cost of care delivered to cancer patients by hospices with the cost of similar care in the traditional health care system.[61] It was found that the average third party payment for care was $1,067 for hospice care during the terminal phase and $2,156 for traditional care during the last two weeks of life. The study also reported that, during the last 12 weeks of life, hospice patients spent less time in hospitals but utilized more home health care services than did patients receiving traditional care. The Hospice Council for Northern Ohio noted that this saved approximately 40 percent on the cost of care and illustrated that hospice care was not simply an additional health care expenditure, but instead replaced traditional patterns of health care.

NOTES

1. 48 Fed. Reg. 56,008 (December 16, 1983).

2. P.L. 97-248, §122.

3. COMM. ON WAYS AND MEANS, THE MEDICARE, UNEMPLOYMENT COMPENSATION, AND PUBLIC ASSISTANCE AMENDMENTS OF 1982 (WMCP: 97-35), 97th Cong., 2d Sess. 22 (1982).

4. 42 C.F.R. §418.20.

5. 42 C.F.R. §418.3.

6. *See supra*, note 3, p.15.

7. 42 C.F.R. §418.24.

8. 42 C.F.R. §418.26.
9. 42 C.F.R. §418.28.
10. 42 C.F.R. §418.30.
11. 42 C.F.R. §418.50.
12. 42 C.F.R. §418.52.
13. 42 C.F.R. §418.54.
14. 42 C.F.R. §418.56.
15. 42 C.F.R. §418.58.
16. 42 C.F.R. §418.66.
17. See supra, note 3, p. 21.
18. 42 C.F.R. §418.60.
19. 42 C.F.R. §418.68.
20. 42 C.F.R. §418.70.
21. 42 C.F.R. §418.80.
22. 42 C.F.R. §418.82.
23. 42 C.F.R. §418.84.
24. 42 C.F.R. §418.86.
25. 42 C.F.R. §418.88.
26. 42 C.F.R. §418.204.
27. See supra, note 3, p. 20.
28. 42 C.F.R. §418.92.
29. 42 C.F.R. §418.94.
30. 42 C.F.R. §418.96.
31. 42 C.F.R. §418.98.
32. 42 C.F.R. §418.100.
33. Comments on the Legislative Intent of Medicare's Hospice Care Benefit, letter to Representative Bill Archer, No. HRD-83-72, July 12, 1983. In MEDICARE AND MEDICAID GUIDE, 33,038.
34. Id.
35. See supra, note 3, p. 18.
36. Id.
37. HOUSE COMM. ON WAYS AND MEANS, MEDICARE HOSPICE REIMBURSEMENT AMENDMENT, H. R. No. 98-333, 98th Cong., 1st Sess., p. 2 (1983).
38. P.L. 98-90.
39. See supra, note 37, p. 3.
40. 42 C.F.R. §418.302.
41. 48 Fed. Reg. 56,008 (December 16, 1983).
42. See supra, note 33.
43. 48 Fed. Reg. 56,016 (December 16, 1983).
44. 48 Fed. Reg. 38,146 (August 22, 1983).
45. 42 C.F.R. §418.302.
46. 48 Fed. Reg. 56,008 (December 16, 1983).
47. 42 C.F.R. §418.302.

48. *Id.*
49. 42 C.F.R. §418.204.
50. 42 C.F.R. §418.302.
51. 48 Fed. Reg. 56,008 (December 16, 1983).
52. 42 C.F.R. §418.400.
53. 42 C.F.R. §418.302.
54. 48 Fed. Reg. 56,008 (December 16, 1983).
55. 42 C.F.R. §418.306.
56. 48 Fed. Reg. 39,871-39,875 (September 1, 1983).
57. 48 Fed. Reg. 56,022 (December 16, 1983).
58. *U.S. to Set Rates for Hospice Care Below Earlier Plan*, Wall Street Journal, December 15, 1983, p. 12.
59. Report Letter, No. 415, MEDICARE AND MEDICAID GUIDE, p. 4.
60. *Id.*
61. Report Letter, No. 408, MEDICARE AND MEDICAID GUIDE, p. 8. This update summarizes the report "Cost Savings of Hospice Care to Third Party Insurers" issued by the Hospice Council for Northern Ohio, Cleveland, Ohio.

Chapter 5

Medicare: End-Stage Renal Disease

The Social Security Amendments of 1972[1] authorized the creation of the end-stage renal disease (ESRD) program under Medicare. These amendments extended Medicare coverage to individuals of any age who require either kidney dialysis or transplantation because of permanent kidney failure and meet certain other eligibility requirements. In order to be eligible for ESRD program benefits under Medicare, a person must be undergoing a regular course of renal dialysis or have had a kidney transplant, must be insured under Social Security at the onset of the disease, and must be either a monthly Social Security beneficiary or the spouse or dependent child of an eligible person.[2]

ESRD, which is the failure of the kidneys to eliminate toxic wastes from the body, afflicts about 70,000 Americans. The disease is fatal unless the patient receives a kidney transplant or undergoes regular dialysis treatments. Most patients begin dialysis while hospitalized for acute kidney failure. After their condition has stabilized, they may be treated as outpatients. Outpatient dialysis treatments may be received at a hospital-based facility, an independent dialysis facility, or at home. Approximately 17 percent of all dialysis patients receive treatment at home, which is substantially less expensive than the other types of dialysis. The remaining 83 percent of all dialysis patients receive treatment in a facility, with 47 percent of these being treated in a hospital and 53 percent being treated in independent facilities.[3]

ESRD MEDICARE PROGRAM

Federal regulations prescribe four objectives for the ESRD program under Medicare:

1. to assist Medicare beneficiaries with ESRD in receiving the care they need

2. to encourage the proper distribution and the effective utilization of ESRD treatment resources while maintaining or improving the quality of care
3. to provide the flexibility necessary for the efficient delivery of appropriate care by facilities and physicians
4. to encourage transplantation or self-dialysis for the maximum practical number of patients who are medically, socially, and psychologically suitable candidates for these treatments[4]

Definitions

ESRD is that stage of renal impairment that appears irreversible and permanent, requiring a regular dialysis program or kidney transplant to maintain life.[5] Federal Medicare regulations recognize three major categories of ESRD services: (1) transplantation services, (2) dialysis services, and (3) self-dialysis and home dialysis training services. There are three subcategories of dialysis services: inpatient dialysis provided to an ESRD patient who is temporarily hospitalized because of a medical need; outpatient dialysis, either staff-assisted dialysis or self-dialysis, at a renal dialysis center or facility; and home dialysis.

Federal Medicare regulations recognize five different types of ESRD facilities:[6]

1. a renal transplantation center, which is a hospital unit approved to furnish surgical and other support services for transplantation. This center must also furnish inpatient dialysis services, or it must have an arrangement with another facility to furnish them.
2. a renal dialysis center, which is a hospital unit approved to furnish the full range of diagnostic, therapeutic, and rehabilitative services needed in the care of ESRD dialysis patients.
3. a renal dialysis facility, either free-standing or hospital-based, which is a unit approved to furnish dialysis services directly to Medicare beneficiaries.
4. a self-dialysis unit, which is a part of either of the three previously described facilities. This unit allows patients, after they have completed an appropriate course of training, to perform the dialysis with little or no professional assistance.
5. a special purpose renal dialysis facility. This type of facility furnishes dialysis services at special locations on a short-term basis to a group of ESRD patients who would otherwise be unable to receive treatment. The special locations must be either special rehabilitative (including

vacation) locations for ESRD patients who are temporarily in residence or locations in need of ESRD facilities for emergencies.

ESRD Network

Federal Medicare regulations require the secretary of the Department of Health and Human Services (HHS) to designate ESRD network areas, each serving a minimum population of 3.5 million people and including at least two renal transplantation centers.[7] The secretary may designate a network area of less than 3.5 million people or with a single renal transplantation center when necessary to achieve ESRD program objectives.[8] The secretary is also required by Medicare regulations to designate a network coordinating council for each network area.[9] Each ESRD facility is "requested" to send a representative to this council. The council's responsibilities include describing and reviewing the ESRD services available in the network area, estimating the future need for ESRD services in the area, and providing this information to the secretary so that it can be used in making decisions on certification of ESRD facilities within the network area.

CONDITIONS OF PARTICIPATION

Federal regulations list a range of conditions that the various renal dialysis providers must meet to participate in the Medicare program.

Utilization and Provider Status

For the purposes of Medicare reimbursement, ESRD facilities are classified according to their utilization rates. On the basis of these rates, the secretary of HHS grants an ESRD facility either unconditional status, conditional status, or the secretary may determine that the facility is not eligible for Medicare reimbursement.[10] An ESRD facility on conditional status is given a period of time to increase its utilization levels to achieve unconditional status or risk exclusion from Medicare reimbursement. Exceptional status is granted at the secretary's discretion when the provider's utilization rate does not meet the minimum acceptable rate, because of its location in an area with a small population base, but its absence would adversely affect the achievement of ESRD program objectives in the area. The ESRD facilities participating in the Medicare program must report their utilization rates for the most recent year of operation and for each of the preceding two calendar years.[11] For purposes of classification, the secretary uses either the utilization rate for the preceding twelve months or the average rate for the preceding two calendar years, whichever is higher.[12]

A renal transplantation center must perform 15 or more kidney transplants each year to achieve unconditional status and 7 to 14 transplants per year to achieve conditional status.[13] A dialysis center or facility that is located within a standard metropolitan statistical area (SMSA) of 500,000 people or more and performs more than 20 percent of its dialyses on outpatients must have 6 or more dialysis stations, and each must perform a minimal average of 4.5 dialyses per week to achieve unconditional status. The same center or facility is given conditional status if it has 6 or more dialysis stations with each performing an average of 4 to 4.5 dialyses per week, or 4 or 5 dialysis stations with each performing a minimal average of 4.5 dialyses per week.

Any facility that is located outside an SMSA or in an SMSA of less than 500,000 people and performs more than 20 percent of its dialyses on outpatients must have 3 or more dialysis stations with each performing a minimal average of 4 dialyses per week to achieve unconditional status. The same facility is given conditional status if it has 2 dialysis stations with each performing a minimal average of 4 or more dialyses per week. A renal dialysis center that performs 20 percent or less of its dialyses on outpatients is given unconditional status if it has 3 or more dialysis stations, provided that each performs a minimal average of 4 dialyses per week. This same renal dialysis center has conditional status if it has 2 dialysis stations, and each performs a minimal average of 4 dialyses per week.

As defined by Medicare regulations, a renal transplantation center and a renal dialysis center must both be units of a hospital.[14] They qualify for Medicare participation under the ESRD program only if the hospital to which they are attached is also an approved provider under Medicare.[15]

Service Needs

The ESRD facility must demonstrate that its services are needed in the network area as a condition for participation in Medicare.[16] It must be shown that there are patients in the network area who need ESRD treatments and that no other qualified provider can meet these needs. These regulations also apply to any expansion of an ESRD facility's treatment capacity.

In the case of *Dialysis Centers, Ltd. v. Schweiker*,[17] a Medicare-approved operator of four kidney dialysis facilities in the Chicago area brought action in federal court seeking to enjoin the secretary's "wrongful" approval of another dialysis facility, which had been requested by Dr. Walid Ghantous, in the Chicago area. Dr. Ghantous had requested advance approval from HHS for an ESRD facility with twenty-eight dialysis stations to serve patients from the suburban area north of Chicago. Network 15, the ESRD network for Illinois, recommended that the secretary of HHS approve the facility, but limit the number of dialysis stations. Approval was eventually given by HHS for a six-station facility on March 26, 1979. Construction was begun on the northwest side of Chicago.

The plaintiff alleged that Network 15 had given advance approval for a facility to serve the suburban area north of Chicago, not the northwest area of Chicago. Hence, the plaintiff argued failure to approve the facility without a new inquiry and a resubmission to Network 15 was arbitrary and capricious, was an abuse of discretion, and violated the relevant statute, regulations, and agency practices. Also, the plaintiff asserted that it would suffer irreparable harm through loss of patients, revenue, and invested capital if the approval of the new facility were permitted to stand. The plaintiff also argued that the agency's wrongful approval violated the plaintiff's due process rights under the Fifth Amendment. The district court dismissed the complaint on the ground that the court lacked jurisdiction on the subject matter.

The plaintiff appealed to the U.S. Court of Appeals, which upheld the district court decision. The appellate court ruled that neither the Social Security Act nor the implementing regulations give an ESRD facility the right to challenge the secretary's approval of another facility under the ESRD program. The court further ruled that no such right is conferred on the plaintiff by the Administrative Procedure Act (APA), since, in order to have standing to sue under the APA, a plaintiff must demonstrate that it has suffered or will suffer an injury and that the alleged injury is within the area of interest regulated by the statute that allegedly has been violated. The court reasoned that, even assuming the plaintiff's loss of patients was sufficient to constitute an injury in fact,

> it is not an injury to an interest intended to be protected by the ESRD program. The stated objectives and obvious purposes of the program are to provide needed treatment to persons suffering from chronic renal disease and to do so as efficiently as possible.[18]

The court of appeals also dismissed Dialysis Center's constitutional arguments. The plaintiff asserted that its business investment had been made in the belief that it would be insulated from competition for patients because the secretary would approve additional ESRD facilities only if it were shown that additional services were needed. The court rejected this expectation as the basis for the due process challenge to the secretary's approval of competing providers because the

> plaintiff concedes that there is no contractual basis, express or implied for its expectation and, as we have already noted, the statute manifests no Congressional intent to protect the financial interests of health care providers. Moreover, plaintiff plainly has no

justifiable expectation or protectable property interest in the continued treatment of specific federally qualified patients, who are free to seek treatment at any approved facility regardless of its location.[19]

The court of appeals thus affirmed the decision of the district court that the plaintiff had not stated a claim upon which relief could be granted.

Administration

Federal regulations require that, in order to participate in the Medicare ESRD program, an ESRD facility must be under the control of an identifiable governing body or designated individuals who have legal authority to administer operations.[20] In addition, the facility must be a member of the network coordinating council and must provide acceptable representation to the council.[21] The ESRD facility and personnel must comply with all applicable federal, state, and local laws and regulations.[22]

Medicare regulations require each facility to have a written long-term program and a written care plan for each patient to ensure that each receives the appropriate type of renal care.[23] The long-term program must specify whether dialysis or kidney transplantation is the appropriate objective of care and which dialysis setting (e.g., home, hospital, self-care, etc.) is preferred for each patient. The patient care plan is based on the nature of the patient's illness, the treatment prescribed, and an assessment of the patient's needs.

The governing board of the ESRD facility must adopt written policies stating the rights and responsibilities of patients.[24] The facility's chief executive officer is responsible for implementing these patient policies. Patients must be fully informed not only of their rights, but also of the services available at the facility, any charges not covered by Medicare, and their medical condition (unless medically contraindicated). Patients must be given the opportunity to participate in planning their treatments and to refuse to participate in experimental research.

Medicare regulations require the ESRD facility to maintain complete medical records on all patients whose care is supervised by its staff, including patients in a self-dialysis unit and patients on home dialysis.[25] A member of the facility's staff must be designated to supervise the medical records, and all records must be kept and preserved in accordance with professional standards and practices.

A renal dialysis facility, which is not required by Medicare regulations to be hospital-based, must have a written agreement with a renal dialysis center, which is required by Medicare regulations to be hospital-based, to provide inpatient care and other hospital services when needed by patients of the renal dialysis facility.[26] Patients are transferred between the two types of ESRD facilities when the attending physician determines it is medically appropriate. Within one working day, the patient long-term program, the patient care plan, and other information useful in the treatment of the patient must be provided to the new ESRD facility.

Staff and Services

Treatment at a renal dialysis facility or a renal dialysis center must be supervised by a director who is a physician.[27] The director need not be a full-time employee, but must plan, organize, conduct, and direct the delivery of ESRD services. The director may also serve as the chief executive officer of the facility. The dialysis facility must have at least one full-time registered nurse responsible for nursing services. Whenever patients are undergoing dialysis, a physician, a registered nurse, or a licensed practical nurse experienced in providing ESRD care must oversee patient care. Also, an "adequate" number of personnel must be present so that the patient/staff ratio is "appropriate" to the level of dialysis care needed.[28] If the facility offers self-care dialysis training, a qualified nurse must be in charge of training.

A renal dialysis facility or a renal dialysis center must provide all the staff and services necessary to perform institutional dialysis. If self-dialysis services are offered, the facility or center must provide all supplies, equipment, and services specified in the patient care policies. In addition, laboratory, social, and dietetic services must be provided to meet the ESRD patient's needs.[29] Laboratory tests must be performed at a Medicare-approved hospital or Medicare-approved independent laboratory, although hematocrit and clotting time tests used to monitor a patient's fluid incident to each dialysis treatment may be performed by the trained staff of the ESRD facility under the direction of a physician. Social services must be provided to help patients and their families adjust to their medical condition; dietetic services, to ensure that the patients have a therapeutic diet that meets the special dietary needs of dialysis patients must also be provided. Medicare regulations state also that ESRD services must be provided in a physical environment that is functional, sanitary, safe, and comfortable for the patients, the staff, and the public.[30]

REIMBURSEMENT LEGISLATION

On July 1, 1973, the Medicare ESRD program began with approximately 11,000 beneficiaries. Studies indicate that the ESRD program has been successful in protecting patients with kidney failure from the catastrophic costs of life-saving care,[31] but the high and rapidly escalating costs of the

ESRD program have placed a burden on the Medicare trust fund. In 1974, the program paid approximately $229 million for dialysis, transplantation, and other services received by Medicare patients. In 1979, there were approximately 42,500 Medicare patients receiving dialysis at a cost of almost $1 billion. By 1985, an estimated 83,800 Medicare patients will receive ESRD program benefits, with payments approaching an estimated $1.6 billion. The annual growth rates in Medicare expenditures for the ESRD program have been high, especially during the 1970s when spending increases exceeded 20 percent annually (see Table I-2).

The End-Stage Renal Disease Program Amendments of 1978[32] were passed primarily to alleviate the problem of these rapidly escalating expenditures. The amendments directed the Health Care Financing Administration (HCFA) to establish methods and procedures for determining the costs incurred by kidney dialysis facilities and to develop a prospective payment method, calculated on a cost-related or other equitable basis, for services provided to ESRD program beneficiaries. Congress wanted this prospective payment mechanism to contain incentives to encourage the efficient and cost-effective delivery of renal dialysis services.

The Omnibus Budget Reconciliation Act of 1981[33] required the HCFA to develop a prospective payment method for outpatient maintenance dialysis that would promote home dialysis. This act required the HCFA, in establishing the prospective mechanism, either to set composite rates for home dialysis and facility dialysis or to develop another method to encourage the utilization of home dialysis.

REIMBURSEMENT REGULATIONS

Reasonable Cost Payments

Prior to the establishment of prospective rates, the Medicare program paid for dialysis services on a retrospective, reasonable cost basis. A hospital-based dialysis facility was paid 80 percent of its reasonable costs, as determined under Medicare's definition of reasonable cost. An independent, or free-standing, dialysis facility was reimbursed 80 percent of the reasonable charge per treatment, as determined under Medicare reimbursement principles on reasonable charges.[34] The remaining 20 percent of the costs was the responsibility of the Medicare patient.

The Medicare payment to both free-standing and hospital-based facilities could not exceed a ceiling of $138 per treatment. This limit did not include the cost of physician services for direct patient care. If a facility included the costs of routine physician services in its expenses for dialysis treatments, the ceiling was raised $12 to $150 per treatment. In addition, the HCFA allowed an extra $20 per treatment for sessions that included training in self-dialysis. Both free-standing and hospital-based facilities could be exempted from these payment limits if they submitted documentation that their costs were higher than the ceiling. For example, an exemption was granted to a facility that served a more seriously ill patient population than average or that had higher costs because of its geographical location.

On December 30, 1977, the secretary of HHS published a series of interim regulations that established the criteria for determining reasonable charges under the ESRD program. Reasonable charges for renal dialysis and kidney transplantation were defined "in terms related to charges or costs prior to July 1, 1973, and to costs and allowances that are reasonable when treatments are provided in an effective and economical manner."[35] The secretary linked the "reasonable charge" required by the Medicare statute to cost because Congress did not define reasonable charge in the statute, saying only that it should not exceed the customary or prevailing charge.[36]

In *Schupak d/b/a Queens Artificial Kidney Center v. Califano*,[37] a provider of outpatient dialysis services sought a preliminary injunction in federal district court to enjoin the secretary from (1) considering cost information in determining the plaintiff's reimbursement rate, (2) requiring the submission of data on the costs of providing dialysis services, and (3) suspending the plaintiff's reimbursement for failure to submit the requested cost information. The provider alleged that the regulations linking reimbursement to costs were illegal because the method was not based on the customary or prevailing charges specified in the statute and, therefore, the secretary had exceeded his authority in developing this method. The provider also asserted that the regulations not only were arbitrary and capricious, but also violated the plaintiff's constitutional right to due process.

In deciding this case, the court referred to *Schupak v. Mathews*,[38] an earlier case in which the plaintiff had challenged the same reimbursement formula defined in earlier regulations. In that case, the court had upheld the substantive validity of the reimbursement formula and the authority of the secretary to relate reasonable charges to costs, on the ground that linking reasonable charges to the cost of services was fully consistent with the intent of Congress. This decision was upheld by the U.S. Court of Appeals for the District of Columbia.

In the case at hand, the court agreed with the earlier decision and concluded

> that the rate of reimbursement for ESRD services and the authority of the Secretary to relate reasonable charge to cost are in full conformity with the mandates of the Social Security Act and the expectations of Congress when it enacted the ESRD program.[39]

Disagreeing with the plaintiff, the court further reasoned that the fact that Congress mentioned only the customary and prevailing charge in the statute could not be "construed as prohibiting the Secretary from prescribing additional criteria, e.g., costs, when [the customary and prevailing factors] do not produce valid results."[40] The court noted that the secretary had the responsibility not only to conserve Medicare funds, but also to protect the resources of Medicare patients who are responsible for 20 percent of the charges. Finally, the court referred to the legislative history of the ESRD amendments and quoted Senator Russell Long:

> with respect to the coverage of kidney dialysis and transplantation, the Secretary would have the authority to define reasonable charges in terms related to the reasonable costs of the treatment provided ... since obtaining customary and prevailing charges for new and complex procedures—many of which will be reimbursed in all instances by the program—would be quite difficult administratively.[41]

The reimbursement formula was upheld.

Before prospective rates were set for dialysis services, the Medicare program used a number of variations to pay for home dialysis.[42] The reason for these variations was that providers could be reimbursed separately for the major components of home dialysis (e.g., supplies, support services, and equipment), whereas these components were lumped together when the Medicare program paid for facility dialysis. The Medicare program sometimes paid for home dialysis under an optional Target Rate Reimbursement Agreement. The ESRD Program Amendments of 1978 (P.L. 95-292) required the HCFA to establish target reimbursement rates for home dialysis for each calendar year. The maximum target rate was limited by statute "to no more than 70 percent of the national average payment for infacility maintenance dialysis services furnished by approved hospital-based and independent facilities during the preceding fiscal year, as adjusted for regional variations and before application of the deductible and coinsurance requirements."[43] If this agreement were used, a dialysis provider furnished all supplies, support services, and equipment to its home dialysis patients and received 80 percent of the comprehensive target rate per treatment from Medicare. Under another payment method, patients or providers were allowed to bill the Medicare program directly for home dialysis equipment and supplies, and Medicare reimbursed them for these costs at 80 percent. Similarly, a free-standing facility, a hospital-based facility, or a state agency may have provided equipment and supplies, receiving payment from Medicare at 80 percent of their costs. Finally, providers may have been reimbursed at 100 percent of the cost of home dialysis equipment if the provider or the state program had an agreement in effect with the HCFA.[44]

Prospective Rate Setting

On February 12, 1982, the HCFA announced preliminary regulations to implement a prospective method for determining Medicare payments for dialysis services.[45] Under the proposed regulations, the Medicare program would establish a prospective rate-setting system for dialysis services in which composite rates were calculated for home and facility treatments. Different rates were to be established for hospital-based and free-standing facilities. Each facility would receive a predetermined payment rate per treatment, adjusted to reflect geographical differences in the cost of labor. The average adjusted payment per treatment for free-standing facilities would be $128; that for hospital-based facilities would be $132. The facility would receive the same rate per treatment for dialysis provided on its own premises as for dialysis provided at the patient's home.

There were to be no year end adjustments to guarantee that the provider recovered its allowable, reasonable costs. If a facility's cost per treatment was less than its Medicare payment, it would retain this difference. If the facility's cost per treatment exceeded the Medicare payment, it would not be able to recover these excess costs unless it was granted an exception. Exceptions to these rates would be granted because of an atypical patient mix, extraordinary circumstances, or medical or paramedical education costs; an exception would also be granted if the provider was an isolated and essential facility.

To calculate the costs of dialysis in facilities, the HCFA selected a sample of 110 facilities from a universe of 825 ESRD facilities that provided in-facility outpatient dialysis services. This universe of providers did not include Veterans Administration and Public Health Service Hospitals, or hospital units without dialysis outpatients.[46] The facilities were then divided into hospital-based (70) and free-standing facilities (40), and these groups were arrayed according to annual costs reported on the Renal Disease Facility Cost and Statistical Questionnaire. These cost reports were then audited by Medicare intermediaries under the supervision of HCFA representatives.

The audited costs were adjusted to exclude cost items not allowed under Medicare regulations. The most significant adjustment to the audited costs of free-standing providers involved compensation to administrators and medical directors. The HCFA set a limit on this compensation at $32,000 per year. The most significant adjustment to the audited costs of hospital-based providers concerned the costs of supplies. The adjustments to costs included adding a factor for routine ESRD laboratory costs for free-standing facilities that did not report these expenses. The preliminary median adjusted cost of free-standing facilities was $108 per treatment, ranging from a low of $80 per treatment to a high of $214 per treatment. The median cost of hospital-based facilities was $135 per treatment with a range of $86 to $277.[47]

After the audits were completed and expenses adjusted, the total costs of each facility were divided by the number of outpatient treatments to yield a cost per treatment. The HCFA calculated for each facility a ratio of labor costs to total costs and applied this ratio to the facility's cost per treatment to yield the labor cost per treatment. To reflect geographical wage differences, the labor cost per treatment was adjusted by the appropriate area wage index.

The sample used to calculate the cost of home dialysis was composed of twenty-three facilities and two state programs, or less than 5 percent of the total number of ESRD facilities that had home dialysis programs. The sample included ten of the thirteen largest home dialysis programs and represented almost 30 percent of all home dialysis patients, however. The facilities in the sample were located in fifteen states and represented all ten of the HHS regions. Representatives of the HHS audit agency visited each of these facilities and reviewed its costs in order to determine the average cost per treatment of home dialysis and to divide these costs into labor and nonlabor components. Because of time constraints, it was not possible to determine if all costs were reasonable and allowable under Medicare principles. The weighted cost per treatment for home dialysis was $97, with $12 per treatment in labor costs and $85 per treatment in nonlabor costs.

To determine the preliminary prospective rate, composites of the home dialysis cost per treatment and the in-facility dialysis (both free-standing and hospital-based facilities) cost per treatment were calculated. The use of composite rates was designed to promote home dialysis, since Medicare would reimburse less expensive home dialysis at the same rate as the in-facility dialysis, thus creating incentives to use less costly methods of treatment. The composite rates were calculated by adjusting the cost per treatment of home and in-facility dialysis by a factor representing the proportion of patients undergoing dialysis at each location. The HCFA used the percentage of home dialysis patients served by hospitals to calculate the composite rate for hospital-based facilities and the percentage of home dialysis patients served by free-standing facilities to calculate the composite rate for free-standing facilities.

To the composite rate for hospital-based facilities an adjustment of $2.10 per treatment was added to reflect the overhead costs of the hospital; furthermore, 105 percent of the median cost was used because the HCFA reasoned that the prospective method may not have captured all the costs of the hospital in providing dialysis services. Both the hospital-based and free-standing facility rates were adjusted by an area wage index, resulting in a range of prospective payment rates. The HCFA thus proposed prospective rates per treatment for free-standing facilities ranging from $109 to $143, with an average of $128. The proposed prospective rates per treatment for hospital-based facilities ranged from $114 to $146, with an average of $132.

When the HCFA announced the final regulations on May 11, 1983, the application of the most recent wage index and the refinement of the prospective method resulted in the average rate per treatment for free-standing facilities falling to $127 and the average rate for hospital-based facilities falling to $131.[48] The new prospective rate-setting regulations became effective on August 1, 1983.

When calculating these payment rates, the HCFA excluded a return on net equity to proprietary providers as an allowable cost under the prospective methodology.[49] Congress gave the secretary of HHS the option of including a return on net equity in making payments to ESRD facilities, but the HCFA reasoned that including a return on equity in the rate would weaken the efficiency incentives of the prospective payment method. Under the prospective rate-setting system, a proprietary provider has the opportunity to earn a profit by keeping expenses below the payment rate. In addition, the HCFA stated that the "new prospective rate structure offers substantial opportunity for additional profit" through transfer of patients to less costly home dialysis.[50]

OUTLOOK

On August 2, 1983, the National Association of Patients on Hemodialysis and Transplantation (NAPHT) filed suit against the secretary of HHS, seeking a preliminary injunction barring the implementation of the prospective method to set Medicare payments for dialysis services.[51] In Count I of the complaint, the NAPHT sought to prevent implementation of the Medicare prospective reimbursement regulations developed by HHS.[52] The NAPHT contended that the prospective system is based on incorrect data concerning the costs of dialysis services and incorrect assumptions about the ability of providers to alter their costs and their patient mix. The plaintiffs argued that, because of these and other defects, the new prospective system is not only arbitrary and capricious, but also violates congressional intent that the payment system promote the efficient, economical, and equitable delivery of dialysis services.

In Count II, the plaintiffs sought to prevent implementation of the Medicare secondary payment regulations,[53] which make employer group health plans the primary payor of benefits for a patient's initial twelve months of eligibility for ESRD program benefits. The regulations state that a Medicare intermediary or carrier is to pay conditional primary benefits only if it "knows from experience or ascertains that" the payments by the employer plan "are substantially less prompt than Medicare's."[54] The NAPHT alleged that the Omnibus Budget Reconciliation Act of 1981 requires Medicare to make conditional primary payments except when an employer group health plan has made payments or when the secretary has determined in advance that payment under an employer group health plan will be as prompt as if the payment were made by Medicare. The plaintiffs argued that the secondary payor regulations do not provide for such determinations and are in conflict with the statute.

In seeking to prevent implementation of the prospective reimbursement regulations (Count I), the NAPHT presented a four-pronged challenge. As summarized by the court, the plaintiffs alleged:

> (1) that the rate setting methodology does not account for barriers to increased home dialysis; (2) that the composite rates are based on inadequate cost information; (3) that the exceptions process erroneously excludes a return on equity; and (4) that the system of reimbursement for physicians is irrationally based and contrary to Congressional intent. In addition, plaintiffs contend that the regulations should provide for a phase-in period.[55]

In the first prong of its attack on the prospective reimbursement regulations, the NAPHT argued that four factors raised barriers to increased home dialysis. First, established patterns of patient referral constrain the ability of many providers to expand home dialysis services. The plaintiffs contended, for example, that free-standing dialysis facilities obtain new patients by referral from general hospitals that have treated these patients for acute kidney failure. Since these hospitals have their own outpatient dialysis facilities, they will attempt to maximize their own number of home dialysis patients in order to take advantage of the incentives built into the prospective composite rate. As a consequence, the plaintiffs maintained, few suitable candidates for home dialysis will be referred to free-standing dialysis facilities, while referrals of patients needing in-facility dialysis will increase.

Second, according to the plaintiffs, the efforts of many providers to increase the number of patients who use home dialysis services are thwarted by certificate-of-need regulations. At least twenty-three states require that providers obtain certificate-of-need approval before they begin home dialysis training programs. The NAPHT asserted that, at best, this process will delay the initiation of home dialysis services for as long as a year and, at worst, will prevent their initiation altogether.

Third, the plaintiffs argued that home dialysis is not a realistic alternative to in-facility treatments for many urban dialysis centers that serve a predominantly poor and inner city patient population. Home dialysis may not be feasible for these patients because they have no spouse or other relative to assist with dialysis treatments, the utility services needed to operate the dialysis equipment are unpredictable, there is not enough space in their home to accommodate the equipment, and they resist dietary restrictions.

Fourth, the plaintiffs submitted that, once patients are accustomed to in-facility dialysis, they "strongly" resist transfer to a home dialysis training program. Given the difficulty of attracting primary home dialysis patients through referral, the NAPHT argued that patient resistance to converting to home dialysis will create additional problems for providers attempting to expand the number of their home dialysis patients. The plaintiffs contended that, since the Medicare composite rate is set below the cost of in-facility treatment, providers unable to expand their number of home dialysis patients will suffer financially. They further maintained that the failure of HHS to adjust the composite rates to compensate for these four barriers to home dialysis makes the regulations arbitrary and capricious.

The defendants responded that Congress was aware of these factors when it instructed HHS to adopt a single reimbursement rate structure for in-facility and home dialysis that was based on the cost experiences of the more efficient providers. Also, Congress assumed that the proportion of home dialysis patients could be increased over time and that the Medicare reimbursement system should encourage this conversion to home dialysis. The defendants argued that the reimbursement regulations rationally implement the statute and that, in reality, the plaintiffs' challenge is to the statute itself. In addition, the defendants pointed out that, although they estimate that 30 to 40 percent of the patient population can undergo dialysis at home, only 17 percent now do so.

Considering this first assault on the prospective reimbursement regulations, the district court decided that

> [t]he rulemaking record reflects that, in developing the reimbursement regulations, HHS considered plaintiffs' concerns, ... and was sensitive to the needs of patients and providers, while mindful of the serious financial problems confronting the ESRD program. In short, HHS has sought to implement Congress' desire for increased efficiencies and strong incentives for home dialysis by setting the composite rate between the in-facility costs per treatment of some facilities ....The Court is persuaded by defendants' argument that to adjust the composite rate to accommodate those facilities would run counter to the Congressional purpose: to increase incentives for home dialysis at the very facilities where the percentage of home patients have been low.[56]

The district court agreed with the NAPHT that individualized adjustments to the composite rate or exceptions for providers unable to break even under the composite rate might ease the transition toward increased home dialysis. The court ruled, however, that "the regulations are not arbitrary and capricious for omitting these particular features."[57]

In the second prong of its attack on the prospective reimbursement regulations, the NAPHT asserted that the composite rates are arbitrary and capricious because they are based on outdated, unreliable, and incomplete data. The plaintiffs argued that the composite rates are based on cost data for dialysis facilities from 1977 through 1979, which contradicts the intent of Congress that reimbursement be based on the costs incurred by providers; the plaintiffs claimed that these cost data should have been adjusted for inflation or updated. The NAPHT further maintained that the cost data used by the HCFA are unreliable not only because they are old, but also because valid dialysis treatment costs equal to 15 percent of audited expenses are excluded from the rate base. Among these excluded costs are a return on equity and compensation to facility administrators and directors above $32,000 per year.

The defendants responded that the total cost per treatment, which they argued is the only relevant cost in developing composite rates, has not increased over time because of greater efficiencies in providing treatment. HHS maintained that adjusting rates for inflation would be contrary to the congressional intent of cost containment and would only guarantee further cost increases. The defendants also pointed out that the Medicare rates may be increased on the basis of annual cost reports from dialysis facilities.

In assessing these arguments, the court re-examined the authorizing statute, which directs the secretary to develop methods and procedures "to determine the costs incurred by providers [of dialysis services] ... on a cost related or other economical and equitable basis."[58] The court decided that the plaintiffs had

> not specified any cost information that the defendants have ignored; rather, they emphasize that defendants were aware of rising labor costs and merely surmise that other costs, such as rent and utilities, must have risen similarly. Based on the record before the Court, the regulations reasonably implement the statute in this regard, and must be upheld.[59]

Referring to the costs that HHS excluded from the rate base, the court again ruled for the defendants. The court noted the HHS' assertion that including a return on equity would weaken efficiency incentives and observed that the statute left the inclusion of this cost center to the secretary's discretion.[60] The court ruled that it "must sustain the agency's determination that return on equity is an inappropriate cost item for Medicare reimbursement [of kidney dialysis]."[61]

In regard to the exclusion of compensation for facility administrators and medical directors above $32,000 per year, the court ruled that facilities are free to pay any salaries they wish, but Medicare is not required to include salaries in excess of $32,000 in the rate base. HHS had pointed out that only 5 percent of the audited facilities paid medical directors salaries in excess of $32,000 per year, and the court ruled "that a limit that covers 95 percent of the audited salaries is reasonable."[62]

In the third prong of its attack on the prospective reimbursement regulations, the plaintiffs alleged that the exceptions process erroneously excludes a return on equity. The statute directs the secretary to provide exceptions to the composite rate due to "unusual circumstances."[63] Looking at the legislative history of the statute, the court concluded that Congress intended

> that the exceptions process would accommodate facilities, usually hospitals, with sicker, more costly patients .... The reimbursement regulations permit an exception when a facility demonstrates reasonable costs that exceed the composite rate due to an "atypical patient mix" or other specified factors.[64]

The NAPHT argued that the exceptions process is really cost-based reimbursement. The plaintiffs further asserted that excluding a return on equity from the exceptions process is arbitrary and capricious because proprietary providers, denied the opportunity to earn any return on their capital investments, will eventually cease providing services.

The defendants responded that proprietary facilities must earn their profit by increasing efficiency, adding that a return on equity is not considered a cost under Medicare reasonable cost principles.[65] Referring to a discussion of legislative intent in regard to a return on equity to proprietary hospitals in *American Medical International, Inc. v. Secretary of HEW*,[66] the defendants stated that the return-on-equity allowance was designed to encourage an increased supply of beds in posthospital care facilities because of a perceived shortage of nursing home beds. The court in *American Medical International* also pointed out that "the return on equity provision is an exception to the usual requirement that reimbursable costs be closely linked to providing medical care."[67] The court in *NAPHT* again ruled for the defendants on this issue, declaring that "[t]he expansion purpose is absent in this case."[68]

In the fourth prong of its attack on the prospective reimbursement regulations, the NAPHT argued that the new regulations, which provide for a single monthly capitation system, are contrary to the intent of Congress to provide two methods for reimbursing physicians and, therefore, are not in accordance with the law. The statute states that "the Secretary shall pay 80 percent of the amounts calculated for such services" on a reasonable charge basis "or" on a monthly fee basis.[69]

The defendants responded that the statute authorizes HHS to reimburse physicians under one or both of these methods. According to the defendants, the legislative history demonstrates "that Congress intended to preserve, rather than restrict, HHS' discretion."[70] Finally, the defendants maintained that the 1981 ESRD program amendments directed HHS to promote home dialysis and that the "Initial Method" (i.e., reasonable charge basis) of physician reimbursement mentioned in the statute is a disincentive to home dialysis.

The court ruled for the plaintiffs, declaring that

> [e]limination of the Initial Method is a drastic and illegal response to this problem. Congress has explicitly endorsed the use of alternative reimbursement methods. Furthermore, as plaintiffs indicate, the operative phrase in the statute is the "Secretary shall pay." ... In contrast, section 1395rr (b) (4) provides that the "Secretary may make payments" for supplies and equipment in one of two ways. This distinction supports the conclusion that Congress has mandated both methods.[71]

The court directed HHS to adapt the Initial Method to satisfy the congressional intent to encourage home dialysis.

The plaintiffs alleged that the new method for calculating physician payments under the monthly capitation payment system, which uses a base multiplier of 12.4 to correspond to the number of dialysis treatments per month plus a monthly examination, is irrational. The plaintiffs argued that, because there is no relationship between the number of dialysis treatments each month and the value and frequency of physician services, the use of the 12.4 base multiplier does not adequately reflect the value of physician services.

The defendants responded that the use of the 12.4 multiplier is a reasonable way to estimate physician involvement in the treatment of the average ESRD patient. HHS noted that the new physician payment method will result in significant decreases in reimbursement rates for physician services during in-facility dialysis, but larger increases in the rates for services to home dialysis patients.[72] Thus, according to the defendants, the new method for calculating reimbursement for physician services promotes home dialysis. The court ruled for the defendants.

In a final challenge to the prospective reimbursement regulations, the plaintiffs argued that the regulations should have allowed for a phase-in period. They maintained that HHS disregarded the limited capacity of dialysis facilities to reduce fixed costs and to increase the number of home dialysis patients. The plaintiffs also asserted that the defendants acted contrary to the intent of Congress when they did not provide for a transitional period.

The court observed that the possibility of a transition period was considered during committee hearings but "no transition period was enacted into the law."[73] The court ruled,

> The reimbursement regulations, effective August 1, 1983, were designed to implement a statute which became effective October 1, 1981. The industry had been on notice of changes in the reimbursement rates since July, 1979. Defendants did allow approximately 75 days after publication of the regulations for adjustment to the new rates and provided that the wage index for the first two years would be limited to protect particularly rural facilities from experiencing immediate adverse effects.... HHS has not acted arbitrarily and capriciously in deciding not to phase in these regulations.[74]

In Count II of the complaint, the plaintiffs challenged the secondary payment regulations on the ground that they do not provide for a determination by the secretary that payments by employer group health plans will be made "as promptly as" Medicare payments.[75] The plaintiffs argued that the plain language of the statute and the legislative history clearly directed the secretary to determine that payments from employer group health plans will be as prompt as those from Medicare; the secondary payment regulations do not comply with congressional intent.

The defendants responded that the statute delegates to the secretary the discretionary power to coordinate Medicare payments with employer group health plan payments. The court refused to defer to the secretary's expertise in exercising this discretionary power, however, observing that the secretary "has relaxed the standard of comparative promptness from the statutory, 'as promptly as' Medicare, to 'substantially less prompt' than Medicare"[76] in the regulations. This relaxation

> disregarded the statutory language and has undermined the statutory objective.... The secondary payment regulations, which provide for secondary payments and require a determination by the intermediary or carrier prior to conditional primary payments, are flatly inconsistent with the statute. While the statute vests the

Secretary with discretion to determine "the point at which Medicare need no longer be the first payor," ... that discretion is circumscribed by the statutory definition of that point: when employer plans pay "as promptly as" Medicare.[77]

The court ruled, therefore, that the secondary payment regulations were "arbitrary, capricious, and not in accordance with law. The Secretary's discretion does not entitle her to rewrite the statute."[78]

National Medical Care (NMC), the nation's largest independent supplier of outpatient dialysis services with over 160 dialysis centers, provides an interesting postscript to the controversy surrounding the Medicare prospective reimbursement policy for dialysis services. For the quarter ending December 31, 1983 (the first full quarter in which the new prospective method was used), NMC increased its earnings per share by almost 14 percent over the corresponding quarter from a year earlier—despite the more restrictive Medicare payment system.[79] Earnings per share for the quarters ending March 31, 1984 and June 30, 1984 increased by almost 17 percent and over 19 percent respectively over the corresponding quarters from the year earlier.[80] NMC's earnings per share for 1984 have been estimated at $1.50 versus $1.26 for 1983, or an increase of 19 percent.[81] As a final note, the W.R. Grace & Co. and a group of investors (including members of NMC's management) agreed to acquire this dialysis services provider for about $360 million in August 1984.[82]

NOTES

1. P.L. 92-603, §299.

2. 47 Fed. Reg. 6,556-6,582 (February 12, 1982).

3. National Assn. of Patients on Hemodialysis and Transplantation, Inc. et al. v. Margaret M. Heckler et al., U.S. District Court, District of Columbia, Civil Action No. 83-2210, June 11, 1984. [Background].

4. 42 C.F.R. §405.2101.

5. 42 C.F.R. §405.2102.

6. 42 C.F.R. §405.2102(e).

7. 42 C.F.R. §405.2110.

8. The ESRD network areas are listed in the Appendix to Subpart U, "Conditions for Coverage of Suppliers of ESRD Services," at 42 C.F.R. §405.2100.

9. 42 C.F.R. §405.2111.

10. 42 C.F.R. §405.2122.

11. 42 C.F.R. §405.2123.

12. 42 C.F.R. §405.2124.

13. 42 C.F.R. §405.2130.

14. 42 C.F.R. §405.2102.

15. 42 C.F.R. §405.2131.
16. 42 C.F.R. §405.2132.
17. 657 F.2d 135 (7th Cir. 1981).
18. *Id.*, p. 138.
19. *Id.*, p. 139.
20. 42 C.F.R. §405.2136.
21. 42 C.F.R. §405.2134.
22. 42 C.F.R. §405.2135.
23. 42 C.F.R. §405.2137.
24. 42 C.F.R. §405.2138.
25. 42 C.F.R. §405.2139.
26. 42 C.F.R. §405.2160.
27. 42 C.F.R. §405.2161.
28. 42 C.F.R. §405.2162.
29. 42 C.F.R. §405.2163.
30. 42 C.F.R. §405.2140.
31. 47 Fed. Reg. 6,556 (February 12, 1982).
32. P.L. 95-292.
33. P.L. 97-35.
34. 42 C.F.R. §405.400, Subpart D (1982) and 42 C.F.R. 405.500, Subpart E (1982).
35. 20 C.F.R. §405.502(e) (1977).
36. 42 U.S.C. §1395 u(b)(3).
37. 454 F.Supp. 105 (1978).
38. No. 75-1109 (D.D.C. 1976).
39. *See* note 37, *supra*, p. 114.
40. *See* note 37, *supra*, p. 115.
41. 118 Cong. Rec. 36,805 (1972).
42. 47 Fed. Reg. 6,557 (February 12, 1982).
43. 47 Fed. Reg. 6,560 (February 12, 1982).
44. 42 C.F.R. §405.690.
45. 47 Fed. Reg. 6,556 (February 12, 1982).
46. 47 Fed. Reg. 6,562 (February 12, 1982).
47. *Id.*
48. 48 Fed. Reg. 21,254 (May 11, 1983).
49. 48 Fed. Reg. 21,261 (May 11, 1983).
50. 47 Fed. Reg. 6,565 (February 12, 1982).
51. National Assn. of Patients on Hemodialysis and Transplantation, Inc. et al. v. Margaret M. Heckler et al., Civil Action No. 83-2210, June 11, 1984, U.S. District Court, District of Columbia.
52. 48 Fed. Reg. 21,254 (May 11, 1983).
53. 48 Fed. Reg. 14,802 (April 5, 1983).
54. 48 Fed. Reg. 14,812 (April 5, 1983).

55. *See* note 51, *supra,* p. 23.
56. *See* note 51, *supra,* p. 26.
57. *See* note 51, *supra,* p. 27.
58. 42 U.S.C. §1395rr(b)(2)(B).
59. *See* note 51, *supra,* p. 30.
60. 42 U.S.C. §1395rr(b)(2)(C).
61. *See* note 51, *supra,* p. 31.
62. *See* note 51, *supra,* p. 32.
63. 42 U.S.C. §1395rr(b)(7).
64. *See* note 51, *supra,* pp. 32-33.
65. 48 Fed. Reg. 21,257 (May 11, 1983).
66. 466 F.Supp. 605 (D.D.C. 1979), *affirmed* 677 F.2d 118 (D.C. Cir. 1981).
67. *Id.,* p. 614.
68. *See* note 51, *supra,* p. 34.
69. 42 U.S.C. §1395rr(b)(3).
70. *See* note 51, *supra,* p. 36.
71. *See* note 51, *supra,* pp. 36-37.
72. 48 Fed. Reg. 21,289 (May 11, 1983).
73. *See* note 51, *supra,* p. 40.
74. *See* note 51, *supra,* p. 41.
75. 42 U.S.C. §1395y(b)(2)(A).
76. *See* note 51, *supra,* p. 43.
77. *See* note 51, *supra,* pp. 44-45.
78. *See* note 51, *supra,* p. 47.
79. 51 STANDARD NYSE STOCK REPORTS 1614 (1984).
80. 55 MOODY'S INDUSTRIAL NEWS REPORTS 2569 (1984); "Digest of Corporate Earnings Reports," *The Wall Street Journal* (August 16, 1984): 16.
81. *See* note 79, *supra.*
82. "Grace and Group to Buy Concern for $360 Million," *The Wall Street Journal* (August 7, 1984): 8.

Chapter 6

Fraud and Abuse in Medicare

The Medicare-Medicaid Anti-Fraud and Abuse Amendments were approved October 25, 1977,[1] after numerous hearings, studies, and investigations undertaken by committees of Congress, the General Accounting Office, and other federal agencies demonstrated that there was a disturbing number of fraudulent and abusive practices associated with the health care financed by the Medicare and Medicaid programs. The disclosures at that time had focused on a broad range of improper activities that were not restricted to one particular class of providers or treatment settings. These activities not only were wasting funds, but also were eroding the financial stability of state and local governments. The activities of those who were defrauding these programs also unfairly called into question the honesty and integrity of the vast majority of practitioners and health care institutions.[2]

Medicare cost the taxpayer approximately $57 billion in 1983.[3] Because these sums are primarily for reimbursement for services rendered, the potential for fraud and abuse is great. To deter waste in these programs, both Titles XVIII (Medicare) and XIX (Medicaid) of the Social Security Act contain criminal provisions.

STATUTES

Section 1877 of the Social Security Act,[4] which describes Medicare, is virtually identical to Section 1909 of the Social Security Act,[5] which describes Medicaid offenses and penalties.

False Statements and Representations

It is a criminal violation knowingly and willfully to make a false statement or representation of a material fact in an application for any benefit or payment.[6] A material fact is one that influences or affects the decision to be made. The phrase *knowingly and willfully* indicates that the misstatement must be made consciously rather than inadvertently. Similarly, it is a criminal violation to make false statements or representations of facts used in determining rights to benefits or payments.[7]

A person also incurs criminal liability by (1) having knowledge of an event affecting (A) his or her initial or continued right to a benefit or payment or (B) the initial or continued right to such a benefit or payment of another individual in whose behalf he or she applied or is receiving benefits or payments, and (2) concealing or failing to disclose this event with a fraudulent intent.[8] The intent may be to gain a greater payment or benefit than deserved or to receive a payment or benefit where none is deserved.

Finally, criminal liability is incurred by a person who, having legitimately applied for a payment for the use and benefit of another, receives and misuses the payment or benefit.[9] This payment or benefit must be knowingly and willfully misused. Misuse, or conversion, is any use that is not for the use or benefit of the other person.

Any person who commits any of these acts in connection with his or her providing health care services for which payment is made under the Medicare and Medicaid law has committed a felony. Upon conviction, the person furnishing the services may be fined not more than $25,000, imprisoned for not more than five years, or both. This crime was upgraded to felony status by a 1977 amendment that also upgraded violations of other provisions of these same statutes to felonies. When these provisions are violated by any person not providing a service, however, the crime is a misdemeanor. Such a person may be fined not more than $10,000, imprisoned for not more than one year, or both.

Illegal Remunerations

A person who knowingly and willfully either solicits or receives, or offers or pays, certain remunerations (e.g., kickbacks, bribes, or rebates) may incur criminal liability.[10] This liability is incurred whether the payment is made directly or indirectly, overtly or covertly, in cash or as an in kind payment.

The provision against solicitation or receipt of unlawful remuneration may be violated in two ways.[11] First, it is illegal to solicit or receive remuneration for referring an individual for a service that the Medicare or Medicaid programs will pay for in whole or in part. Second, it is unlawful to solicit or receive remuneration for purchasing, leasing, ordering, or arranging for—or recommending purchasing, leasing, or ordering—any goods, facility, service, or item for which payment may be made in whole or in part from Medicare or Medicaid funds.

The provision against offering or paying illegal remuneration may also be violated in two ways.[12] First, the offer or payment of remuneration to induce another to refer an individual for the arranging or furnishing of a service that may be paid for in whole or in part from Medicare and Medicaid funds is unlawful. Second, the statute is violated when the remuneration is offered or paid to induce another to purchase, lease, order, or arrange for—or recommend purchasing, leasing, or ordering—any goods, facility, service, or item for which payment may be made from Medicare or Medicaid funds.

Persons who violate the statute on illegal remunerations in any listed manner commit a felony. This felony is punishable by a fine of not more than $25,000, imprisonment for not more than five years, or both.

These restrictions do not apply in two instances. A discount or other reduction in price obtained by a provider of services or other entity under Medicare or Medicaid is lawful if the reduction in price is properly disclosed and appropriately reflected in the cost claimed or charges made by the provider or entity. Amounts paid by the employer to a bona fide employee for employment in providing items of service are also permissible.

False Statements or Representations with Respect to Institutions

The knowing and willful making of false statements or representations regarding the conditions or operation of any institution or facility in order that such institution or facility may qualify (for either certification or recertification) as a hospital, skilled nursing facility, intermediate care facility (Medicaid only), or home health agency as defined under Medicare or Medicaid is a criminal violation.[13] Conviction of this offense is a felony punishable by up to $25,000 in fines, five years in jail, or both.

Violation of Assignment Terms

Medicare may enter into contracts with carriers, requiring each carrier to take necessary action to ensure that payments made on a charge basis are reasonable and not higher than the charge applicable for a comparable service and under comparable circumstances to the policyholders and subscribers of the carrier. With some exceptions, payments will be made on the basis of assignments. Such assignments must provide that the reasonable charge is the full charge for the service and the person furnishing the service will not charge for the service if payment cannot be made because it is excluded from coverage.

To the extent that these carriers knowingly, willingly, and repeatedly violate the terms of such assignments, they shall be guilty of a misdemeanor.[14] Upon conviction, they may be fined not more than $2,000 or imprisoned for not more than six months.

REGULATIONS

Prosecution for crimes is beyond the regulations of the Department of Health and Human Services (HHS) and the Health Care Financing Administration (HCFA). Civil penalties may be imposed, however, for fraud and abuse in connection with administrative regulation of the Medicare program. Consequences of fraud and abuse are set forth in several places in the federal regulations, and detailed procedures for hearings and reviews have been established.[15]

Definitions

The regulations contain the word *convicted* in several instances. It means that a judgment of conviction has been entered by a federal, state, or local court. The definition applies even if an appeal from that judgment is pending. The use of the word *exclusion* means that items or services furnished by a specific practitioner, provider, or other supplier of services are not reimbursable under Medicare.

The word *furnished* refers to items and services provided directly by or under the direct supervision of a practitioner, either as an employee or in his or her capacity as a practitioner, a provider, or other supplier of services. The term does not refer to services ordered by one party but provided by or under the supervision of and billed for by another.

A *practitioner* is a physician or other health care professional who is licensed under state law to practice his or her profession and may be eligible to receive reimbursement under the Medicare program. A *provider* is a hospital, a skilled nursing facility, or a home health agency. A provider is also a clinic, rehabilitation agency, or public health agency for the limited purposes of furnishing outpatient physical therapy or speech pathology services.[16] Professional standards review organizations (PSROs) also play a role in the administration of the Medicare program.[17]

Exclusion and Suspension

Practitioners, providers, and other suppliers of services may be excluded from participation in the Medicare program,[18] even when there is no criminal prosecution. Payment will not be made through Medicare for items or services furnished if the HCFA determines that the practitioner, provider, or other supplier of services has (1) knowingly and willfully made or caused to be made any false statement or misrepresentation of a material fact in a request for payment under Medicare or for use in determining the right to payment under Medicare, (2) furnished items or services that are substantially in excess of the beneficiary's needs or that do not meet professionally recognized standards of health care, or (3) submitted or caused to be submitted bills or requests for payment that are substantially in excess of customary charges or cost.[19]

A determination that the items or services furnished were excessive or of unacceptable quality is made on the basis of reports, including sanction reports, from the following sources:[20]

1. the PSRO for the area served by the practitioner, provider, or other supplier of services
2. state or local licensing or certifying authorities
3. peer review committees of fiscal agents or contractors
4. state or local professional societies
5. other sources deemed appropriate by the HCFA

This allowance may be waived on the ground that the beneficiary and the practitioner, provider, or other supplier of services could not reasonably be expected to know that payment would not be made for a particular item or service. Excess charges may also be paid if justified by unusual circumstances.[21]

When the HCFA proposes to deny reimbursement or to terminate a provider agreement, it sends written notice of its intent. Within thirty days, the aggrieved party may submit a written argument or may request in writing an opportunity to submit evidence orally.[22] If the party is eventually excluded or terminated, the HCFA sends a notice stating

1. the reason for the decision
2. the date it becomes effective
3. the extent of its application
4. the earliest date the HCFA will accept a request for reinstatement
5. the requirements and procedures for reinstatement
6. the avenues of appeal available

The decision and notice constitute an "initial determination" and a "notice of initial determination" for purposes of the administrative appeals procedure. The HCFA also gives notice of exclusion or termination and the effective date to the public, beneficiaries, and selected other entities.[23]

In determining the length of the exclusion, the HCFA considers

1. the number and nature of the program violations and other related offenses
2. the nature and extent of any adverse impact the violations have had on beneficiaries
3. the amount of any damage incurred by the Medicare program
4. any mitigating circumstances
5. any other facts bearing on the nature and seriousness of the violations or related offenses
6. any previous sanctions of the excluded party under the Medicare or Medicaid program[24]

Any party may also be suspended from participation in the Medicare program after conviction of a criminal offense related to involvement in the Medicare or Medicaid program.[25] Such conviction must have occurred since October 25, 1977. Suspension would likewise apply to (1) practitioners; (2) suppliers that are wholly owned by a convicted individual; (3) individuals who are employees, administrators, or operators of providers; and (4) any other individuals who in any capacity are receiving payment for providing services under Medicare.[26] The practitioner is given a written notice to be effective fifteen days after its date. The written notice sets forth (1) the reason for the suspension, (2) the duration of the suspension and the factors considered in setting the duration, (3) the requirements and procedures for reinstatement, and (4) the appeal rights.[27]

The effect of suspension is similar to that of exclusion. Like an exclusion notice, the suspension notice specifies the earliest date on which reinstatement may be sought. Factors considered are

1. the number and nature of the program violations and other related offenses
2. the nature and extent of any adverse impact the violations have had on beneficiaries
3. the amount of damages incurred by the Medicare, Medicaid, and the social services programs
4. any mitigating circumstances
5. the length of the sentence imposed by the court
6. other facts bearing on the nature and seriousness of the program violations
7. any previous sanctions of the suspended party under the Medicare or Medicaid programs[28]

Appeal and Reinstatement

The practitioner may appeal a suspension on three narrow grounds: (1) whether he or she was actually convicted; (2) whether the conviction was related to Medicare, Medicaid, or social services programs; (3) whether the length of the suspension is reasonable.[29] Hearings are conducted in accordance with the procedures set forth in the regulations.[30] Any party to the hearing dissatisfied with the decision is entitled to request an appeals council review of the decision.[31] A suspended party may then seek judicial review of the final decision.

An excluded practitioner, provider, or other supplier of services, either excluded or suspended, may request reinstatement at any time after the date specified in the notice. This may be done by submitting to the HCFA or authorizing the HCFA to obtain (1) statements from private health insurers that there have been no questionable claims submitted during the period of exclusion or suspension; (2) statements from peer review bodies, probation officers where appropriate, or professional associates as required by the HCFA attesting to their belief, supported by facts, that the violations will not be repeated; and (3) a statement from the affected party setting forth the reasons that reinstatement is appropriate.

The HCFA will not grant reinstatement unless it is reasonably certain that the violations that led to the exclusion or conviction will not be repeated. In making this decision, the HCFA considers, among other factors, (1) whether the applicant has been convicted in federal, state, or local courts for activities related to program participation and (2) whether the state or local licensing authority has taken any adverse action against the party since the date of the exclusion or suspension.[32]

Notice of Action on Requests for Reinstatement

When a request for reinstatement has been approved, the HCFA will give notice. It will give written notice to the excluded or suspended party, specifying the date on which program participation may resume. Second, it will give notice to the public and, as appropriate, to Title V state agencies, state Medicaid agencies and fraud control units, hospitals, skilled nursing facilities, home health care agencies, medical societies or associations, contractors, health care prepayment plans, health maintenance organizations, PSROs, the state or local licensing or certifying authority, and other affected organizations.[33]

When a request for reinstatement has been denied, the HCFA notifies the party in writing. Within thirty days after the date of the notice, the excluded or suspended party may submit documented evidence and written arguments against the continued exclusion or suspension, or a written request to present oral evidence or arguments to an HCFA official.

If no additional evidence is submitted within thirty days or if, after evaluating the additional evidence, the HCFA still denies reinstatement, it will send written notice to confirm the denial and indicate that a subsequent request for reinstatement will not be accepted until six months after the date of confirmation. If the additional evidence causes the HCFA to approve reinstatement, it will specify the date when program participation may be resumed and will notify the public and the appropriate agencies and institutions that would have been notified had the request been initially approved.[34]

The HCFA will also reinstate a suspended party whose conviction has been reversed or vacated. When reinstatement is made following reversal or vacating of convictions, the HCFA will make payments either to the party or the beneficiary for claims that would have been covered by Medicare except for the suspension.

Abuse

Although the HCFA cannot convict persons for violations of its regulations, the Medicare and Medicaid laws allow the HCFA to make exclusions for abuse, defined in the Medicaid regulations as

> Provider practices that are inconsistent with sound fiscal, business or medical practices, and result in unnecessary cost to the Medicaid-Medicare program, or in reimbursement for services that are not medically necessary or that fail to meet professionally recognized standards for health care.[35]

Therefore, even though a provider of services may not be criminally liable, there may still be abuse. The following have been suggested as examples of abuse:

- unnecessary service
- breach of assignment agreement
- gang visits
- improper billing practices
- routine waiver of coinsurance and deductibles
- failure to maintain adequate accounting records to substantiate costs
- excessive compensation to owners and administrators or owner-related employees[36]

CASES

The cases that have been decided under these statutes seem to be consistent with the intent of Congress.

False Statements or Representations

In a case originating in the state of Arkansas, *United States v. Huckaby*,[37] a nursing home owner had been convicted of concealing and failing to disclose the actual level of care that the nursing home provided to Medicaid recipients in order to gain greater benefits. In Arkansas, the condition of the patient determined the level of care classification. The higher the care classification, the greater the reimbursement received by the nursing home.

Apparently, the fact that the statements were false was not contested in *Huckaby*, but the defendant claimed that the government had not shown her intent to violate the statute. Since the employee primarily responsible for preparing the service evaluation forms had been fired, apparently for not filing false forms, and new forms had been prepared at the direction of the defendant, the court relied on circumstantial evidence to uphold the conviction. Courts invariably base their conclusions on appearances rather than the uncorroborated statements of defendants.

Aside from a falsehood committed knowingly and willfully, the laws require that the falsehood be material. In *United States v. Adler*,[38] a Missouri case involving Medicare and Medicaid claims, the court set forth the test for "materiality":

> The test for determining the materiality of the falsification is whether the falsification is calculated to induce action or reliance by an agency of the United States—is it one that could affect or influence the exercise of government function—does it have a natural tendency to influence or is it capable of influencing agency decision.[39]

Apparently relying on the last part of the definition, the physician on trial in *Adler* claimed that the government must show that the claim presented could lawfully be paid and that otherwise the claim in question was not material. The court did not agree with this argument and affirmed the conviction.

An earlier case, *United States v. Radetsky*,[40] involved a physician who billed the government for services that were not compensable under the Medicare regulations. The court had decided that, even if the physician had not performed the services, they were not material since the agency would not pay for them in any case. At least one court has held that the materiality of a false statement should be decided by the court as a question of law rather than by the jury.[41]

The court in *Adler*, however, said that a statement is material if it has a tendency to induce government to act and places the claimant (provider or practitioner) in a position to receive government benefits. The court reasoned that, if providers could submit claims that should not be paid in hopes that they would be paid by mistake, the number of noncompensable claims would increase and claims that slip through would not be subject to the criminal provisions of the statutes. Health care providers must ensure not only that submitted claims are truthful, but also that the services involved are compensable under Medicare or Medicaid.

A false statement that enhances the value of an otherwise lawful claim may also be criminal. In *United States v. Edgewood Health Care Center*,[42] a conviction was upheld for the reasons stated in *Huckaby*. Patients were alleged to be housed in a west wing, a certified skilled nursing facility, when they were actually maintained in the east wing, an intermediate care facility. The costs of care for the east wing patients were not reimbursable under Medicare and were reimbursable only at a much lower rate under Medicaid. The nursing home thereby benefitted from the misrepresentation, even though some patients would have qualified for some benefits in any case.

Even though the 1977 Medicare and Medicaid anti-fraud amendments seem to be fairly comprehensive, providers of services may still be charged under other federal statutes, such as mail fraud[43] and making false statements.[44]

Illegal Remuneration

By far the most reported prosecutions under the offenses and penalties provisions of Medicare and Medicaid have involved illegal remuneration. Much of the potential confusion arises from the definition of "kickbacks" and "bribes" prior to the 1977 anti-fraud amendments.

One of the early cases, *United States v. Porter*,[45] was decided on the statute as written prior to the 1977 amendments. In that case, the Fifth Circuit Court of Appeals defined a "kickback" as "the secret return to an earlier possessor of part of a sum received."[46] In *Porter*, physicians were "reimbursed" up to $35 by certain laboratories for blood samples from Medicare patients sent to those laboratories. The fee that Medicaid would have paid these physicians directly would not have exceeded $6 for this service. Since these physicians never had the money that was being "returned" to them, their convictions were overturned. The *Porter* court's restrictive definition of kickback found support in another case, *United States v. Zacher*,[47] which suggested that "the receipt of supplemental payments when a patient was eligible for Medicare rather than private insurance would not, without more, constitute a bribe."[48] In essence, the court in the *Porter* case seemed to be saying that the laboratory lawfully came into possession of the money received for performing blood tests. The physicians were not raising prices to the patients to pay the laboratories and later having this money kicked back to them. Arguably, the definition of "kickback" in *Porter* is still more restrictive than the *Zacher* court's definition of bribe.

The opinion of the Fifth Circuit Court of Appeals in *Porter* has not enjoyed wide acceptance. The Seventh Circuit Court of Appeals in *United States v. Hancock and Palombi*[49] came to a different conclusion. There chiropractors were charged with soliciting and receiving kickbacks in Medicare and Medicaid cases. The laboratory used by the defendants for the testing of blood and tissue specimens from the Medicare and Medicaid patients billed the patient insurer or state agency handling Medicare and Medicaid claims. The defendants contended that the funds they received from the laboratory were handling fees. The Seventh Circuit Court of Appeals indicated that it could not agree with the Fifth Circuit. The Seventh Circuit defined kickback as "a percentage payment ... for granting assistance by one in a position to open up or control a source of income."[50] Consequently, the convictions were affirmed. Other courts have followed this reasoning.[51]

The 1977 amendment speaks in terms of remuneration and includes kickback, bribe, and rebate within that definition. Therefore, it appears that the form of remuneration is not important. Under this statute as amended, a 15 percent rebate proposal in exchange for the referral of Medicare and Medicaid business was found to violate the statute.[52] Similarly, a 10 percent cash rebate on Medicare and Medi-Cal (California Medicaid) collections and a discount on private patient billings to a person to induce that person to refer laboratory work was also held to be a violation.[53] Extracting sizeable cash payments and liquor was also held to be in violation of this statute.[54]

One of the underlying reasons for outlawing kickbacks, bribes, and rebates is to contain the cost of medically related services. In some instances, a kickback may be paid if it could not raise the cost of the medical service. In *United States v. Ruttenberg*,[55] however, the court concluded that kickbacks are illegal even if they could not increase the costs of insurance. Therefore, providers and practitioners should be alert to possible violations, even when the costs to Medicare or Medicaid for the service will not be increased.

OUTLOOK

According to a report of the Office of the Inspector General (OIG)[56] there were $32.1 million involved in recommended financial adjustments in HCFA programs during the second six months of Fiscal Year 1983. The OIG intensified its efforts to detect health care fraud, establishing a case review committee for each region. Their priorities are set by OIG offices involved with health care investigations, but the committees determine the procedures to be employed and allocate resources. "The decision to concentrate resources on health care cases was affirmed during this period by some of the heaviest sentences and penalties ever obtained by the OIG," according to the report.[57]

Fraud and abuse in programs the size of Medicare may far exceed losses from typical property crimes. Therefore, there is likely to be a greater emphasis on prosecution for white collar crimes in the future. At least fifteen states have racketeering statutes, several being enacted very recently. Although these statutes are normally associated with organized crime, their wording is such that they also apply to cases of fraud and abuse in Medicare and Medicaid. This entire movement suggests much closer scrutiny of fraud and abuse in Medicare and Medicaid in the near future.

NOTES

1. P.L. 95-142.
2. 1977 U.S. CODE CONG. & AD. NEWS 3046, 3047.
3. DEP'T OF HEALTH & HUMAN SERVICES, REPORT OF THE INSPECTOR GENERAL, January 1982-Sept. 30, 1982. MEDICARE AND MEDICAID GUIDE, 32,891.
4. 42 U.S.C. §1395nn.
5. 42 U.S.C. §1396h.
6. 42 U.S.C. §1395nn(a)(1).
7. 42 U.S.C. §1395nn(a)(2).
8. 42 U.S.C. §1395nn(a)(3).
9. 42 U.S.C. §1395nn(a)(4).
10. 42 U.S.C. §1395nn(b).
11. 42 U.S.C. §1395nn(b)(1).
12. 42 U.S.C. §1395nn(b)(2).
13. 42 U.S.C. §1395nn(c).
14. 42 U.S.C. §1395nn(d).
15. 42 C.F.R. §405, Subpart 0.
16. An employee might be included in this definition by criminal statutes. *See* North Carolina v. Beatty, 308 S.E.2d 65 (N.C. 1983), holding that a pharmacist-manager who had no proprietary or stock interest in the pharmacy was subject to the state's medical fraud statute.
17. 42 C.F.R. §420.2.
18. 42 C.F.R. §420.101.
19. *Id.*
20. 42 C.F.R. §420.101(b).
21. 42 C.F.R. §420.101.
22. 42 C.F.R. §420.105.

23. 42 C.F.R. §420.107.
24. 42 C.F.R. §420.114.
25. 42 C.F.R. §420.122. The secretary of HHS is granted authority to suspend physicians convicted of criminal offenses under 42 U.S.C. §1395y(e)(1). *See* Michienz v. Harris, 634 F.2d 345 (6th Cir. 1980), in which the court denied an injunction requested by suspended practitioners.
26. 42 C.F.R. §420.122.
27. 42 C.F.R. §420.123.
28. 42 C.F.R. §420.125.
29. 42 C.F.R. §420.128.
30. 42 C.F.R. §§405.1531, 405.1533, 405.1534, 405.1540, 405.1541, and 405.1543-405.1558.
31. 42 C.F.R. §§405.1559-405.1595.
32. 42 C.F.R. §420.132.
33. 42 C.F.R. §420.134.
34. 42 C.F.R. §420.134(a)(2).
35. 42 C.F.R. §433.203.
36. MEDICARE AND MEDICAID GUIDE, 13,895, annot. 17.
37. 698 F.2d 915 (8th Cir. 1982), *cert. denied*, 103 S.Ct. 1526.
38. 623 F.2d 1287 (8th Cir. 1980).
39. *Id.*, at 1291.
40. 535 F.2d 556 (10th Cir. 1976), *cert. denied*, 429 U.S. 820 (1976).
41. United States v. Abadi, 706 F.2d 178 (6th Cir. 1983), *cert. denied*, 104 S.Ct. 86.
42. 608 F.2d 13 (1st Cir. 1979).
43. 18 U.S.C. §1341.
44. *See, e.g.*, United States v. Simon, 510 F.Supp. 232 (E.D. Pa. 1981); United States v. Gordon, 548 F.2d 743 (8th Cir. 1977).
45. 591 F.2d 1048 (5th Cir. 1979).
46. 591 F.2d 1054.
47. 586 F.2d 912 (2d Cir. 1978).
48. 591 F.2d 1053.
49. 604 F.2d 999 (7th Cir. 1979).
50. *Id.*, at 1002.
51. *See, e.g.*, United States v. Taport, 625 F.2d 111 (6th Cir. 1980), *affirming* United States v. Weingarden, 468 F. Supp. 410 (E.D. Mich. 1979).
52. United States v. Duz Mor Diagnostic Laboratory, Inc., 650 F.2d 223 (9th Cir. 1981).
53. United States v. Fekri, 650 F.2d 1044 (9th Cir. 1981).
54. United States v. Perlstein, 632 F.2d 661 (6th Cir. 1980).
55. 625 F.2d 173 (7th Cir. 1980).
56. OFFICE OF THE INSPECTOR GENERAL, DEP'T OF HEALTH & HUMAN SERVICES, ATTACKING FRAUD, ABUSE, AND WASTE IN HEALTH AND HUMAN SERVICES (1983), 33,521.
57. *Id.*

Part II

The Medicaid Program

Created by the Social Security Amendments of 1965,[1] the Medicaid program is a cooperative federal-state effort to provide medical care to the poor who are aged, blind, or disabled, or who are members of families with dependent children. The program, jointly financed by the federal and state governments, is designed and administered primarily by the states, acting within federal guidelines. Because the states determine eligibility requirements and the scope of benefits, both vary widely from state to state. Unlike the Medicare program, which is a health insurance program for the elderly, the Medicaid program is linked to the welfare system. Eligibility for Medicaid benefits is determined by a number of factors, but the income levels and the financial resources of the beneficiaries are the most important criteria.

COVERAGE

Participating Medicaid programs must serve the categorically needy, defined as persons who receive cash payments under the Aid to Families with Dependent Children program and the aged, blind, or disabled who receive benefits under the Supplemental Security Income program. Federal law gives state programs the option of also serving the medically needy. These individuals have slightly greater incomes or financial resources than do the categorically needy, but are unable to pay for medical care. As Figure II-1 illustrates, twenty state programs limit coverage to the categorically needy, while the remaining states include the medically needy as well. (Effective January 1, 1984, the Oregon Medicaid program covered medically needy children under age 18 and pregnant women.)

138   LEGAL ASPECTS OF HEALTH CARE REIMBURSEMENT

Figure II-1 Medicaid: Medically and Categorically Needy

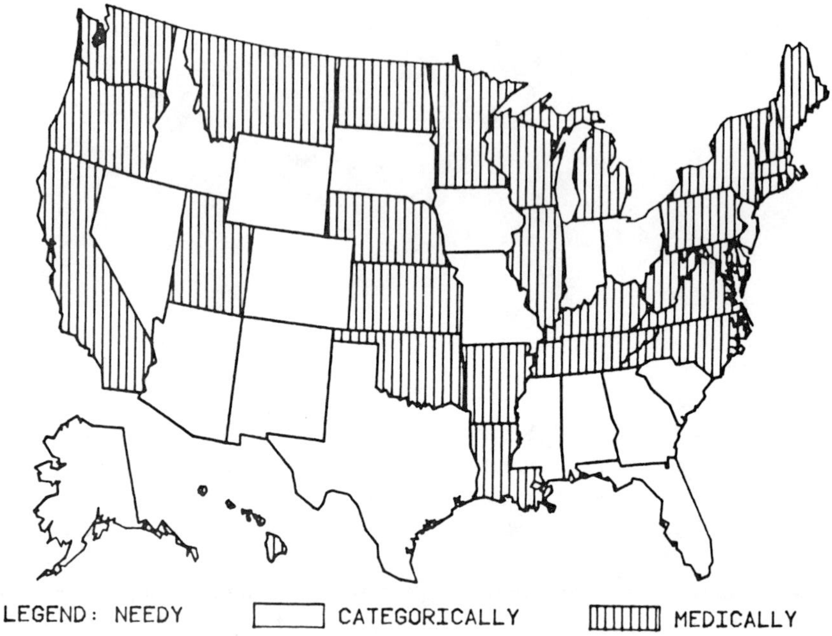

LEGEND: NEEDY   ☐ CATEGORICALLY   ▒ MEDICALLY

Source: Medicare and Medicaid Guide, "State Charts," ¶15,550.

Federal law requires state Medicaid programs to cover

- inpatient and outpatient hospital services
- rural health clinic services
- laboratory and x-ray services
- skilled nursing facility services for beneficiaries 21 years and older
- early and periodic screening, diagnosis, and treatment for individuals under age 21
- family planning services and supplies for beneficiaries of childbearing age
- physician services
- home health care services
- nurse-midwife services
- transportation to medical care

Federal law allows state programs to cover additional services for the categorically needy, such as dental services, prescribed drugs, eyeglasses, intermediate care facility services, and physical therapy services. States that cover the medically needy are given flexibility in determining which services to cover for these beneficiaries, but they may not provide more services for the medically needy than they provide for the categorically needy.

FINANCING

As mentioned earlier, the federal and state governments finance the Medicaid program together. A federal medical assistance percentage (FMAP) is calculated to determine the federal share of each state's Medicaid expenditures. If a state's per capita income equals the national average per capita income, for example, the federal share of that state's Medicaid expenditures equals 55 percent. For states with per capita incomes above the national average, the FMAP declines from 55 percent, but it never falls below 50 percent, the minimum federal share. For states with per capita incomes below the national average, the FMAP increases from 55 percent to a maximum federal share of 83 percent. During 1984, Mississippi had the highest FMAP (77.63 percent), and several states had the lowest FMAP (50 percent).

The Omnibus Budget Reconciliation Act of 1981[2] mandated reductions in federal Medicaid payments below the level each state is entitled to receive by 3 percent in Fiscal Year 1982, 4 percent in Fiscal Year 1983, and 4.5 percent in Fiscal Year 1984. The states could reduce these cutbacks in federal payments if they undertook specified cost containment actions, however. For example, these annual cutbacks were reduced by one percentage point if the state had an operating hospital cost review program. They were reduced by another one percentage point if the state sustained an unemployment rate greater than or equal to 150 percent of the national average during the quarter preceding the quarter to which the cut applies, and by still another one percentage point if the state recovered through anti-fraud and abuse controls an amount equal to 1 percent of federal payments.

These reductions in federal payments, combined with a decrease in tax revenues as a result of the severe economic contraction of 1981-1982 have caused severe fiscal problems for many state Medicaid programs. A survey taken in April, 1983 revealed that four states have reduced the amount, scope, and duration of covered services, while an additional twelve states are considering such action.[3] Eight states have taken action to require co-payments or to alter their current co-payment structure, and twenty states are considering similar proposals. Four states have limited or reduced hospital payments, and sixteen states are debating similar action. Two states have limited or decreased payments to nursing homes, and eight other states are considering reimbursement limitations.

The potential complexity of federal-state financing of Medicaid payments to providers became clear when the Medicaid program in Massachusetts overpaid twenty-seven nursing homes that later filed for bankruptcy. The Health Care Financing Administration (HCFA) estimated that the federal share of these overpayments was more than $5 million; after administrative appeal and renegotiation, however, the federal share of overpayment was reduced to $3.7 million. The federal government wanted to reduce federal payments to the Massachusetts Medicaid program to offset this amount of overpayment. The Commonwealth of Massachusetts, seeking judicial review and declaratory and injunctive relief from this decision, filed suit in federal court.[4]

The Massachusetts Medicaid program, using a retroactive payment system for long-term care as part of its state plan, makes provisional payments to providers at interim rates based on payments to providers in previous years. At the end of the year, a final rate for providers is calculated, based on actual costs of care. If the final rate is greater than the interim rate, the provider receives additional payments. If the final rate is lower than the interim rate, the Massachusetts Medicaid program recovers the difference. In this dispute, the interim rate to the twenty-seven nursing homes exceeded their final rate. When these providers later filed for bankruptcy, the issue became whether the Massachusetts Medicaid program should be required to refund to the federal government the federal share of the excess payments at that time or whether the program should be required to remit the refund only after obtaining repayment from the provider.

The court noted that there was no case law on this subject to provide guidance in this conflict and that the Medicaid Act itself is "ambiguous." The court explained that the Medicaid statute permits the secretary of Health and Human Services (HHS) to reduce federal contributions to recover overpayments,[5] but certain payments are not to be considered overpayments until the state recovers the money from the provider.[6] Neither the statute nor implementing regulations define overpayment, however. The court declared that the federal government failed to provide any evidence which established that payment by a state program at a higher interim rate than the final rate constitutes an overpayment under the Medicaid statute.

The court reasoned that "to place the full burden of unrecoverable Medicaid payments on the states would be inconsistent with the general scheme of the Medicaid program, which was intended to function as a partnership between the states and the federal government."[7] The district court cited the U.S. Supreme Court decision in *Harris v. McRae*[8] as establishing that "the cornerstone of Medicaid" is joint federal-state financial cooperation. The Supreme Court stated that nothing in the Medicaid statute or its legislative history

> suggests that Congress intended to require a participating state to assume the full costs of providing any health service in its Medicaid plan. Quite the contrary, the purpose of Congress in enacting Title XIX [Medicaid] was to provide federal financial assistance for all legitimate state expenditures under an approved Medicaid plan.[9]

The district court ruled in the case at hand that, when a state makes a payment to a provider at an interim rate in compliance with a federally approved state plan and the interim rate through no fault of the state is higher than the final rate, the federal government cannot rule the interim rate "improper." If the state recovers the excess payment from the provider, the federal share of that recovery can be considered an overpayment. However, until "recovery occurs ... HHS is not entitled to treat its payments to a state at an interim rate in excess of the final rate as overpayments."[10] The district court ruled for the Commonwealth of Massachusetts and declared that the plaintiff's interim payments to the bankrupt nursing homes were not overpayments within the meaning of the Medicaid statute.

COST SHARING

The Tax Equity and Fiscal Responsibility Act (TEFRA) of 1982[11] allowed states to alter cost-sharing requirements significantly for Medicaid beneficiaries. Prior to the enactment of this statute, state Medicaid programs were not allowed to impose cost sharing on mandatory services provided to the categorically needy. The states were permitted, although not required, to impose cost sharing on optional services provided to the categorically needy and on all services provided to the medically needy, however. Under the TEFRA, states may impose cost-sharing charges, such as deductibles, copayments, or co-insurance, on both the categorically and medically needy for any service covered by the states.[12] Federal law prohibits cost sharing, however, in the following cases:

1. services to Medicaid beneficiaries under age 18
2. services to pregnant women
3. inpatient services in a hospital, long-term care facility, or other medical institution if the beneficiaries are required to spend all of their income, except a personal needs allowance, for medical care
4. emergency hospital services to prevent death or serious impairment of a beneficiary's health

5. family planning services
6. services of a health maintenance organization provided to categorically needy beneficiaries

Federal regulations limit the amount of cost sharing that state programs can impose on Medicaid participants. Any deductible for noninstitutional services cannot exceed $2 per month per family for each period of Medicaid eligibility.[13] For example, if Medicaid eligibility is certified for three months, the maximum deductible imposed on that family for that period of eligibility is $6. Any co-insurance rate on noninstitutional services cannot exceed 5 percent of the payment that the Medicaid program makes for the service. Any copayments on noninstitutional services cannot exceed 50¢ for a state payment of $10 or less; $1 for a state payment of $10.01 to $25; $2 for a state payment of $25.01 to $50; and $3 for a state payment of $50.01 or more. The state Medicaid program cannot require a maximum deductible, co-insurance, or copayment charge for each admission into an institution that exceeds 50 percent of the state payment for the first day of care.[14] Furthermore, the state Medicaid programs must have a cumulative maximum amount for all deductible, co-insurance, or copayment charges that it imposes on any family during a specified time period.[15]

TOTAL MEDICAID SPENDING

Payments to intermediate care facilities became the largest Medicaid expenditure category in 1981, surpassing payments for hospital care (Table II-1). By 1985, an estimated 29¢ of every $1 of Medicaid expenditures will go to intermediate care facilities; 42¢ of every $1 will go to nursing homes when payments to skilled nursing facilities are added to this figure. If payments for inpatient hospital care are added, better than $2 of every $3 of Medicaid expenditures will go to pay for institutional care services during 1985.

Medicaid payments to intermediate care facilities have grown rapidly, averaging an estimated 18.5 percent per year between 1975 and 1985 (Table II-2). Unless the growth rate in payments for institutional care can be contained, state Medicaid programs will continue to face fiscal problems. Given rising program expenditures and declining federal contributions, the state programs will be forced to reduce the scope and duration of covered services, decrease reimbursement levels, tighten eligibility standards, and increase cost sharing to remain financially solvent.

Table II-1 Major Medicaid Spending Categories (Millions)

Year	Total Medicaid	Hospital	Skilled Care	Intermediate Care*
1985 (E)	$40,762	$10,325 (25%)	$5,389 (13%)	$11,975 (29%)
1984 (E)	$37,209	$ 9,264 (25%)	$5,051 (14%)	$10,940 (29%)
1983 (E)	$34,285	$ 8,567 (25%)	$4,753 (14%)	$10,033 (29%)
1982	$29,906	$ 7,822 (26%)	$4,383 (15%)	$ 8,587 (29%)
1981	$27,284	$ 7,203 (26%)	$4,160 (15%)	$ 7,417 (27%)
1980	$23,301	$ 6,271 (27%)	$3,709 (16%)	$ 6,198 (27%)
1979	$20,462	$ 5,650 (28%)	$3,368 (16%)	$ 5,272 (26%)
1978	$17,975	$ 4,988 (28%)	$3,097 (17%)	$ 4,285 (24%)
1977	$16,276	$ 4,603 (28%)	$2,687 (17%)	$ 3,518 (22%)
1976	$14,135	$ 3,938 (28%)	$2,488 (18%)	$ 2,791 (20%)
1975	$12,292	$ 3,411 (28%)	$2,446 (20%)	$ 2,216 (18%)

*Includes intermediate care facilities for the mentally retarded.

Note: The percentage following each expenditure amount describes the percent the spending level for each service is of total Medicaid spending during that year.

Source: Estimates for 1985, 1984, and 1983 were obtained from U.S. Department of Health and Human Services, Health Care Financing Administration, Office of Financial and Actuarial Analysis; data for 1982-1975, from U.S. Department of Health and Human Services, Health Care Financing Administration, Office of Policy, Planning and Research, *Medicaid State Tables—Recipients, Payments, and Services,* Fiscal Years 1975-1982.

Table II-2 Medicaid: Major Spending Categories and Annual Cost Increases

					Institutional Long-Term Care			
Year	Total Medicaid	Annual Increase (%)	General Hospital	Annual Increase (%)	Skilled Care	Annual Increase (%)	Intermediate Care*	Annual Increase (%)
1985 (E)	$40,762	9.5	$10,325	11.5	$5,389	6.7	$11,975	9.5
1984 (E)	$37,209	8.5	$ 9,264	8.1	$5,051	6.3	$10,940	9.0
1983 (E)	$34,285	14.6	$ 8,567	9.5	$4,753	8.4	$10,033	16.8
1982	$29,906	9.6	$ 7,822	8.6	$4,383	5.4	$ 8,587	15.8
1981	$27,284	17.1	$ 7,203	14.9	$4,160	12.2	$ 7,417	19.7
1980	$23,301	13.9	$ 6,271	11.0	$3,709	10.1	$ 6,198	17.6
1979	$20,462	13.8	$ 5,650	13.3	$3,368	8.8	$ 5,272	23.0
1978	$17,975	10.4	$ 4,988	8.4	$3,097	15.3	$ 4,285	21.8
1977	$16,276	15.1	$ 4,603	16.9	$2,687	8.0	$ 3,518	26.0
1976	$14,135	15.0	$ 3,938	15.5	$2,488	2.0	$ 2,791	25.9
1975	$12,292		$ 3,411		$2,466		$ 2,216	
Average Annual Increase 1975–1985		12.8		11.8		8.3		18.5

*Includes intermediate care facilities for the mentally retarded.

Source: Estimates for 1985, 1984, and 1983 were obtained from U.S. Department of Health and Human Services, Health Care Financing Administration, Office of Financial and Actuarial Analysis; data for 1982–1975 were obtained from U.S. Department of Health and Human Services, Health Care Financing Administration, Office of Policy, Planning and Research, Medicaid State Tables—Recipients, Payments, and Services, Fiscal Years 1975–1982.

NOTES

1. P.L. 89-97.
2. P.L. 97-35.
3. INTERGOVERNMENTAL HEALTH POLICY PROJECT, GEORGE WASHINGTON UNIVERSITY, RECENT AND PROPOSED CHANGES IN STATE MEDICAID PROGRAMS: A FIFTY STATE SURVEY, *April 1983* (1983).
4. Commonwealth of Massachusetts v. Margaret Heckler, U.S. District Court, District of Massachusetts, Civ. No. 82-1048-G, January 13, 1984. In MEDICARE AND MEDICAID GUIDE, 33,593.
5. 42 U.S.C. §1396b(d)(2).
6. 42 U.S.C. §1396b(d)(3).
7. *See* note 4, *supra*, at p. 9856.
8. 448 U.S. 297, 308-309 (1981).
9. *Id.*, at 308-309.
10. *See* note 4, *supra*, at p. 9857.
11. P.L. 97-248.
12. 42 C.F.R. §447.53.
13. 42 C.F.R. §447.54(a).
14. 42 C.F.R. §447.54(c).
15. 42 C.F.R. §447.54(d).

Chapter 7

Medicaid: Inpatient Hospital Reimbursement

The Medicaid program will spend an estimated $10.3 billion for inpatient hospital care during 1985, with 5½¢ of every $1 spent on this type of care coming from the Medicaid program. Expenses for inpatient hospital care will also absorb a major share of the Medicaid budget—an estimated 25 percent during 1985.[1] Medicaid payments for inpatient hospital care will grow an average 11.8 percent per year between 1975 and 1985.

The federal and state governments have adopted various policy innovations to attempt to control these rising costs. Of particular importance to future Medicaid reimbursement policies for hospital care is the new diagnosis-related group (DRG) method adopted by Medicare to determine reimbursement payments. If the DRG system proves successful in cost containment, this Medicare method, together with the DRG systems developed by Medicaid programs in New Jersey, Pennsylvania, Utah, and Washington, may become the hospital reimbursement model for other state Medicaid programs. As of April 1984, at least twenty-seven states were considering the adoption of a DRG rate-setting system.

Federal regulations require that, in order to participate in the Medicaid program, a hospital must meet the participation requirements for Medicare.[2] To participate in both the Medicare and Medicaid programs, the hospital must conform to all relevant state and local laws governing the licensure of hospitals and must be approved by the state or local agency responsible for hospital licensure.[3] (See Acute Care Hospital, Chapter 2.)

LEGISLATIVE HISTORY OF MEDICAID REIMBURSEMENT

Before 1972, state Medicaid programs were required by the federal government to pay for hospital care on the basis of Medicare reasonable cost reimbursement principles. The 1972 amendments to the Social Security Act permitted states to develop their own reasonable cost payment system for hospital care, subject to approval by the secretary of what was then the

Department of Health, Education and Welfare.[4] No payment made under the state's own definition of reasonable cost could exceed the level of reimbursement calculated under Medicare principles, however.

Congress came to view reasonable cost reimbursement, resulting in a retrospective cost-based payment, as inflationary.[5] With rising hospital costs and reductions in the federal contributions to the Medicaid program placing states in a fiscal squeeze, Congress decided that the states needed greater flexibility in paying for hospital care. The Omnibus Budget Reconciliation Act of 1981[6] amended the Social Security Act to require that, effective October 1, 1981, state Medicaid programs reimburse hospitals with rates that are "reasonable and adequate to meet the costs" incurred by "efficiently and economically operated" hospitals. The legislative history demonstrates that Congress intended "to give states greater latitude in developing and implementing alternative reimbursement methodologies that promote the efficient and economical delivery of such services."[7] In addition, Congress wanted the states to use adequate payment levels in order to attract a "sufficient" number of providers to ensure that all Medicaid patients would receive high-quality hospital care. Congress noted that, in several states, many physicians refused to treat Medicaid patients because of low Medicaid fees.[8] Therefore, Congress wanted payment rates to be set at a level that would attract a "majority" of the hospitals in each state into Medicaid participation.

Congress also stated in developing the Omnibus Budget Reconciliation Act that state Medicaid programs should recognize the "special costs" incurred by hospitals that treat a large number of Medicaid patients and other patients not covered by third party payors. The Medicaid programs should also consider the mix of cases, recognizing the complexity and severity of disease in patients treated by the hospital. In reviewing the hospital reimbursement methods used by the states, Congress directed the secretary of the Department of Health and Human Services (HHS)

> to analyze the impact the reimbursement methodology has on access to care for Medicaid beneficiaries, on differentials in payment levels between Medicare and Medicaid, and on the financial viability of institutions whose patient populations are disproportionately composed of Medicaid patients or patients without third party coverage.[9]

FEDERAL REGULATIONS

State Medicaid programs must reimburse hospitals with rates that are "reasonable and adequate" to meet the costs incurred by hospitals that are operated efficiently and economically in conformance with state and federal laws, regulations, and quality and safety standards.[10] Medicaid payments for inpatient hospital services cannot exceed the hospital's customary charges,[11] nor can they exceed "in the aggregate" the amount that would be paid for care under Medicare reimbursement principles.[12]

Adhering to the intent of Congress as expressed by the statute and in its legislative history, federal regulations declare that the methods and standards used by state Medicaid programs to calculate payment rates "must take into account the situation of hospitals which serve a disproportionate number of low income patients with special needs."[13] Also, the reimbursement methods and standards used by state programs must recognize that payments for an "inappropriate level of care" will be made at lower rates, reflecting the level of care actually provided;[14] for example, the cost of care for a Medicaid recipient who must be kept in the hospital longer than medically necessary because there is no bed available in a skilled care or intermediate care facility is reimbursable at a lower rate than that for inpatient hospital care. In addition, the state Medicaid programs must use sufficiently high payment rates for hospital care to "assure that recipients have reasonable access" to care of "adequate" quality, taking into account geographical location and travel time.[15]

State Medicaid programs must submit to the secretary of HHS the average proposed payment rate for hospital care, as well as the rates for skilled and intermediate nursing home care.[16] The states must include the amounts by which the new rates are higher or lower than the previous rates. In addition, the state Medicaid programs must estimate the short-term and long-term effects that the new rates will have on the availability of care, the type of care delivered, the extent of provider participation, and the degree to which costs are covered in hospitals that serve a disproportionate number of low-income patients with special needs. State programs must give public notice of any significant proposed change in its methods and standards for setting payment rates for inpatient hospital services, unless the change is required by court order or the change is necessary to conform to Medicare reimbursement methods or levels.[17]

Under federal regulations, each state Medicaid agency must require hospitals to file uniform cost reports.[18] The state agencies must also provide for periodic audits of the financial and statistical records of participating hospitals.[19]

STATE REIMBURSEMENT POLICIES

The state Medicaid programs have adopted a variety of payment mechanisms to pay for inpatient hospital care (Table 7-1). Although the state programs have not been required by the federal government to reimburse hospitals for inpatient care on the basis of Medicare principles since 1972, Table 7-1 illustrates that many states continue to use either Medicare reasonable cost principles or modified Medicare reasonable cost principles in 1984.

Table 7-1 Medicaid Hospital Reimbursement Factors: 1984

	Limited Days of Paid Care		Method of Payment*	Prospective Payment	Adoption of Medicare DRG System	Average Payment per Stay (1983)
	Per Year	Per Spell of Illness/Stay				
Alabama	12	12	1	Yes	No	$1,331
Alaska	None	None	3	Yes	No	
Arizona			7	7	No	
Arkansas	Other	Other	1	U.C.†	U.C.	$1,495
California	None	None	4	4	No	
Colorado	None	None	3	Yes	No	
Connecticut	None	None	1	U.C.	U.C.	$1,418
Delaware	None	None	1	No	U.C.	$1,667
Florida	45	45	3	Yes	U.C.	$1,936
Georgia	None	None	3	Yes	No	$2,342
Hawaii	None	None	1	No	No	$2,208
Idaho	40	40	2	No	U.C.	
Illinois	None	None	2	Yes	U.C.	
Indiana	None	None	1	No	U.C.	$1,203
Iowa	None	None	3	Yes	U.C.	$2,209
Kansas	None	None	1	Yes	No	$1,742
Kentucky	None	14	2	Yes	U.C.	$ 947
Louisiana	15	15	2	No	U.C.	$1,714
Maine	None	None	2	Yes	No	$1,992
Maryland	None	20	3	Yes	No	
Massachusetts	None	None	2	Yes	No	$2,194
Michigan	None	18‡	2	Yes	U.C.	$2,963
Minnesota	None	None	2	Yes	U.C.	
Mississippi	15 (7/1/84)		3	Yes		
Missouri	None	None	2	Yes	U.C.	$2,250
Montana	None	None	1	Yes	U.C.	$1,667 (per case)

Table 7-1 continued

	Limited Days of Paid Care Per Year	Limited Days of Paid Care Per Spell of Illness/Stay	Method of Payment*	Prospective Payment	Adoption of Medicare DRG System	Average Payment per Stay (1983)
Nebraska	None	None	3	Yes	U.C.	$1,868
Nevada	None	None	3	Yes	No	
New Hampshire	None	None	2	No	U.C.	$1,461
New Jersey	None	None	5	Yes	No	$1,606
New Mexico	None	None	1	No	No	$1,344 (per recipient)
New York	None	20[‡]	1	Yes	U.C.	$3,159 (1982)
North Carolina	None	None	2	Yes	No	$1,765
North Dakota	None	None	1	No	U.C.	$1,364
Ohio	None	30 (1983)	1	Yes	U.C.	$2,662
Oklahoma	60	10[‡]	2	Yes	No	$2,005
Oregon	18	18	2	Yes	U.C.	$1,576
Pennsylvania	None	None	5 (7/1/84)	Yes	No	
Rhode Island	None	None	2	Yes	U.C.	
South Carolina	12	None	1	No	U.C.	$1,547
South Dakota	None	None	1	No	U.C.	$1,237
Tennessee	14	14	2	Yes	U.C.	$1,599
Texas	120	30	1	No	No	$ 978
Utah	None	None	6	Yes	Yes	$2,417
Vermont				Yes	No	
Virginia	21	21	2	Yes	No	$2,261
Washington	None	None	5 (10/1/84)	Yes	No	$1,278
West Virginia	20	None	1	No	U.C.	$1,430
Wisconsin	None	None	2	Yes	U.C.	$1,655
Wyoming	None	None	1	No	U.C.	

*Method of payment:
1. Pre-DRG, Medicare reasonable cost principles.
2. Modified Pre-DRG, Medicare reasonable cost principles.
3. Other

Table 7-1 continued

4. "In 1982 California enacted a Selective Provider Contracting Program that involves competitive bidding for prospective rates, generally on a per diem basis. Now (May, 1984) the California Medical Assistance Commission negotiates the rates and terms of the contracts and the California Department of Health Services implements and manages the contract. Many hospitals, however, are still under the Medicare, retrospective cost based system." Survey, California Department of Health Services.
5. The state's own DRG system.
6. Medicare's DRG system.
7. The Arizona Health Care Cost Containment System (AHCCCS), a three-year experimental Medicaid program, utilizes a competitive bidding process to retain contractors who assume responsibility for provision of the complete range of AHCCCS services on a prepaid capitated basis.

†Under consideration.

‡Extensions beyond limit granted with Medicaid approval.

Source: Reprinted with permission from *HOSPITALS*, published by American Hospital Publishing, Inc., copyright September 1, 1984, Vol. 58, No. 17.

A survey of the state programs taken for this book showed that twenty-seven states of the forty-nine responding considered adopting the new Medicare DRG system in early 1984; four states have adopted some form of a DRG-based payment system. This low utilization of the DRG system may be due to the newness of the Medicare system and, as one state Medicaid administrator observed, to the differences in age, health status, and care needs between Medicare and Medicaid patients. Given these differences, the Medicare DRG rates may be too costly for the state Medicaid programs to use as a basis for reimbursement for hospital care provided to Medicaid recipients.

Thirty-three states adopted a prospective rate-setting system, and only fifteen states used a retrospective payment system to pay for inpatient hospital services for Medicaid recipients during 1984. Of the fifteen states using retrospective payments, Arkansas and Connecticut reported that they were considering the use of a prospective mechanism. In addition to the thirty-three states using prospective rate setting, California uses a prospective rate to reimburse hospitals in areas of the state covered by its bidding system. The California program responded to the survey that it is also considering using this rate-setting system "experimentally" for hospitals not already receiving a prospective payment.

REASONABLE AND ADEQUATE LITIGATION

Alabama

The Medicaid program in Alabama developed an alternate prospective reimbursement method, effective October 1, 1981, that distinguishes among the education, capital, and operating costs that hospitals expect to incur in providing care to Medicaid patients. The Alabama method differs from the Medicare reasonable cost method by, among other things, limiting the amount of reimbursement permitted for the capital and operating costs incurred by hospitals. Providers with an average unused capacity exceeding 50 percent of their available licensed beds receive less than full reimbursement for capital costs. The reimbursement limitation for operating costs is determined by dividing hospitals into classes based on licensed bed size and rural or urban locations, calculating the mean operating costs for hospitals within each class, and limiting reimbursement for each hospital's operating costs to the mean operating costs for its class plus one standard deviation. HHS approved the plan under the reasonable cost standards.

The Alabama Hospital Association and ten Alabama hospitals filed suit in federal district court to enjoin implementation of the plan.[20] Congress had revised the federal standards for hospital reimbursement by reducing the threshold of permissible payment rates away from reasonable cost to a new standard of "reasonable and adequate." The plaintiffs alleged in *Alabama Hospital Association* that the new Alabama plan was invalid under the new "reasonable and adequate" standard. Because HHS had not reviewed Alabama's method under the new standards, the district court temporarily enjoined implementation of the method, pending completion of the proceedings before the court. HHS subsequently approved the plan under the new standards, concluding that Alabama gave satisfactory assurances of compliance with the reasonable and adequate standard. Following a trial on the merits, the district court held that HHS had properly approved Alabama's alternate reimbursement plan and dissolved its temporary injunction.

The plaintiffs appealed this ruling by the district court to the U.S. Circuit Court of Appeals for the Eleventh Circuit.[21] They argued that HHS' approval of Alabama's alternate reimbursement plan could not stand because (1) HHS failed to promulgate standards that define the efficient cost standard, (2) Alabama did not submit to the federal government information required by federal regulations, (3) the Alabama plan did not take into account the plight of hospitals serving a disproportionate number of poor patients, and (4) the plan does not reduce rates for patients receiving an inappropriate level of care. The appellate court rejected the first three arguments and accepted the fourth.

The court of appeals noted that Alabama's alternate reimbursement system had first been approved under the previous reasonable cost standard, "a standard which is more generous from the appellant's perspective." The Court reasoned that, "because the new 'efficient cost' standard [reasonable and adequate] is designed to lower the threshold of permissible reimbursement rates, rates properly approved under the reasonable cost standard will satisfy the new efficient cost standard."[22] According to the court, the Alabama Hospital Association did not challenge that the plan was properly approved under the reasonable cost standard, nor did it offer plausible reason why, after approving the Alabama plan under the reasonable cost standard, which was more restrictive to the state's discretionary power, HHS should reach a different decision when applying the new efficient cost standard designed to give the states more discretion in rate setting.

The appellate court also dismissed the plaintiffs' objections that the Alabama plan does not allow reimbursement for bad debts and telephone services, costs that the plaintiffs argued must be incurred by efficiently and economically operated hospitals. Noting that the Medicare reimbursement method also does not generally allow reimbursement of these costs, the court observed that Congress intended "to move away from the inflationary Medicare reimbursement methodology.... Congress intended the efficient cost standard to reduce, not increase, the permissible level of reimbursement below that available under Medicare principles."[23]

In dismissing the plaintiffs' first argument, then, the court ruled that HHS' alleged error in failing to define the efficient cost standard was a "harmless error." The court saw no reason "to require HHS to refine an analysis when, seen in light of the appellants' own contentions, refinement would appear unnecessary, duplicative and wasteful."[24] For similar reasons, the court dismissed the plaintiffs' second argument, i.e., that the state failed to submit to HHS information required by federal regulations, as a harmless error.

With regard to the plaintiffs' argument that the Alabama plan does not take into account the plight of hospitals serving a disproportionate number of poor patients, the court noted that the Alabama Medicaid program had amended its plan to address this issue. The plaintiffs did not challenge the adequacy of this amendment, but urged the court to hold that the unamended plan violates the federal Medicaid statute. The plaintiffs reasoned that Alabama may rescind this amendment. The court of appeals rejected this argument as moot, citing a U.S. Supreme Court ruling that, unless there is a reasonable expectation that the alleged violation will recur, the issue is moot.[25] The court of appeals concluded that the Alabama Hospital Association and its co-plaintiffs "may, without undue difficulty, assert their objections against the unamended plan if and when the state rescinds the amendment."[26]

The court of appeals accepted the plaintiffs' argument that the plan did not provide for reduced reimbursement rates for patients who received an inappropriate level of care. The court noted that the Medicaid statute expressly requires this policy[27] and that HHS erred in approving Alabama's plan when it did not contain this provision. The court remanded the case to district court so that an appropriate remedy could be found, but remarked that because the plan's general structure had been upheld, the district court may allow the plan to operate while it remedies the failure to include a provision concerning payments for inappropriate levels of care.

Wisconsin

In Wisconsin, the Medicaid program pays a retrospective "all-inclusive rate" per discharge to each hospital, which is calculated using a reasonable cost method for a base year. A federally defined "hospital cost index" is applied to each hospital's rate per discharge for the base year to calculate the payment rate for the final settlement year. The Wisconsin program submitted assurances to HHS that its hospital payment method, approved on July 19, 1982, took inflationary cost increases into account and that the rates established by the method complied with the reasonable and adequate standard.

On April 30, 1982, the Wisconsin legislature delayed by three months Medicaid rate increases scheduled to take effect on or after July 1, 1982, and before July 1, 1983. Estimating that this freeze would reduce Medicaid payments to its 141 members by approximately $4 million, the Wisconsin Hospital Association sought in federal court preliminary and permanent injunctive relief to prevent the Wisconsin Medicaid program from enforcing this freeze on reimbursement rates for hospital care.[28]

The association made two main arguments against the freeze. First, the plaintiffs asserted that a freeze is arbitrary and, therefore, cannot be said to comply with the reasonable and adequate standard required by federal law. Arguing that the state plan approved by HHS provided for rate increases to reflect inflation, the plaintiffs claimed that a freeze denying these inflationary increases is unreasonable and in violation of the reasonable and adequate standard contained in the Social Security Act. Citing the Supremacy Clause of the U.S. Constitution, the plaintiffs noted that any state statute violating a federal statute is invalid.

In its second argument against the freeze, the Wisconsin Hospital Association contended that the freeze violated orders of the court that had been given in an earlier dispute, in which the association had challenged the state plan on the ground that it failed to provide reasonable payment rates to Medicaid providers. That lawsuit had been settled by an Amended Stipulation adopted by the present court in an order signed on July 21, 1982. This Amended Stipulation stated that the plaintiffs were to be reimbursed for services provided to Medicaid patients "in accordance with the State Plan." The Amended Stipulation also modified and clarified the state plan with the effect of increasing reimbursement rates.

The defendants responded to the plaintiffs' motion by arguing that, when the Wisconsin Hospital Association agreed to the Amended Stipulation, it was aware of the freeze enacted May 1, 1982. The defendants further contended that, since the association accepted the benefits of the new state plan "with full knowledge of the imminent freeze," the plaintiffs should be estopped from challenging the freeze. The defendants also argued that the freeze is consistent with the reasonable and adequate standard.

The court found

> that a rate freeze is inherently unreasonable. . . . The State itself made assurances to the USDHHS that its state plan "granted rate increases to participating providers based on inflationary increases for a federally defined hospital market basket." . . . Thus the state itself takes the position that rate reimbursement based on increases in the Hospital Cost Index provides a reasonable and adequate rate. . . . It cannot at the same time support the position that an arbitrary freeze, which ignores inflationary increases, continues to be reasonable and adequate.[29]

The court also disagreed with the defendants' estoppel argument, remarking that the dates cited by the defendants did "not tell the full story." After reviewing earlier negotiations and agreements between the parties, the court noted:

> Thus, it is clear that while no mention of a Medicaid freeze was ever made until April 15, 1982, the State and WHA had reached an agreement, which provided increased benefits to the hospitals under the Amended State Plan well before April 15. That agreement was signed on February 24, 1982.[30]

The court ruled that, while it "is sympathetic to the Wisconsin Legislature in its efforts to contain the high costs of medical care, the court cannot approve"[31] the freeze on hospital payment rates. "If the State wishes to continue to participate in the Medicaid program it must find cost saving methods which do not violate federal law."[32] Having found that the freeze violates federal law and is unconstitutional under the Supremacy Clause and having rejected the defendants' estoppel argument, the court granted summary judgment in favor of the Wisconsin Hospital Association. The court permanently enjoined the Wisconsin Medicaid program from implementing the freeze on hospital reimbursement rates.

The U.S. Court of Appeals for the Seventh Circuit reversed this district court ruling and remanded the case for further proceedings.[33] The appellate court noted that, when a state Medicaid program makes assurances that its hospital rates are reasonable and adequate,

> the state does not certify that these rates are only or barely adequate. It is not therefore for a court to conclude, without further analysis and consideration of evidence, that any other rate is by definition unreasonable or inadequate. In general, rates required to meet a standard of reasonableness may fall within a zone of reasonableness. [34]

The appellate court decided that the reviewing court must examine "the individual effects of this particular freeze in order to determine whether the resulting rates are adequate and reasonable."[35] For example, the appellate court wanted the district court to consider whether the freeze would affect the quality of care, whether the number of Medicaid patients would decrease, or whether hospitals would operate as before with only reduced profits.

On remanding the case, the appellate court presented important principles to be observed. First, the revised state plan should be submitted to HHS so that the secretary's determination can provide guidance to the district court in evaluating the reasonableness and adequacy of the Medicaid rates as affected by the freeze. Second, the plaintiffs have the burden of demonstrating that the rates resulting from the freeze have an adverse impact on hospital services, finances, or other relevant factors in order to show the rates to be unreasonable and inadequate. Third, the district court should note that "the reasonableness of a rate increase may presumably cover a zone and is not necessarily defined by a single point."[36]

California

On October 1, 1981, the California legislature enacted, effective immediately, a 6 percent cap on increases in Medicaid payments for inpatient hospital services. The California Hospital Association, the United Hospital Association, and a number of individual hospitals brought action in federal district court against state and federal officials, challenging California's Medi-Cal (Medicaid) plan for implementing this cap.[37]

The court ruled that the assurances given by the California Department of Health Services to HHS that the 6 percent cap met the reasonable and adequate standard were not based on a proper finding of fact. To the contrary, the court found that the assurances were based "upon an effort to develop the best case" for the amendment. Only those factors favorable to the 6 percent cap had been considered and equally relevant but unfavorable factors had been intentionally ignored by the California Department of Health Services. In preparing supporting documents for the 6 percent cap, five indicators which made the best case for the amendment were included and another three to five indicators which did not support the cap or even contradicted the other indicators were ignored. The adoption of the 6 percent cap without considering all the relevant factors to determine if the proposed rates meet the reasonable and adequate standard was ruled to be "arbitrary and capricious and inconsistent with law." The court enjoined implementation of the 6 percent cap "until such time as the state DHS, after considering all relevant factors, makes a finding in compliance with statutory and regulatory requirements"[38] that the rates meet the reasonable and adequate standard. On March 28, 1983, this judgment was affirmed by the U.S. Court of Appeals for the Ninth Circuit.[39]

Pennsylvania

Magee-Womens Hospital challenged in federal district court the Pennsylvania Medicaid program's enforcement of an amendment to its state plan before the amendment had been approved by HHS.[40] Because of federal cutbacks, the Pennsylvania Department of Public Welfare had been forced to limit increases in its Medicaid budget, resulting in new regulations that imposed a 10 percent ceiling on increases in interim Medicaid rates.

In October 1982, Magee-Womens Hospital began operation of a new maternity wing, the construction of which had increased the hospital's interest and depreciation expenses for 1982-1983. The plaintiff had anticipated reimbursement from the welfare department for Medicaid's share of these increased costs, but the new wing had increased expenses beyond 110 percent of the previous year's costs. Although the new regulations made provisions for the reimbursement of expenses associated with capital expenditures, these payments were not included in the interim rates.

The welfare department began implementing the 110 percent ceiling on increases in interim rates, even though the new regulations had not received approval from HHS. The plaintiff, seeking a declaratory judgment that new regulations were invalid and an injunction against their enforcement, contended that new regulations are not enforceable without final approval from HHS. The defendants countered by arguing that the Social Security Act does not require prior approval. The issue before the court was "whether

Congress required approval by the Secretary prior to the enforcement of any amendments to a state's Medicaid plan."[41]

To resolve this issue, the court reviewed the Medicaid statute and its recent history. Until the 1981 amendments were enacted, the Medicaid statute had explicitly required approval by HHS before the states could enforce any amendments to their state plan. The court observed that the 1981 amendments deleted this explicit requirement of prior approval "though its inclusion would have been a simple matter for Congress. We conclude that the deletion of the prior approval requirement is persuasive evidence that Congress intended to change the meaning of the statute."[42] Therefore, the court held that approval by the secretary is not required before a state can enforce amendments to its state Medicaid plan and denied the plaintiff's motion for a preliminary injunction.

LIMITS TO PAID CARE

In an effort to control Medicaid expenditures for inpatient hospital services, seventeen states have established limits to the number of reimbursed days of care on either a per illness/stay or per year basis (see Table 7-1). The Oklahoma program, for example, pays for up to ten days per stay, with extensions when medically necessary, up to a maximum of 60 allowable days per year. The limit to the number of paid days of care per year ranges from a low of twelve paid days in South Carolina and Alabama to no limit in thirty-five states. The limit to the number of paid days per illness/stay ranges from a low of ten days in Oklahoma (with extensions granted when medically necessary) to no limit in thirty-two states. Figure 7-1 illustrates the geographical distribution of state Medicaid programs that limit the number of reimbursed days of hospital care. States with such limits tend to be concentrated in the southern United States.

On December 21, 1981, Charleston Memorial Hospital, the South Carolina Hospital Association, and other South Carolina hospitals filed suit in federal district court seeking declaratory and injunctive relief from the reductions in both inpatient and outpatient coverages implemented by the South Carolina Department of Social Services (Medicaid) on July 1, 1981.[43] The plaintiffs alleged that, although the South Carolina Medicaid program did not reduce its reimbursement rate, the reductions in the number of reimbursed inpatient days to twelve per year and reimbursed outpatient days to eighteen days per year were actually an issue of reimbursement, not coverage, because they ultimately decreased the compensation hospitals received for inpatient and outpatient services. According to the plaintiffs, the level of coverage was no longer "sufficient in amount, duration, and scope to achieve its purpose,"[44] and the reductions were improper because they were based on budgetary

Figure 7-1 Medicaid: Limits to Paid Days/Inpatient Hospital Care: 1984

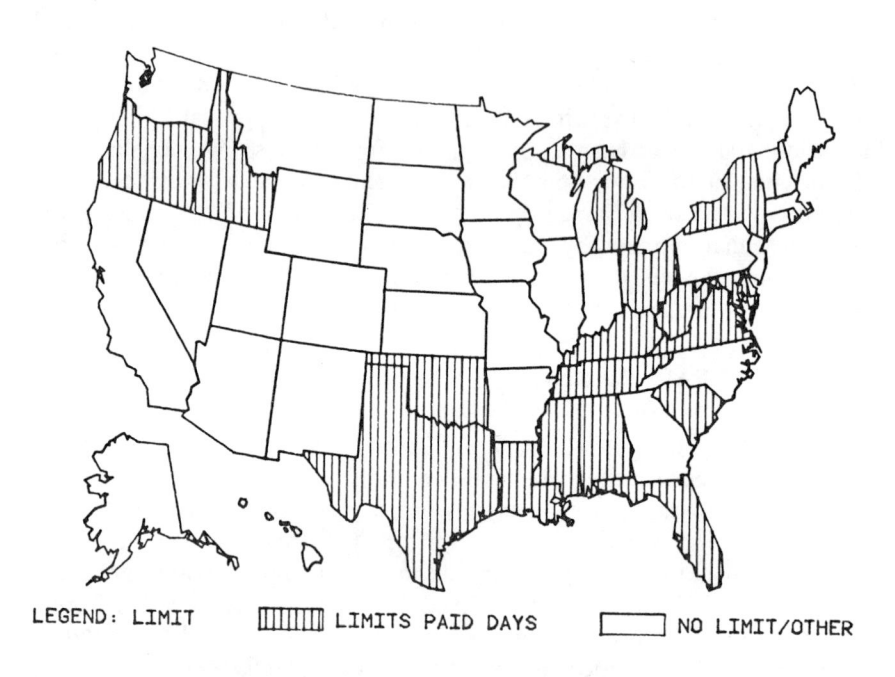

LEGEND: LIMIT   ▦ LIMITS PAID DAYS   ☐ NO LIMIT/OTHER

Source: Data compiled from author's survey of state programs.

---

constraints. The plaintiffs further alleged that the reductions were invalid because (1) the state plan did not take into account the plight of hospitals that serve a disproportionate number of low income patients, (2) the plan did not have reimbursement rates that were reasonable and adequate to meet the costs of economically operated hospitals, and (3) the reimbursement rates were not adequate to ensure that Medicaid recipients would have reasonable access to high-quality inpatient services. The plaintiffs also charged that the reductions violated federal procedural requirements because the South Carolina Medicaid program had not given public notice of the reductions and the reductions took effect before HHS approved them. In a final allegation, the plaintiffs charged that the reductions deprived them of property without due process of law, since the Hill-Burton Act required them to participate in the Medicaid program in exchange for Hill-Burton benefits and Medicaid compensation in South Carolina was inadequate to cover their costs.

On December 28, 1981, the district court entered a preliminary injunction against implementation of the reductions until a hearing could be held to determine the legality of the reductions. After the hearing, the district court dissolved the preliminary injunction and denied all relief sought by the plaintiffs.

The plaintiffs appealed this decision to the U.S. Court of Appeals for the Fourth Circuit.[45] The appellate court, deciding against the plaintiffs, ruled that the reductions in the number of covered days per year did not violate the substantive requirements of federal law. In agreeing with the district court's ruling that the reductions were decreases in coverage, not in levels of reimbursement, the court cited *Virginia Hospital Association v. Kenley*,[46] in which the court had ruled that an amendment to the Virginia state plan limiting inpatient hospital services to twenty-one days was an issue "merely" of coverage.

The court of appeals agreed with the district court that the level of service would meet the needs of most Medicaid recipients. A limit of twelve inpatient hospital days would meet the needs of 88 percent of the Medicaid recipients requiring inpatient care, and a limit of eighteen outpatient days would meet the needs of 99 percent of the Medicaid recipients requiring outpatient care in South Carolina.

Again citing *Virginia Hospital Association*, in which a limit of twenty-one days had been found rationally related to the state's legitimate interest in guaranteeing the fiscal solvency of its Medicaid program, the court rejected the plaintiffs' allegation that the reductions were unreasonable because they were based solely on budgetary considerations. The plaintiffs had cited *Alabama Nursing Home Association v. Harris*[47] in which the court had decided that budgetary problems did not excuse a state from complying with federal Medicaid requirements. The court of appeals in *Charleston Memorial Hospital* ruled that *Alabama Nursing Home* did not apply, however, because the South Carolina Medicaid program was "not seeking to escape compliance" with federal law but only to reduce inpatient and outpatient hospital services "to a level that is fiscally feasible but still satisfies federal requirements."[48] The appellate court agreed with the district court that the South Carolina plan met the requirements of federal substantive law.

The court of appeals also agreed with the district court that the reduction in covered days did not violate federal procedural law. In the district court's opinion, the federal procedures that the plaintiffs asserted the South Carolina Medicaid program should have followed[49] applied only to reductions in rates of reimbursement and changes in reimbursement method, not to changes in coverage. In response to the plaintiffs' procedural complaint that the reductions were implemented before HHS had approved them, the South Carolina Department of Social Services countered that the issue was moot because HHS had since reviewed the changes and found them in compliance with federal law. The court of appeals agreed that this procedural allegation was moot.

The district court had ruled that the plaintiffs failed to offer any significant evidence to support their due process/Hill-Burton argument; stating that this finding is "not clearly erroneous," the court of appeals ruled it was bound by the district court's conclusion.

The Idaho Supreme Court and federal district court have upheld the Idaho Medicaid program's policy of not reimbursing providers for hospital care beyond twenty days per stay.[50] The Idaho Supreme Court made a distinction between "hospitalization" and "medical treatment," ruling that the state Medicaid program is not required to pay for hospitalization beyond twenty days, but is required to pay for medical treatment without any time limit. A trial court must decide which services provided beyond the limit of twenty days are hospitalization and which services are medical treatment in order to determine which services are Medicaid reimbursable. The federal district court ruled that the Medicaid program in Idaho acted within the law in limiting reimbursed acute inpatient hospital care to twenty days per stay. (See *Children's Memorial Hospital v. Illinois Department of Public Aid* in the Illinois section below for a related case on limits to lengths of stay.)

STATE REIMBURSEMENT METHODOLOGIES

Federal statutes and regulations have authorized the secretary of HHS to permit the Medicaid and Medicare programs to develop experimental reimbursement methods. In 1967, the Social Security Act was amended to permit demonstration projects to determine if reimbursement systems other than retrospective, reasonable cost systems could contain Medicaid and Medicare costs without adversely affecting the quality of care.[51] In 1972 amendments to the Social Security Act allowed the secretary of HHS to authorize experiments and demonstration projects to assess the merits of prospective rate setting.[52] In October 1982, the Health Care Financing Administration (HCFA) issued the general criteria used in determining whether new demonstration projects for statewide hospital reimbursement systems should be approved.[53] To obtain approval for a state rate-setting demonstration project, new projects must include DRGs as the units of payment. Many state Medicaid programs have taken advantage of these statutes to develop innovative reimbursement methods to pay for inpatient hospital services.

New Jersey

The use of DRGs for Medicaid reimbursement was pioneered in New Jersey. The experiment, which began on January 1, 1980, initially covered 26 hospitals, added coverage of another 40 hospitals during 1981, and further expanded to cover an additional 43 hospitals in 1982; thus, all acute care hospitals in New Jersey were included by the end of 1982.

In the New Jersey experiment, patients are assigned to one of 467 DRGs, according to primary and secondary diagnoses, surgical procedures, age, sex, and discharge status. A specific per case payment rate is calculated for each DRG,[54] based on medical discharge abstracts, patient billing records, and uniform hospital financial and statistical data.[55] The major cost centers are the direct costs of patient care, which include expenses for nursing and ancillary services; institutional costs, which include operating costs for managerial, educational, and maintenance services; and general service costs.

Hospitals are divided into groups based on teaching, minor teaching, or nonteaching status, as well as urban or rural location. An average direct patient care cost per DRG is calculated for each group of hospitals, serving as an incentive standard. Each hospital's base rate for each DRG is a combination of its group standard and its own direct patient care costs. This base rate is adjusted for inflation, multiplied by expected patient volume, and added to other DRG costs to yield the reasonable patient care costs for inpatient services.

Each hospital's general service costs are allocated to direct patient care costs and institutional cost centers using standard step-down accounting procedures. The costs of direct patient care and the institutional expenses are combined with allowances for uncompensated care, working capital needs, capital costs for the facility, and personal health allowances to develop a preliminary cost base. A revenue budget is developed for each hospital from this preliminary cost base, allowing hospitals to structure their charges and calculate the bills for patients in the different DRGs. A final review of patients' bills and the audited financial statement of the hospital at the end of the year reveals the differences between revenues collected and the approved budget. Any discrepancy is reconciled in the next year's rates. Hospitals that are dissatisfied with their rates may appeal through the Hospital Rate Setting Commission.

Mississippi

In 1981, the Medicaid program in Mississippi implemented, with the approval of the secretary of HHS, an alternative reimbursement method for inpatient hospital services that sets a prospective per diem rate for each hospital participating in the Medicaid program. The rate is based on each hospital's Medicaid costs for the previous year, adjusted to exclude costs disallowed under the Medicare program.[56] Each hospital is assigned to one of five classes, based on its number of licensed beds. Within each of these five classes, a limit is set prospectively on the per patient day reimbursement level.

The allowable costs are categorized into three cost centers: capital expenses, education expenses, and operating expenses. The capital cost component is calculated by dividing a hospital's total allowable capital costs related to the care of Medicaid patients by the number of Medicaid inpatient days. Reimbursement for the capital cost component is reduced if the hospital's occupancy rate falls below specified levels for its class of care, however. The education cost component is calculated by adjusting the hospital's education expenses in the prior year by the hospital industry inflation rate. Then each hospital's inflation-adjusted education costs are divided by its actual number of Medicaid inpatient days.

The operating cost component is calculated by determining the Medicaid program's share of each hospital's operating costs for the prior year and making an adjustment for the hospital industry inflation rate. These costs are then divided into labor and nonlabor categories and divided by the number of Medicaid inpatient days. The per diem labor cost is adjusted by the Standard Metropolitan Statistical Area (SMSA) Wage Index published in the *Federal Register* to reflect variations in labor costs between urban and rural areas in Mississippi. The adjusted labor and nonlabor per diem costs are then arrayed from the lowest to the highest with the comparable cost figures for other hospitals in the same class and the 80th percentile figure is calculated. This figure serves as a cost ceiling for operating costs within each class. Hospitals with per diem operating costs below the 80th percentile figure receive full reimbursement of their allowable operating costs; hospitals with operating costs above the ceiling receive the 80th percentile rate. Any hospital with allowable per diem costs that exceed the ceiling may appeal its rate to the Mississippi Medicaid Commission if certain conditions are present.

In 1981, the Mississippi Hospital Association and twelve Mississippi hospitals sought a preliminary injunction in federal district court to prevent the Mississippi hospital reimbursement plan from being implemented on July 1, 1981.[57] The plaintiffs argued that the secretary of HHS failed to comply with his obligation to review and approve the Mississippi plan and that the plan failed to reimburse the reasonable costs of care. The district court found, however, that the secretary's analysis of the similarities and differences between the Mississippi plan and Medicare principles was sufficient "to support the Secretary's ultimate decision that Mississippi's alternative reimbursement plan as a whole reimburses 'reasonable cost' as required by statute."[58] Furthermore, the district court ruled that the 80th percentile limitation used in the plan is not so arbitrary or restrictive that this method would result in less than the reasonable cost of care.

The plaintiffs also asserted that, because of the classification system used in the plan, the prospective limitation on per patient day payments, and the link between occupancy rates and reimbursement rates, the plan failed to reimburse providers for the reasonable costs of care as required by federal statute. In response to the plaintiffs' criticism of the classification system, the district court stated: "although the court might disagree with the wisdom of a classification system based solely on the number of licensed beds within a facility, we are unable to conclude such a classification system is irrational."[59] The court decided that, given the safeguards afforded to participating hospitals by the appeals process of the Mississippi plan, the classification system is a "rational method of grouping hospitals for the purpose of comparing and dealing with similarly situated hospitals."[60] With regard to the plaintiffs' criticism of the use of occupancy rates to adjust reimbursement payments for capital costs, the district court observed that testimony during the trial indicated that this was designed to reduce unnecessary capacity and unnecessary expansion. For this reason, the court stated it was "unable" to conclude that this method was irrational or would result in reimbursement levels less than reasonable cost.

On these grounds, the district court denied the preliminary injunction requested by the plaintiffs. The court did agree, however, with the plaintiffs' assertion that the Mississippi plan's denial of reimbursement for legal costs and fees incurred by providers in suits against federal and state agencies administering the Medicaid program was invalid. The court ruled that federal procedures for making such a change had not been followed, nor was a rational reason for the change given.

The Mississippi Hospital Association and its co-plaintiffs appealed this decision upholding the validity of the Mississippi plan to the court of appeals.[61] The Mississippi Medicaid program filed a cross appeal of the district court's decision to invalidate the provision of the state plan that disallowed the reimbursement of providers' legal costs in litigation with federal and state agencies administering the Medicaid program.

The appeals court, in upholding those parts of the decision in favor of the Mississippi Medicaid program, ruled that the burden was on the Mississippi Hospital Association "to establish that the plan is arbitrary or capricious, or in violation of federal law, and this they have not done."[62] In addition, the court of appeals ruled for the Mississippi Medicaid program by reversing the district court's ruling that the plan could not disallow litigation costs. The appellate court found that there were no procedural violations in developing this regulation and that the disallowance of litigation costs had a rational basis. In summary, the decision of the court of appeals stated that:

A state of limited resources, in the face of federal cutbacks, has adopted a plan to make the most of its Medicaid funds. The plan complies with flexible federal substantive and procedural requirements and cannot be described as arbitrary or capricious.[63]

The Mississippi Hospital Association has decided not to appeal the case to the U.S. Supreme Court.

New York

In 1983, the Medicaid, Medicare, and Blue Cross programs in New York state began to use a uniform prospective rate-setting method to calculate per diem payment rates for inpatient hospital care.[64] Under a waiver of Medicare and Medicaid reimbursement rules,[65] this experimental method will be used through 1985. The goal of the approach, as described by the director of the Office of Health Systems Management of the New York State Department of Health (NYSDH), is the attainment of " 'financial stability for the hospital industry while at the same time promoting cost containment and overall increased efficiency in hospital operation.' "[66] To achieve this objective, the reimbursement method is designed to account for and control all sources of hospital revenue.

The Medicare, Medicaid, and Blue Cross programs account for approximately 80 percent of all payments for hospital care in New York, with private insurance, self-insured groups, and self-pay patients accounting for the remaining 20 percent.[67] To make the cost containment system workable and to prevent hospitals from recouping losses incurred in the provision of care to some groups of patients by charging higher rates to other groups, it was necessary to control the rates paid by all groups of patients. The NYSDH already regulated Medicaid payment rates and, through state laws regulating insurance, Blue Cross payment rates. The waiver from the federal government permitted the NYSDH to control Medicare rates in New York. As a result, the NYSDH has established one method of hospital reimbursement for major third party payors, such as Medicare, Medicaid, and Blue Cross, and another for all other payors. All other payors must pay rates that are 12 to 15 percent higher than the rates paid by the major third party payors.

The 1983 rates for the major third party payors were based on the 1981 financial and statistical data that every hospital in New York state filed with local Blue Cross Plans. These cost reports were then desk-audited by the local Blue Cross Plans, key punched for data processing, and forwarded to Blue Cross and Blue Shield of Greater New York. The reported costs were then allocated to various areas, such as inpatient care, emergency room care, and clinic care. The allocated inpatient expenses, adjusted to include only

Medicaid-allowable costs, became the basis for the 1983 prospective Medicaid per diem rates for hospital payments. In calculating the prospective rate, the NYSDH took into account capital expenses, certain "add-on" expenses, and operating expenses (e.g., routine costs, ancillary costs, and professional costs). Ceilings were established for each of the operating cost centers.

To calculate these ceilings, hospitals were grouped according to several factors, including teaching status, the case and patient mix, the number of beds, and the percentage of occupancy. Ceilings were established for routine costs and length of stay at 107½ percent of the average routine per diem costs of the peer group. Ceilings for the costs of ancillary services were set at 105 percent of the peer group's average weighted costs per discharge. The increase in professional costs was limited to the increase in the state geographical wage indicator for the one of five regions of New York in which the hospital is located. Costs that exceeded these ceilings were disallowed after adjustment for case mix difference, but the total percentage disallowance was limited to the percentage of costs disallowed in 1982.

As the first step in calculating the overall prospective rate, the Medicaid program's share of total allowable operating costs, based on the rate at which Medicaid recipients utilized these services, was determined. This amount was then adjusted by an inflation factor to bring the 1981 base year costs to 1983 levels. These projected costs were next divided by the number of 1981 patient days to yield a per diem operating cost. If necessary, the number of 1981 patient days was inflated to meet minimum utilization requirements.

Second, the capital cost component of the overall prospective rate was calculated. The capital costs incurred by hospitals during 1981 were adjusted to include only those expenses allowed by Medicaid; they were not adjusted by an inflation factor. Again, the Medicaid program's share of these capital costs was determined by the rate at which Medicaid patients utilized care. These allowable capital costs allocated to Medicaid were then divided by the number of 1981 patient days to yield a capital cost per diem. Profit-making hospitals also received a return on investment.

The operating and capital cost per diem rates were then combined to form a single per diem rate for each facility. Add-ons to this prospective rate were allowed. An allowance of 1 percent was added to the prospective rate, for example, for use at the hospitals' discretion. Add-ons for bad debt and charity care, for participation in a financially distressed hospital pool, and for a transition fund were also allowed. The prospective rates for 1984 and 1985, the final two years of the three-year experiment, are also based on the 1981 period, with adjustments made for significant cost changes. The Commissioner of Health in New York must certify that these prospective rates are reasonable and adequate to meet the costs incurred by efficiently and economically operated hospitals.

In December 1983, Sebastian Rebaldo, on behalf of the United Optical Workers Insurance Fund, filed action in federal district court, seeking declaratory and injunctive relief against implementation of the New York experimental plan's provision that hospital rates charged to self-insured groups, such as the Fund, must be 12 to 15 percent higher than the rates charged to the Medicare, the Medicaid, and the Blue Cross programs.[68] The plaintiff argued that, since this provision restricts the right of an employee welfare benefit plan to negotiate with hospitals for reduced rates, it conflicts with and is preempted by the federal Employment Retirement Income Security Act of 1974 (ERISA).

The ERISA is a comprehensive body of federal law designed to promote and protect the interest of employees and their beneficiaries in pension and welfare benefit plans. It defines an employee welfare benefit plan as "any plan, fund or program that provides medical, surgical or hospital care or benefits for contingencies such as illness, accident, disability, death or unemployment."[69] All parties to the action agreed that the plaintiff's Fund is covered by the terms of the ERISA. The dispute revolved around the ERISA's preemption provision and its "savings clauses." The plaintiff argued that the ERISA preempts this provision of the New York plan, while the defendants argued that the provision escapes preemption under two of the ERISA's savings clauses. One savings clause, they argued, exempts state laws that regulate insurance from the ERISA preemption; the other savings clause, the defendants asserted, forbids construing the ERISA's preemption provision so as to alter, amend, or modify federal law.

The federal district court ruled that the provision is preempted by the ERISA and, therefore, cannot be enforced against funds such as that administered by the plaintiff. The court stated that, with certain exceptions, the ERISA preempts any state laws that "relate" to any ERISA-covered employee benefit plan. The ruling by the district court noted that the scope of the preemption provision was defined by the U.S. Supreme Court in *Shaw v. Delta Airlines*,[70] in which the Supreme Court announced that "the breadth of [the ERISA's] pre-emptive reach is apparent from that section's language. A law 'relates to' an employee benefit plan, in the normal sense of the phrase, if it has a connection with or reference to such a plan."[71] The Supreme Court declared in *Shaw* that requiring multistate plans (such as Rebaldo's Fund) to comply with varying state regulations would increase the costs and decrease the efficiency of administering the plan, thereby reducing benefits to participants.

The district court observed that the ERISA's legislative history had been given "considerable attention" in *Shaw*. The Supreme Court quoted the ERISA's sponsors in Congress as saying that the act reserved to federal authority "the sole power to regulate the field of employee benefit plans."[72]

The sponsors also expected the statute to eliminate any threat of conflicting or inconsistent state and local regulation. Furthermore, the Court declared in *Shaw* that interpretations of the ERISA's savings clauses should be narrowly construed.

The district court determined that the New York plan provision adversely affects the administration of self-insured plans because the higher rates they must pay for hospital care reduce the breadth of coverage for their beneficiaries. In addition, the New York experimental reimbursement method imposes local conditions on the administration of plans such as the United Optical Workers Insurance Fund. The Fund, in order to "best conserve its assets, ... might well find it practical to operate separate plans in separate states," causing higher administrative costs.[73] The court ruled that it "is bound to comply with the express congressional intent to displace all state action in the field of private employee benefit programs and subsection 2807-a.6(b) trenches upon that protected area."[74]

The court did not agree with the defendants' arguments that the provision escapes preemption under two of the ERISA's savings clauses. Noting the Supreme Court's direction that specific exceptions to the ERISA's preemption rule are to be narrowly construed, the district court decided that the two savings clauses mentioned by the defendants did not apply to the case at hand. The court enjoined enforcement of the New York plan's provision against self-insured funds on March 13, 1984. The defendants filed an appeal of this decision with the Second Circuit Court of Appeals on April 30, 1984.

Minnesota

In order to implement a statutory directive to limit the growth of payment rates for inpatient hospital care,[75] the Minnesota Department of Public Welfare developed a prospective inpatient hospital reimbursement method that pays a flat rate per admission for each hospital. This rate is calculated by multiplying the base year allowable costs (1981) for each hospital by the current year's hospital cost index. To this product is added the hospital's allowable pass-through costs, and that sum is divided by the number of Medicaid admissions. This payment per admission, unique to each hospital, covers all inpatient services delivered to Medicaid patients at the facility.

Each hospital's base year costs are identified on the 1981 Medicare/ Medicaid cost reports. From these costs are deducted any malpractice insurance costs and any capital costs allocated to the Medicaid program. The Department of Public Welfare uses the Hospital Cost Index to calculate weighted average inflation estimates of health expense categories in Minnesota, adding 1 percent to reflect changes in technology. To the extent possible, the welfare department attempts to capture regional differences in the expense categories on the Index. Pass-through costs, such as depreciation, rents and leases, property taxes, license fees, interest, and malpractice insurance, are not subject to adjustment by the Hospital Cost Index.

This prospective method has ease of calculation and administration, but all capital costs are passed through for reimbursement. In this respect, the Minnesota method lacks the efficiency incentives of the Mississippi plan, for example, which links the level of capital reimbursement to the hospital's occupancy rates to reduce idle capacity and to discourage unnecessary expansion. To offset the dangers of unnecessary expansion, to some extent, the Minnesota plan does not reimburse providers for the capital costs of projects that have not been granted a certificate of need.

Virginia

The Virginia Medicaid program sets a prospective reimbursement rate for hospital operating costs incurred in providing inpatient care; the rate is determined for each hospital based on the Medicare definition of allowable costs, adjusted for inflation. Depreciation costs, capital interest costs, and education costs approved according to Medicare standards are passed through for payment and are not part of the prospective rate for operating costs.

Under the Virginia system, each hospital is placed in one of seven bed size categories:

1. rural, under 100 beds
2. rural, 101-170 beds
3. rural, 171 or more beds
4. urban, under 100 beds
5. urban, 101-400 beds
6. urban, 401-600 beds
7. urban, 601 or more beds

The Medicaid payment rate for each hospital cannot exceed the lowest of its customary charges or the prospective payment and ceiling placed on operating costs for the bed size class in which the hospital is placed. The class ceiling is the median prospective rate of each bed size grouping.

Each hospital with a Medicaid utilization rate over 8 percent can increase its operating costs ceiling by 1 percent for each percentage point of utilization between 8 percent and 30 percent. In other words, a hospital with a Medicaid utilization rate of 19 percent could increase its ceiling by 11 percent; a hospital with a Medicaid utilization rate of 30 percent could increase its ceiling by 22 percent. Hospitals that operate below their initial or raised ceiling may share in the difference as a profit.

Michigan

The Michigan Medicaid program reimburses hospitals at the lesser of their customary charges to the general public or their reimbursable costs of providing inpatient services.[76] Payment rates are determined on the basis of Medicare-allowable cost principles and cost reporting forms. In addition, the Michigan program uses an incentive reimbursement system for hospitals that elect and qualify for incentive payments. The Michigan incentive program is complex, relying on two complementary cost limitation methods. One method, the Individual Hospital Limitation on Expenditures (IHLE), limits the rate of growth for each hospital's total inpatient costs based on a "triennially rolling three year base period." The other method, the Individual Hospital Operating Cost Limitation (IHOCL), establishes a unit cost limit based on the most recently submitted cost reports.

To calculate the IHLE, the Michigan Medicaid program updates each hospital's included cost basis by using the Hospital Cost Index. Included costs are defined as the Medicare-allowable costs less "excluded costs," the latter consist of allowable capital and certain nonrecurring expenses that are passed through in the amount incurred during the prospective year. The Hospital Cost Index contains not only an inflation factor, but also factors to adjust for volume, case mix, and intensity. This intensity factor measures changes in the quantity and quality of services delivered due to changes in technology. Budget reviews may be requested to determine the appropriate rate of change in the included costs if a hospital has significant changes from the base period to the prospective year in the services it provides. If any changes result from the budget review, they are reflected in a modified Hospital Cost Index. The IHLE is then defined as the included cost basis adjusted by the Index, plus the excluded costs from the prospective year and a rollover of the incentive (if any) from the prior fiscal year.

The IHOCL is also used to limit each hospital's total inpatient costs. In the calculation of the IHOCL, each hospital's adjusted operating cost limit is multiplied by its total inpatient days. To this product are added the pass-through costs for the prospective year, consisting of the excluded costs and education costs. Each hospital's operating cost limit is the adjusted per patient day operating cost at the 75th percentile for its class of hospitals.

There are seven classes of hospitals, four urban and three rural bed size categories. The classwide per patient day operating costs are adjusted to reflect the inflation and intensity factors of the Hospital Cost Index, area wage levels, case mix, and high Medicaid volume. An individual hospital's area wage level adjustment is based on its specific proportion of labor costs to total operating costs and the Medicare area wage level indexes. The case mix adjustment is based on the hospital's number of patient days and the statewide relative cost per patient day in the 398 List A diagnosis groups defined by the Commission on Professional and Hospital Activities. The high Medicaid volume adjustment is a 1 percent increase in the operating cost limit for each percentage point that the hospital's number of Title V and Title XIX patient days exceeds 25 percent of total inpatient days.

Hospitals that have kept their costs within the Medicaid limitations on total hospital costs and have not requested a budget review may receive their allowable costs plus an incentive payment. The incentive is set at 50 percent of the difference between the IHLE and the allowable costs incurred by the hospital. It cannot exceed 5 percent of the Medicaid payment, nor can the hospital's reimbursement with the incentive bonus exceed the IHOCL or the federal limits on hospital costs.

The program's determination of reasonable and efficient costs is the lower of the IHLE, the IHOCL, or total allowable costs. A hospital's reimbursable cost is the "program share" of the reasonable and efficient cost (i.e., the fraction of inpatient allowable costs allocated to the program over total inpatient costs as determined from the hospital's cost report). The Medicaid program in Michigan has concluded that "as a result of the stringency of Michigan's own unit (IHOCL) and rate of growth (IHLE) limits to costs, the federal limits are not expected to be a factor in the state's reimbursement to hospitals either on an individual basis or in the aggregate."[77]

Illinois

The Medicaid reimbursement method used by the Illinois Department of Public Aid (IDPA) to pay for hospital care has been challenged in a number of court cases. In *Illinois Hospital Association v. Illinois Department of Public Aid*,[78] for example, the Illinois Hospital Association sought a preliminary injunction to prevent the IDPA from reimbursing hospitals with "shortfall rates" rather than the "final rates" earlier approved as reasonable and adequate for Fiscal Year 1984. The IDPA had been forced to use the shortfall rates rather than the final rates because of budget constraints faced by the Illinois government.

For Fiscal Years 1982 and 1983, the Illinois General Assembly and the IDPA developed and implemented Medicaid payment methods for inpatient hospital care consistent with the federal "reasonable and adequate" efficient cost standard. Hospitals were paid interim Medicaid rates. The Illinois statutes mandated a reconciliation adjustment at the end of the year, however, so that each hospital received an overall Medicaid payment equal to the final rate level calculated by the IDPA. On April 1, 1983, IDPA published proposed rules to become effective July 1, 1983, in which a new Medicaid rate-setting method for hospital reimbursement during Fiscal Year 1984 was described. The new rules no longer established an interim rate to be adjusted for reconciliation, but rather established one final rate. These rules, in compliance with the reasonable and adequate standard, were adopted as proposed.

While the Illinois General Assembly debated the 1984 state budget, the IDPA issued an "urgent notice" on June 13, 1983 to Medicaid providers, summarizing the Medicaid program changes that would occur if the General Assembly did not increase taxes. On June 14, 1983, IDPA issued a second "urgent notice" to hospitals, describing the proposed rate-setting method for hospital reimbursement in Fiscal Year 1984 and estimating the Medicaid revenues that the hospitals would receive with and without a tax increase. In this notice, the IDPA also said, "Insufficient funds are available to pay the full final reimbursement rate during fiscal year 1984. Without a tax increase, it will be necessary to defer 23.5 percent of the final reimbursement rate into later years."[79] The IDPA notified the hospitals that they would be reimbursed at lesser "interim rates" calculated to "equal the final rates adjusted according to the proportion of available funds (approved by the legislature) to the funds necessary to provide for payments at the final rates."[80] The unaffordable portion of payments at the final rates was to be deferred to later years, subject to the availability of funds in those years. For Fiscal Year 1984, hospitals were assured of payments only at the shortfall rates and not, the court observed, "at the Final Rates IDPA determined were necessary to conform to the statutory mandate (the reasonable and adequate standard) under its own rate setting methodology."[81] The court also noted that there were no assurances to providers that they would ever receive payment at the final rates.

On July 5, 1983, the Illinois General Assembly appropriated $543.9 million for Medicaid payments for inpatient hospital care during 1984, which was $147 million less than the amount needed to fund reasonable and adequate reimbursement at the final rates calculated by IDPA. The court noted that the appropriation for inpatient hospital care during Fiscal Year 1984 actually declined from the $692 million appropriated in Fiscal Year 1983, despite an inflation rate of 7.1 percent. The court also observed that eighteen hospitals would suffer losses of over $1 million each, solely because of the shortfall rates.

After the Illinois Hospital Association began its legal action against the Illinois Medicaid program, the IDPA notified HHS that a request for funds would be submitted to the Illinois General Assembly to pay the deferred portion of the 1984 final payments. The court observed that the IDPA hopes to obtain in 1985 what it has not yet obtained for fiscal year 1984.... IDPA now seeks to "assure" that the Final Rates for fiscal year 1984 will be paid by July, 1985. That "assurance" lacks any factual basis in legislative developments, remains unspecified in time and is in reality only an assurance that a request will be made.[82]

The court further noted that hospitals cannot borrow money against an assurance of a request for funds and that they cannot plan and manage their financial affairs based on the promise of a request for funds without assurance of payment.

The IDPA argued that its deferment of payment was consistent with the law because statutes do not require full reimbursement during the fiscal year in which the services are provided. The court rejected this argument, distinguishing between a payment plan in which a portion of an assured payment is simply deferred and a payment plan (such as the IDPA's) in which there is no assurance that the deferred payment will ever be paid. The court went on to rule that, even if a state plan guaranteed making these deferred payments, the plan would violate the federal standards contained in the Social Security Act unless the deferred payments compensated hospitals for their costs in financing the deferred payments to the extent that payments received are less than current cash needs.

In determining whether to issue the preliminary injunction, the court evaluated four criteria: (1) whether the plaintiffs demonstrated a reasonable likelihood that they will succeed on the merits; (2) whether the plaintiffs will suffer irreparable harm for which there is no adequate remedy of law, (3) whether the threatened injury to the plaintiffs outweighs the threatened harm that the injunction may pose to the defendants, and (4) whether issuance of the injunction will disserve the public interest.

The court ruled that the plaintiffs "demonstrated far more than a reasonable likelihood of success on the merits."[83] Since the proposed shortfall rates were 23.5 percent less than the original final rates that, according to the IDPA, met the reasonable and adequate standard, the court ruled that the shortfall rates were "by definition" unreasonable and inadequate. Citing *Alabama Nursing Home Association v. Harris*,[84] the court noted that Medicaid payment rates may not be based solely on budgetary needs. The court also noted that, if states could evade federal requirements simply by failing to appropriate sufficient funds to meet them, the states could rewrite congressional standards. Referring to *California Hospital Association v. Schweiker*,[85] and *Wisconsin Hospital Association v. Reivitz*,[86] this court observed that federal courts "enjoined states' impositions of limitations on

Medicaid reimbursement rates based on budgetary considerations rather than compliance with the [Social Security] Act's standards."[87]

The court also ruled that the harm to the plaintiffs is substantial, citing the fact that the shortfall rates make it impossible for many Illinois hospitals to maintain the availability, quality, and scope of services necessary to serve their communities. The court concluded that the harm that would come to the plaintiffs if the injunction were not issued outweighed any harm that would come to the IDPA if the injunction were issued. The court further ruled that the plaintiffs demonstrated that issuance of the injunction would not disserve the public interest because the injunction would preserve the plaintiffs' ability to provide health care to Medicaid patients in Illinois.

The court ordered the IDPA to pay each Illinois hospital participating in Medicaid at the final rate "for all unpaid claims for inpatient services to Medicaid recipients during fiscal year 1984."[88] Any changes proposed by the IDPA that would adversely affect the amounts, rates, or timing of payments required to conform to this ruling needed prior approval by the court. Subsequently, the court modified its order so that hospitals had to be paid at the final rates for services provided on or after December 6, 1983, the date of the original ruling.[89] This modification was made because the Eleventh Amendment to the U.S. Constitution prohibits retroactive monetary settlements in suits against states in federal courts.

In an out-of-court settlement announced on May 14, 1984, the Illinois Medicaid program agreed to stop deferring hospital payments to later fiscal years.[90] The agreement, resulting from the district court ruling in *Illinois Hospital Association*, requires that the entire amount of Medicaid reimbursement for inpatient care be paid in the normal course of business. The agreement also allows increases in some outpatient rates and adjustments of inpatient rates during Fiscal Year 1985 to reflect inflation.

In *Children's Memorial Hospital v. Illinois Department of Public Aid*,[91] another provider challenged the IDPA's reimbursement methods for hospital care. Children's Memorial Hospital argued that the reimbursement method used by the Illinois Medicaid program was based on DRGs that are too broad to allow efficiency comparisons. Also, the plaintiff contended that, in practice, the method improperly equates Children's Memorial, a freestanding pediatric facility, to other teaching hospitals.

During Fiscal Year 1983, the IDPA adopted a new mechanism for determining the maximum number of days of reimbursable inpatient care a hospital could provide to Medicaid recipients. Various ailments requiring medical treatment were divided into 214 primary diagnosis groups (PDGs). In addition, hospitals were divided into three groups: rehabilitative, major teaching, and other. A maximum number of reimbursable Medicaid days was established at the 80th percentile of the length of stay for each PDG within each hospital category. The method was designed primarily to reduce the overutilization of hospital care by denying Medicaid payments to those providers that on the average keep their patients for lengths of stay beyond the 80th percentile for specified diagnosed ailments.

Children's Memorial, a highly specialized hospital that treats only pediatric patients and often provides care for rare or complex conditions, was classified as a major teaching hospital. Approximately 25 percent of its patients receive care as Medicaid beneficiaries. Under the rule establishing the new mechanism, Children's Memorial would be allowed Medicaid payment for 16,099 days of care during Fiscal Year 1983, which it projected would be exhausted in mid-March 1983. Neither party to the challenge disputed these facts. Children's Memorial moved for a preliminary injunction prohibiting the enforcement of this rule, as well as the imposition of a ceiling on Medicaid spending levels to hospitals at $797.5 million for inpatient, outpatient, and clinic services during Fiscal Year 1983.

In deciding to grant or deny preliminary injunctive relief, the court applied the same four criteria that had been applied in *Illinois Hospital Association.* Noting that the HCFA had approved the IDPA's hospital reimbursement method as meeting the federal reasonable and adequate standard, the court remarked it must give "substantial deference" to the interpretation of a statute by an agency charged with its administration. This court declared that it must not defer to an agency's interpretation of a statute, however, if there are compelling indications that the agency is wrong. The court then addressed the merits.

The court ruled that Children's Memorial failed to show any likelihood of success in challenging the $797.5 million ceiling on Medicaid spending for hospital care in Fiscal Year 1983 on the ground that it in itself violated the federal reasonable and adequate standard. According to the court, Children's Memorial had to show that the ceiling causes hospitals or Children's Memorial itself to be reimbursed at less than the economic and efficient level mandated by federal law; the plaintiff failed to establish this.

The court then turned to the challenge by Children's Memorial of the 80th percentile formula. The plaintiff argued not only that the formula is based on DRGs too broad to allow efficiency comparisons, but also that Children's Memorial is improperly equated with other teaching hospitals. The defendants responded by describing the 80th percentile formula as an effective mechanism for identifying inefficient providers, by claiming that there is no evidence to overcome the presumption of the formula's validity implied in HCFA's approval of the method, and by suggesting that Children's Memorial is an inefficient provider.

The court disagreed with the plaintiff's challenge to the percentile formula itself, reasoning that a percentile formula may be a reasonable way to identify inefficient providers.... Illinois has attempted to classify diagnoses and treatments and hospital settings in such a way that overutilization can be identified. Where lengths of hospital stays for the same treatment under the same circumstances exceed a certain fairly determined point, there may be some indication a provider is not restricting treatment to what is medically required.[92]

The court noted, however, that the critical element to a percentile formula based on lengths of stay is "that comparisons must be made between like treatments in like settings."[93] The court ruled that the IDPA's formula does not classify Children's Memorial with "like treatments in like settings," defeating the purposes of the reasonable and adequate standard.

The court observed that Children's Memorial deserves special status because it is a free-standing pediatric facility.

Children's Memorial treats, and regularly has referred to it, complex cases other hospitals typically do not or cannot handle. Any "efficiency" system based on average hospital stays for the universe of all patients is obviously inapplicable to Children's Memorial's special circumstances.[94]

Noting that Children's Memorial had no patients in 65 of the 214 PDGs, almost no patients in 64 other PDGs, and 93.4 percent of its patients in the remaining 85 groups, the court remarked that the plaintiff is being penalized by the 80th percentile formula not because of inefficiency but "because its patients fall into the more complex ends of the more complex primary diagnostic groups."[95] The court ruled that Children's Memorial had presented compelling evidence that the use of the 80th percentile formula to reimburse it for care it provided is arbitrary and irrational.

The court decided that Children's Memorial made an adequate showing of the need for injunctive relief, demonstrating irreparable damage to the patients, physicians, and hospital if an injunction were not issued. In terms of balance of harms, the court declared that the threatened injury to the plaintiff far outweighs any threatened harm an injunction may cause Illinois. The preliminary injunction does not disserve the public interest, according to the court, but actually advances the national public interest as articulated in the federal reasonable and adequate standard. The court specifically limited the injunctive relief to enjoining the IDPA from enforcing the Medicaid designated maximum number of reimbursable days for Children's Memorial for Fiscal Year 1983 as calculated with the 80th percentile formula. The court emphasized it was not objecting to the new system in general, but only to its application to Children's Memorial.

California

The California Medi-Cal (Medicaid) program has developed two methods to pay for inpatient hospital care. In selected areas of the state, only those hospitals that enter into negotiated and competitively bid contracts are reimbursed for providing inpatient services to Medi-Cal patients.[96] Until the contractual approach is introduced into the area, hospitals are reimbursed with an all-inclusive rate per discharge.[97] The contractual approach is implemented in an area when 100 percent of the projected bed capacity needed for Medi-Cal recipients can be contracted.

Hospitals in a geographical area are notified of the opportunity to contract to provide inpatient services for Medi-Cal patients. The California Medical Association Commission has the authority to negotiate, seek competitive bids, and use other procurement methods in dealing with hospitals interested in participating in Medi-Cal. Factors about each hospital that are considered by the Commission include, but are not limited to

- patient access
- utilization controls
- ability to provide quality services efficiently and economically
- ability to deliver or arrange needed specialty services
- protection against fraud and abuse
- factors that reduce costs, promote access, or enhance the quality of care
- ability to provide tertiary services on a regional basis
- recognition of the variations in severity of illness and complexity of care
- existing labor management collective bargaining agreements

The commission is directed by the California plan to "select the most cost-effective hospitals" and to contract with a sufficient number of hospitals to "provide adequate bed capacity for Medi-Cal patients in the area." The plan states that the willingness of the provider to enter into a contract guarantees the reasonableness and adequacy of the rates to meet the costs of efficiently and economically operated hospitals. The contracting provider may be paid on a capitation or prepayment basis, a combination of the two methods, or other methods "the California Medical Assistant Commissioner determines to be feasible."

Judicial review is available to resolve disputes relating to terms, performance, or termination of contracts; an alternate remedy is administrative review of contract disputes. All hospitals participating in the contractual process continue to submit uniform Medi-Cal cost reports. Periodic audits or reviews of the contracting hospitals' performance in terms of efficiency and quality of care are conducted. Reimbursement to a contracting hospital cannot exceed its customary charges to the general public or the aggregate amount that would be paid to the provider under Medicare principles of payment.

In areas of California where the contractual method is not in effect, hospitals are reimbursed with an all-inclusive rate per discharge, which is calculated by a retrospective, cost-based system under Medicare reimbursement principles. The rate paid to the hospital is the lesser amount calculated by four different approaches:

1. each hospital's customary charge
2. each hospital's allowable costs, calculated under Medicare reimbursement principles
3. each hospital's all-inclusive rate per discharge adjusted annually to reflect changes in price, case mix, patient volume, and items allowed because of adjustments and appeals
4. the median all-inclusive rate per discharge at the 60th percentile for the peer group to which the hospital is assigned

Medi-Cal payments for fixed costs, including capital costs, are reduced when the hospital's average annual occupancy rate falls below 55 percent of its licensed bed capacity. New, rural, or sole community hospitals are exempted from this occupancy standard.

OUTLOOK

The Medicaid program's treatment of each hospital's capital costs remains a reimbursement issue of concern. Many state Medicaid programs continue to reimburse capital costs on a reasonable cost basis, even if they use a prospective rate-setting method. The Minnesota program passes capital costs through the prospective method for reasonable cost reimbursement, for example. Reimbursing the reasonable cost of capital expenses offers little incentive to providers to contain these costs.

Congress has scheduled hearings on the effects that mergers and acquisitions in the hospital and nursing home industries have on capital costs (see Outlook, Chapter 2). These hearings may produce changes in federal policy guidelines on the treatment of capital costs for Medicaid reimbursement purposes. Furthermore, the payment of hospital capital costs under a Medicare prospective payment method by October 1, 1986, may serve as an example to state Medicaid programs in their efforts to contain costs.

Many state programs have set limits to the number of reimbursed days of care a Medicaid patient can receive either on an annual or per illness basis in order to contain Medicaid hospital payments. Federal and state courts have ruled that this is permissible as an issue of coverage and does not violate the substantive requirements of federal law. As of 1984, seventeen states have set limits on the number of days of hospital care per recipient reimbursed by Medicaid. In attempts to contain growing Medicaid expenditures for hospital care, state programs can develop reimbursement methods that include cost containment incentives, restrict the coverage of hospital services, or do both.

NOTES

1. Department of Health and Human Services, Health Care Financing Administration, Office of Financial and Actuarial Analysis.
2. 42 C.F.R. §440.10(a)(3)(iii).
3. 42 C.F.R. §405.1020.
4. 42 U.S.C. §1396a(a)(D).
5. HOUSE COMM. ON THE BUDGET, REPORT ON THE OMNIBUS RECONCILIATION ACT OF 1981, Report 97-158 (Vol. II), 97th Cong., 1st Sess., p. 293 (1981).
6. P.L. 97-35, §2173.
7. REPORT ON THE OMNIBUS RECONCILIATION ACT, note 5, *supra*, p. 293.
8. *Id.*, p. 294.
9. *Id.*, p. 297.
10. 42 C.F.R. §447.250.
11. 42 C.F.R. §447.271.
12. 42 C.F.R. §447.253(b)(1)(ii)(C)(2).
13. 42 C.F.R. §447.253(b)(1)(ii)(A).
14. 42 C.F.R. §447.253(b)(1)(ii)(B).
15. 42 C.F.R. §447.253(b)(1)(ii)(C).
16. 42 C.F.R. §447.255.
17. 42 C.F.R. §447.205.
18. 42 C.F.R. §447.253(b)(1)(ii)(C)(2)(d).
19. 42 C.F.R. §447.253(b)(1)(ii)(C)(2)(e).
20. "Alabama Hospital Association v. Rebecca Beasley," U.S. Court of Appeals, Eleventh Circuit, No. 81-7965, April 14, 1983, In MEDICARE AND MEDICAID GUIDE, 32,821.
21. *Id.*
22. *Id.*, at p. 9155.
23. *Id.*, at p. 9156.

24. *Id.*
25. 440 U.S. at 631, 99 S.Ct. at 1383.
26. *See* note 20, *supra*, p. 9157.
27. 42 U.S.C.A. §1396a(a)(13)(A).
28. Wisconsin Hospital Association et al. v. Linda Reivitz, U.S. District Court, Eastern District of Wisconsin, No. 83-C-1055, January 11, 1983. In MEDICARE AND MEDICAID GUIDE, 32,380.
29. *See* note 20, *supra*, pp. 9895-9896.
30. *See* note 20, *supra*, pp. 9896-9897.
31. *See* note 20, *supra*, p. 9897.
32. *Id.*
33. Wisconsin Hospital Ass'n et al. v. Linda Reivitz et al., U.S. Court of Appeals, Seventh Circuit, No. 83-1725, May 8, 1984. In MEDICARE AND MEDICAID GUIDE, 33,966.
34. *Id.*, at p. 9299.
35. *Id.*, at p. 9300.
36. *Id.*, at p. 9303.
37. California Hosp. Ass'n v. Schweiker, 559 F. Supp. 110 (1982).
38. *Id.*, at 117.
39. 705 F.2d 466 (9th Cir. 1983).
40. Magee-Womens Hosp. v. Heckler, 562 F. Supp. 483 (1983).
41. *Id.*, at 484.
42. *Id.*, at 485.
43. Charleston Memorial Hosp. et al. v. Virgil L. Conrad, U.S. District Court, District of South Carolina, Civ. Action No. 81-2759-1, April 16, 1982. In MEDICARE AND MEDICAID GUIDE, 31,958.
44. 693 F.2d 328 (1982).
45. 693 F.2d 324 (1982).
46. 427 F. Supp. 781 (E.D. Va. 1977).
47. 617 F.2d 388 (5th Cir. 1980).
48. 693 F.2d 330 (1982).
49. 42 C.F.R. 447.254.
50. University of Utah Medical Center v. Bonneville County, 96 Idaho 432, 529 P.2d 1304 (1974); Idaho Corp. of Benedictine Sisters v. Dr. John Marks, U.S. District Court, Idaho, No. 1-72-169, August 29, 1973. Both in MEDICARE AND MEDICAID GUIDE, 14,531.85.
51. P.L. 90-248, §402.
52. P.L. 92-603, §222.
53. 47 Fed. Reg. 44,612 (October 8, 1982).
54. State of New Jersey, Division of Medical Assistance and Health Services, Department of Human Services, survey, January 1984.
55. MEDICARE AND MEDICAID GUIDE, 13,770.
56. This description of the hospital reimbursement method used by the Mississippi Medicaid program was taken from the background section of Mississippi Hosp. Ass'n, Inc. et al. v. Heckler, 701 F.2d 511 (1983).
57. Mississippi Hosp. Ass'n v. Schweiker, U.S. District Court, No. WC81-89-LS-P, July 1, 1981. In MEDICARE AND MEDICAID GUIDE, 31,422.

58. *See* note 57, *supra*, p. 9127.
59. *See* note 57, *supra*, p. 9128.
60. *Id.*
61. 701 F.2d 517 (1983).
62. *Id.*, at 517.
63. *Id.*, at 524-542.
64. Office of Health Systems Management, Department of Health, State of New York, *1983 New York Prospective Hospital Reimbursement Methodology.* In MEDICARE AND MEDICAID GUIDE, 13,770.62.
65. Permitted by P.L. 90-248, §402.
66. Sebastian Rebaldo v. Mario Cuomo, U.S. District Court, Southern District of New York, 83 Civ. 8707 (WCC), March 13, 1984 [Facts]. In MEDICARE AND MEDICAID GUIDE, 33,665.
67. *Id.*
68. N.Y. PUBLIC HEALTH LAW, §2807-a.6(b). *Refer to* Sebastian Rebaldo v. Mario Cuomo, U.S. District Court, Southern District of New York, 83 Civ. 8707 (WCC), March 13, 1984.
69. 29 U.S.C. §1002(1).
70. 103 S.Ct. 2890 (1983).
71. *Id.*, at 2899.
72. *Id.*, at 2901.
73. *See* note 66, *supra*, at p. 10,145.
74. *Id.*, at p. 10,150.
75. MINN. STAT. §256.966, amended 1983 MINN. LAWS, ch. 312, art. 5, §§6, 39.
76. Department of Social Services, State of Michigan, State Plan under Title XIX of the Social Security Act, Attachment 4.19 A, June 20, 1983.
77. *Michigan's Prospective Reimbursement for Inpatient Hospital Services Provided to Medicaid Recipients.* Michigan Department of Social Services, Medical Services Administration, Paul Allen, Director. Survey Response, February 8, 1984.
78. 576 F. Supp. 360 (1983).
79. *Id.*, at 363.
80. *Id.*
81. *Id.*, at 363-364.
82. *Id.*, at 366.
83. *Id.*, at 367.
84. 617 F.2d 388 (5th Cir. 1980).
85. 559 F. Supp. 110 (1982).
86. *See* note 28, *supra.*
87. *See* note 78, *supra*, at 368.
88. *See* note 78, *supra*, at 372.
89. Illinois Hosp. Ass'n v. Illinois Dep't. of Public Aid, in MEDICARE AND MEDICAID GUIDE, 33,511.
90. Governor's Office News Release, May 14, 1984. In MEDICARE AND MEDICAID GUIDE, Report Letter No. 427, p. 8.
91. 562 F. Supp. 165 (1983).
92. *Id.*, at 172.

93. *Id.*
94. *Id.*, at 173.
95. *Id.*
96. Department of Human Services, State of California, Attachment 4.19-A of the California Medicaid plan. In MEDICARE AND MEDICAID GUIDE, 32,257.
97. *Id.*, 15,560.

Chapter 8

Medicaid: Long-Term Care Reimbursement

The Medicaid program has become the largest government purchaser of long-term care in the United States, with an estimated 44¢ of every $1 spent on nursing home care expected to come from the Medicaid program during 1985. Expenditures for these health care services also absorb the largest share of the total Medicaid budget, expected to account for 42 percent of total Medicaid spending during 1985.[1] The 1965 amendment (Title XIX) to the Social Security Act, which created the Medicaid program, required each state to reimburse providers for skilled care services in order to participate in the program. In 1971, Congress gave state programs the option of including intermediate care services in their range of covered services. All state Medicaid programs except Arizona reimburse intermediate care facilities for the care they provide to Medicaid patients. In fact, by 1981 payments for intermediate care became the largest category in the Medicaid budget, and these payments will grow at an estimated 18.5 percent average annual rate between 1975 and 1985.

THE SKILLED NURSING FACILITY

The 1972 amendments to the Social Security Act created a single definition of skilled nursing facilities (SNFs), effective July 1, 1973, for both the Medicaid and Medicare programs. Before this, the term *skilled nursing home* applied to Medicaid and the term *extended care facility* applied to Medicare. The care provided by an SNF is now defined as

> services provided directly by or requiring the supervision of skilled nursing personnel, or skilled rehabilitation services, which the patient needs on a daily basis, and which as a practical matter can only be provided in a skilled nursing facility on an inpatient basis.[2]

For a complete discussion of federal standards and requirements for SNFs see the Medicare chapter on skilled nursing facilities.

When the 1972 amendments became effective, an SNF certified to participate in Medicare became eligible to participate in Medicaid, and vice versa.[3] Although states cannot set lower Medicaid standards for SNFs than those established by the federal government, states can require higher standards through statute and regulation. If a state requires higher standards for SNFs, these standards apply to both the Medicaid and the Medicare programs in that state.

THE INTERMEDIATE CARE FACILITY

Federal law recognizes an intermediate care facility (ICF) as a state-licensed institution that provides a level of health care less intensive than that provided by an SNF or a hospital. Because of their mental or physical condition, however, the patients must require a level of care that goes beyond simple room and board, and that can be made available only by institutional facilities.[4] In the ICF, patient care focuses on preventive medicine and preservation of the patients' health status. In contrast, at the SNF, patient care focuses on therapeutic and rehabilitation services, control of prescribed medication, and continuous patient observation. Although Medicaid pays for intermediate care, Medicare does not. Like SNFs, ICFs must meet minimum federal health and safety regulations before they can be certified as providers under Medicaid.

The Social Security Act gives the secretary of the Department of Health and Human Services (HHS) the authority to prescribe standards for care, safety, and sanitation in ICFs. These standards are listed in the *Code of Federal Regulations*.

Health Services

The ICF must provide each resident with health services that include treatment, medications, diet, and other health services prescribed or planned for the patient on a 24-hour basis each day.[5] The ICF must have a registered nurse, a licensed practical nurse, or a vocational nurse for each day shift who is employed on a full-time basis to supervise the administration of the ICF's health services.[6] A written health care plan must be developed and implemented for each resident according to the instructions of the attending or staff physician. The plan must be reviewed and revised at least quarterly, sooner if required by the resident's health status.[7] The ICF must provide nursing care for each resident that allows the patient "to achieve and maintain the highest possible degree of function, self care, and independence."[8]

Responsible ICF staff members must be on duty and "awake 24 hours a day to take prompt, appropriate action in case of injury, illness, fire, or other emergency."[9] The ICF is required to have policies and procedures to ensure that the health care of each patient is under the continuing supervision of a physician. The physician must see the resident whenever necessary, but at least once every sixty days unless the physician decides this is not necessary and records the reason for that conclusion.[10]

Medications

The ICF must employ a licensed pharmacist or have a formal arrangement with a licensed pharmacist who advises the ICF on ordering, storing, administering, disposing, and keeping records of drugs.[11] All medication administered to the resident must be ordered by the attending or staff physician.[12] The ICF must have written policies and procedures for controlling medication dosage, including automatic stop orders when the physician does not include in the orders a limit on the length of time that the medication is to be administered or the number of doses. Also, the attending physician must be notified that the medication is being stopped.[13] A registered nurse must review medications for each resident monthly and notify the physician if modifications are necessary. The staff or attending physician must review quarterly the medications that residents receive.[14] Before they are allowed to administer medications, staff members must have completed a state-approved training program in the administration of medications. The ICF can allow a resident to self-administer medication only if the attending physician gives permission.[15]

Rehabilitative Services

The ICF must provide rehabilitative services for residents as required by their health status. These rehabilitative services must maintain and improve the resident's ability to function independently, prevent as much as possible the advance of progressive disabilities, and restore maximum function. These services must be developed in consultation with the attending physician and be provided by qualified therapists or assistants in accordance with accepted professional practices.[16] The ICF may provide these services directly or may make arrangements for qualified outside agencies to provide them.

Meal Service

The ICF must serve three meals or their equivalent every day at regular times. No more than fourteen hours can elapse between a substantial evening meal and breakfast. Food must be procured, stored, prepared, distributed, and served under sanitary conditions.[17] An ICF staff member must be trained or experienced in food management or nutrition. This person must plan menus that meet the nutritional needs of residents, following the orders of the attending physician; supervise meal preparation and service to ensure that the menu plan is followed; and have menus planned by a professional dietician or reviewed and approved by the attending physician for those residents who require medically prescribed special diets. The ICF must keep for thirty days a record of each menu served.[18]

Social Services and Activities Programs

The ICF must provide social services for each resident or must arrange for qualified outside agencies to provide them. One staff member, who is qualified by training or experience, must be designated to arrange social services and integrate social services into the other elements in the plan of care. These services must be provided under a written plan of care that is placed in the resident's record and re-evaluated periodically.

The ICF must also provide an activities program designed to encourage each resident to maintain normal activity and to return to self-care. One staff member, who is qualified by training or experience, must plan independent and group activities for each resident. These activities are to be developed according to the resident's needs and interests, incorporated into the resident's overall plan of care, reviewed with the resident at least quarterly, and changed as needed. The ICF must provide adequate recreation areas with sufficient equipment and resources to support the activities program.[19]

Safety Standards

The ICF must comply with the health care occupancy provisions of the 1981 *Life Safety Code* of the National Fire Protection Association. If the secretary of HHS concludes that the state has enacted a fire and safety code that adequately protects ICF residents, however, this state code may be used instead of the *Life Safety Code*.[20] An ICF with fifteen beds or less may be governed by the residential occupancy requirements of the *Life Safety Code* rather than the health care occupancy provisions, if the ICF is involved primarily in treating patients for alcohol and drug abuse and a physician certifies that each resident is ambulatory, engaged in an active program leading to independent living, and capable of following directions and taking action for self-preservation in emergency situations.[21]

The state may waive specific provisions of the *Life Safety Code* if the waiver does not adversely affect the health and safety of the residents and if compliance with specific provisions of the code would result in an "unreasonable hardship" for the ICF. Any waiver is granted according to the guidelines established by the Health Care Financing Administration (HCFA). No facility of two or more stories that is not fire-restrictive and is participating in Medicaid under a waiver of construction type or height may have blind, nonambulatory, or physically handicapped residents above the street level floor. Exceptions may be made if the ICF is of protected noncombustible construction as defined in the *Life Safety Code*, has a full sprinkler system (Type II, III, or V), or achieves a passing score on the Fire Safety Evaluation System.[22]

Environmental and Safety Standards

Living areas in the ICF must be designed and equipped for the comfort and privacy of each resident. All corridors used by residents must have handrails.[23] Each resident's room must have or be conveniently located near toilet and bathing facilities, contain a bed and other suitable furnishings for each resident, have no more than four beds, and be equipped with a calling device. In addition, there must be at least 100 square feet for a resident in a single room and at least 80 square feet for each resident in a multiresident room. The space and occupancy requirements may be waived for an existing building if strict enforcement of these requirements would cause an unreasonable hardship on the ICF or if the waiver serves the needs of residents and does not adversely affect their health and safety.[24] The ICF must have enough linen for the proper care and comfort of the residents, and each bed must have clean linen.[25] The ICF must supply sufficient hot water to meet the needs of residents; all plumbing fixtures must have control valves that automatically regulate the temperature of hot water used by residents.[26]

MEDICAID REIMBURSEMENT LAW

The statute that created the Medicaid program in 1965 did not specify the method of reimbursement to be used by the state programs in paying for nursing home care. The state programs were free to develop their own reimbursement formulas, with only the general restriction that the payment rates should not "exceed reasonable charges consistent with efficiency, economy, and quality of care."[27] The result was a variety of payment methods with a wide range of per diem rates.[28]

Reasonable Cost-Related Reimbursement

The U.S. Congress became concerned that the lack of uniformity in state Medicaid reimbursement policies may have caused some states to pay too much for care and other states to pay too little to guarantee the delivery of quality care.[29] As a result, Congress amended the Social Security Act so that, effective July 1, 1976, all state Medicaid programs were required to reimburse nursing homes on a "reasonable cost-related basis."[30] The statute also directed the secretary of the Department of Health, Education and Welfare (HEW, later HHS) to develop regulations to guide the states in developing their reasonable cost-related methods of payment. The federal government would then approve any reasonable cost-related plan developed by the states if the payment method complied with these guidelines.

Under the regulations developed by HEW, the state plans were required to

1. prescribe procedures for cost finding and cost reporting by long-term care providers
2. provide for audits to verify the reasonableness of the cost reports furnished by providers
3. define allowable costs
4. establish methods and standards to calculate reasonable cost-related payments
5. mandate that the state pay the reasonable cost-related rate to providers who deliver care under the requirements of the state plan[31]

HEW, however, did not release these guidelines until July 1, 1976—the date on which all states were mandated by Congress to begin reasonable cost-related payments. This delay in turn prevented the states from submitting their reimbursement plans to the federal government for approval in a timely fashion.

The secretary of HEW responded to these delays by agreeing not to impose sanctions against states that were not in compliance with the statutory requirement until January 1, 1978. All states were encouraged, however, to meet each requirement of the regulations as soon as possible.[32] The ultimate impact of this decision was to delay the effective implementation date of reasonable cost-related reimbursement beyond the July 1, 1976, date mandated by Congress to the January 1, 1978, date set by the secretary of HEW.

The decision by the secretary spawned considerable legal action. For example, the Alabama Nursing Home Association (ANHA) brought suit in federal district court against HEW and its secretary during 1977, charging that the method of reimbursement used by the Alabama Medicaid program did not comply with the federal statute mandating reasonable cost-related payment.[33] Specifically, the ANHA challenged the secretary's decision to delay implementation of this reimbursement method beyond the date set by Congress. The district court noted that Congress had specified July 1, 1976, as the implementation date for reasonable cost-related payments and that the regulations developed by the secretary have "a later effective date. A clearer inconsistency is difficult to imagine. Consequently, the regulation, insofar as it sets an effective date other than July 1, 1976, is invalid."[34] The district court ruled for the ANHA.

The principal defense used by the state of Alabama was that the state legislature had not appropriated sufficient funds to pay for reasonable cost-related reimbursement. The district court ruled, however, that "inadequate funding does not excuse failure to comply with federal standards."[35] The court added that there is "no provision, express or implied, in the Social Security Act permitting a state to alter federal standards to suit its budgetary needs."[36] Citing the U.S. Supreme Court decision in *Rosado v. Wyman,*[37] the district court ruled that, since state participation in the Medicaid program is voluntary and the state accepts federal funds, it must follow federal statutes. The court concluded:

> If a state could evade the requirements of the [Social Security] Act simply by failing to appropriate sufficient funds to meet them, it could rewrite the congressionally imposed standards at will. The conditions which Congress laid down for state participation in Medicaid and other programs would be utterly meaningless.... Consequently, Alabama must meet the statutory requirements so long as it remains in the Medicaid program, regardless of budgetary considerations.[38]

Additional suits were brought in other federal district courts.[39] The outcomes were similar to that in *ANHA*: the action by the secretary in delaying the effective implementation of Medicaid reasonable cost-related reimbursement for nursing home care beyond the July 1, 1976, date set by Congress was held to be invalid.

In March of 1977, the Florida Nursing Home Association (FNHA) brought suit against the secretary of HEW and the Florida Department of Health and Rehabilitative Services, challenging the delay in implementing reasonable cost-related reimbursement.[40] In addition, the FNHA sought payments retroactive to July 1, 1976, equal to the difference between the reasonable cost-related payments that they should have received with reasonable cost-related reimbursement and the payments that they actually received from Medicaid. This challenge was critical because of the potentially large retroactive payments involved nationwide. The U.S. District Court for the Southern District of Florida, basing the decision on its earlier decision in *Golden Isle Convalescent Center, Inc. v. Califano*,[41] held that the delay in implementing reasonable cost-related reimbursement was invalid. The court consolidated these two cases to decide if the nursing homes could receive retroactive payments from the Florida Medicaid program. The district court ruled that the Eleventh Amendment of the U.S. Constitution, which prohibits retroactive monetary relief against a state in federal court, barred the retroactive payments sought by the FNHA.

The decision was appealed to the U.S. Court of Appeals for the Fifth Circuit. This court agreed that the secretary of HEW could not delay implementation of reasonable cost-related reimbursement, but reversed that part of the ruling concerning the retroactive relief sought by the FNHA. The court of appeals ruled that the Eleventh Amendment prevented retroactive monetary relief against a state in federal court unless "consented to by the state." The appellate court further ruled that Florida had, by two actions, waived its Eleventh Amendment immunity. First, Florida law contained a "general waiver of sovereign immunity" which declared that its Department of Health and Rehabilitative Services "is a 'body corporate' with the capacity to 'sue and be sued.' "[42] Second, the appellate court found a specific waiver of immunity under the Eleventh Amendment in a Medicaid agreement in which the Department of Health and Rehabilitative Services agreed to

> recognize and abide by all state and federal laws, regulations, and guidelines applicable to participation in and administration of the Title XIX Medicaid program. ... By contracting with appellants to be bound by all federal laws applicable to the Medicaid program, the state has expressly waived its Eleventh Amendment immunity and consented to suit in federal court regarding any action by providers alleging a breach of these laws.[43]

This appellate court decision on immunity was, in turn, appealed to the U.S. Supreme Court. Stating that its ruling was controlled by its earlier decision in *Edelman v. Jordan*,[44] the Court ruled that the lower appellate court had erred when it reached its decision allowing retroactive relief. In *Edelman v. Jordan*, the Supreme Court had established the proper standard for a waiver of Eleventh Amendment immunity by a state. The Court ruled in that case that "we will find waiver only where stated 'by the most express language or by such overwhelming implications from the text as [will] leave no room for any other reasonable construction.' "[45] The mere fact that a state participates in a federal program and receives federal aid "is not sufficient to establish consent on the part of the state to be sued in the federal courts."[46]

The Supreme Court ruled that the decision of the lower appellate court in *FNHA* was inconsistent with the *Edelman* decision. In reaching this conclusion, the Supreme Court stated that the mere fact that the Florida Department of Health and Rehabilitative Services had agreed to obey federal law in administering the Medicaid program

> can hardly be deemed an express waiver of Eleventh Amendment immunity. This agreement merely states a customary condition for any participation in a federal program by the state, and *Edelman* already established that neither such participation in itself, nor a concomitant agreement to obey federal laws, is sufficient to waive the protection of the Eleventh Amendment.[47]

Because of the doctrine of *stare decisis*, Justice Stevens voted with the majority to use *Edelman* to overturn the appellate court's decision in *FNHA*; however, he thought *Edelman* had been incorrectly decided. Justice Stevens' overriding concern was

> the potential damage to the legal system that may be caused by frequent or sudden reversals of direction that may appear to have been occasioned by nothing more significant than a change in the identity of this court's personnel. Granting that a zig-zag is sometimes the best course, I am firmly convinced that we have a profound obligation to give recently decided cases the strongest presumption of validity.... The presumption is an essential thread in the mantle of protection that the law affords the individual. Citizens must have confidence that the rules on which they rely in ordering their affairs—particularly when they are prepared to take issue with those in power in doing so—are rules of law and not merely the opinions of a small group of men who temporarily occupy high office.... For me, the adverse consequences of adhering to an arguably erroneous precedent in this case are far less serious than the consequences of further unravelling the doctrine of *stare decisis*.[48]

The Supreme Court's decision to deny retroactive payments to nursing homes for revenues lost as a result of the delay in implementing reasonable cost-related reimbursement had considerable financial implications for the Medicaid program. HEW estimated that Medicaid spending for nursing home care would have increased by $202 to 302 million had the reasonable cost-related payments requirement been implemented from July 1, 1976, to June 30, 1977.[49]

Reasonable and Adequate Reimbursement

Passed in December 1980, the Omnibus Reconciliation Act[50] eliminated from federal law the requirement that state Medicaid programs pay for nursing home care on a reasonable cost-related basis, effective as of October 1, 1980. Section 962, also known as the Boren Amendment, allowed states to develop less costly reimbursement methods, with assurances to the secretary of HHS that the new plans are "reasonable and adequate to meet the costs which must be incurred by efficiently and economically operated facilities" complying with federal and state quality and safety standards.[51] According to the report of the Senate Finance Committee, the state Medicaid programs had never been entirely pleased with reasonable cost-related reimbursement because it restrained their administrative and fiscal discretion.[52] The states were also dissatisfied with the complex federal regulations governing implementation, because they forced the states to rely heavily on Medicare's more expensive definition of reasonable cost-related payments, which "are inherently inflationary and contain no incentives for efficient performance."[53] The states also claimed that the statutes and regulations restricted their ability to innovate and develop reimbursement methods that would encourage providers to be more efficient. Therefore, given the increasing financial burdens facing state Medicaid programs, Congress eliminated the reasonable cost-related requirement and gave the state Medicaid programs more flexibility in establishing reasonable and adequate reimbursement systems for long-term care.

Reasonable and Adequate Litigation

Nebraska

The Nebraska Health Care Association filed suit in federal district court to contest these new federal and state Medicaid policies for reimbursing providers of long-term care on the ground that nursing homes are not adequately compensated for care delivered to Medicaid recipients.[54] Specifically, the association argued that the failure of HHS to define the phrase "efficiently and economically operated facilities" allows HHS to use subjective and unannounced criteria when it decides if state payment rates satisfy the requirements of the federal law and policy.

The court observed that the legislative history reveals that Congress had two reasons for passing the Boren Amendment. "First, 'Congress intended that states set their own reimbursement rates without stifling and expensive federal oversight of the methodology used, as has been the case. . . . Probing beyond the bottom line to the underlying rate setting methodology is not required under the new standard.' "[55] Second, Congress wanted to reduce Medicaid program costs by allowing the states to develop payment systems that promote efficiency.

The court in *Nebraska Health Care Association* noted that defining

> the term "efficiently and economically operated facility" is crucial. The costs for such a facility are used to calculate the payment for all other facilities in the state, and two different definitions could produce dramatically different payment schedules.[56]

According to the court, however, it is not the responsibility of the secretary of HHS to define the phrase. In fact, if the secretary defined it, the secretary "in effect would determine what payments the state would have to make,"[57] which would directly conflict with the intent of Congress and the Boren Amendment to allow the states "to determine their own methods for calculating proper payments and to reduce their current payment levels."[58] The secretary is to intervene in state rate setting, under the Boren Amendment, "only when a state abuses the flexibility bestowed upon it by Congress . . . .As I read the statute, the Secretary is to invoke her intervening power when she perceives that the quality of care being provided to nursing home patients is inadequate."[59] Concluding that the failure of the secretary of HHS to impose a "crucial definition" is neither arbitrary nor capricious and is consistent with congressional intent, the judge dismissed the United States and Margaret Heckler, Secretary of HHS, from the action.

In order to promote efficiently and economically operated nursing homes, the Nebraska Medicaid program uses minimum occupancy rates in calculating a facility's reimbursement rate. For example, a nursing home's total allowable cost apportionment is computed on the basis of the actual occupancy rate or 85 percent of total licensed bed days, whichever is greater. For new construction, whether it involves an entire facility or bed additions, the basis for these computations is the greater of actual occupancy or 50 percent of total licensed bed days available during the first year of the newly constructed facility's operation, beginning with the first day of patient care provided.

Applying this occupancy rate method in final rate calculations, the Medicaid program determined that Haven Home, a Nebraska nursing home, had been reimbursed in excess of $50,948.59 in interim payments for 1979. Haven Home appealed this decision to the Nebraska district court, which affirmed the determination of overpayment. Haven Home appealed this district court decision to the Nebraska Supreme Court.[60]

The Nebraska Supreme Court noted that state Medicaid programs have been granted flexibility to experiment and calculate payment rates that they find adequate to reimburse efficiently and economically operated facilities. The court presumed that the Medicaid rates are valid and that the challenging party has the burden of proof if they are not. In this case, Haven Home failed to prove to the court that the rates were invalid.

> This court may not substitute its judgment for that of the DPW [the Nebraska Medicaid program] in determining which method or methods are preferable in reimbursements.... The DPW is not obliged to justify why it arrived at an 85 percent minimum occupancy requirement instead of one set at 80 percent or 90 percent.[61]

The Court concluded that

> the record is conspicuously absent of any evidence that the minimum occupancy requirement is not rationally related to the state's interest. The reason for the occupancy requirement is obvious. Certain fixed expenses continue, irrespective of the number of occupants. If there is an unusually low occupancy rate private patients and the state (on behalf of the welfare recipients) pay a disproportionate share of the expenses.[62]

In conclusion, the Nebraska Supreme Court cited *Mississippi Hospital Association, Inc. v. Heckler*[63] as a similar case in which a U.S. court of appeals had ruled that a minimum occupancy rate did not violate federal law. Since the Nebraska occupancy policy was properly promulgated under federal and state law and did not violate the Equal Protection Clause or Supremacy Clause of the U.S. Constitution, the Nebraska Supreme Court affirmed the ruling of the district court that upheld the overpayment decision in *Haven Home*.

Minnesota

Minnesota has an Equalization Statute that prohibits a nursing home from receiving Medicaid payments unless it agrees in writing that it will refrain from charging private (non-Medicaid) patients more than the Medicaid charge for similar services plus the lesser of the percentage differential between the private rate and the Medicaid rate in effect on April 13, 1976, or 10 percent of the current Medicaid rate.[64] In other words, the Equalization Statute allows nursing homes that participate in the Minnesota Medicaid program to charge private patients a maximum of 10 percent more than they charge Medicaid patients. The law also requires that, if a nursing home has exceeded this differential since April 13, 1976, it must return the amount collected in excess of the allowable differential to the private pay patient or to that person's representative by July 1, 1977. The Equalization Statute, passed in 1976, was amended in 1977 to include the retroactive payback provision.

The Minnesota Association of Health Care Facilities challenged the Equalization Statute and the adequacy of the Minnesota Medicaid reimbursement system for long-term care. The Minnesota Hospital Association challenged the retroactive payback provision of the Equalization Statute. These lawsuits were tried together in *Minnesota Association of Health Care Facilities, Inc. v. Minnesota Department of Public Welfare.*[65] The plaintiffs challenged the Equalization Statute, the payback provision of this statute, and the Minnesota Medicaid reimbursement system on substantive and procedural grounds. The plaintiffs contended that the enforcement and implementation of these Minnesota provisions violate not only federal law, but also their constitutional rights.

The U.S. District Court ruled that the Equalization Statute, its payback provision, and Minnesota's prospective Medicaid payment system are valid under the U.S. Constitution and federal Medicaid law. The court reasoned that, because Medicaid participation is voluntary, the nursing home providers could not establish that the limits on charges to private patients, coupled with Medicaid payments that were allegedly too low, resulted in unconstitutional deprivation of property. In addition, the plaintiffs failed to prove that the Medicaid rates were less than reasonable and adequate payment for an efficiently and economically operated facility or to establish a right to subsidize Medicaid patients by charging private patients at rates that are above the statutory limits. In rejecting the plaintiffs' challenge to the law, the court stated,

> Not only is the Private Pay Law [Equalization Statute] a reasonable exercise of the state's police powers—the state has the duty to protect those in need of nursing home services—obviously a group which the legislature could reasonably conclude was desperately in need of protection—but also plaintiffs are in a heavily regulated industry and could have foreseen—and in fact did foresee—this legislation.[66]

This decision by the district court was appealed by the plaintiffs.[67] The U.S. Court of Appeals for the Eighth Circuit ruled on August 28, 1984 that the basic equalization statute was constitutional, affirming the decision by the district court. The appellate court, however, reversed the lower court and invalidated the retroactive portion of the equalization statute, ruling that it was an unconstitutional impairment of contracts. The court reasoned "[b]ecause of its retroactivity, the statute imposes totally unexpected liability on nursing homes for charges that were permitted by law when collected. This [retroactive payback provision of the] statute goes too far because it disrupts settled and completed financial arrangements under contracts made in reliance on existing law. The retroactive payback provision is invalid."[68]

In a related case, Highland Chateau, a 111-bed nursing home in which all beds had been licensed by the Minnesota Department of Health and certified for participation in Medicaid, attempted to avoid the requirements of Minnesota's Equalization Statute by dividing its facility into two separate wings—one for private patients and the other for Medicaid patients. The nursing home notified state agencies that it intended to decertify all but 44 beds from Medicaid participation. Highland Chateau contended that only these beds, located in the wing of the nursing home certified for participation in Medicaid, were subject to the Equalization Statute. The nursing home filed suit in Minnesota District Court, challenging the implementation of the Equalization Statute.[69] The Minnesota Department of Public Welfare moved that the court grant summary judgment against Highland Chateau.

The court agreed with the Department of Public Welfare and dismissed all the plaintiff's actions. Reasoning that the Equalization Statute applies to the entire nursing home, the court concluded that, if the plaintiff's interpretation of the law prevailed, the Equalization Statute

> might well become meaningless. Every nursing home in Minnesota could easily avoid the requirements of the law by decertifying as much of the nursing home as possible . . . .The express language of the law provides that the equalization requirement applies to the licensed nursing home, not the certified portion of it.[70]

The court further concluded that the Equalization Statute does not violate the constitutional standards of the Equal Protection, Due Process, or Contract Clauses.

MEDICAID REIMBURSEMENT POLICIES

In a survey of state programs compiled for this book, it was found that twenty-eight states used some form of reasonable cost-related reimbursement for skilled care, sixteen states used a payment system allowing reasonable and adequate rates for skilled care, and two states used a payment system classified as "other" for skilled care during 1984. Oklahoma responded that it was in the process of revising its payment system, and the experimental program in Arizona does not reimburse providers for long-term care. Three states did not respond to the survey. The survey also revealed that twenty-seven states paid for intermediate care with the reasonable cost-related method, seventeen states paid for intermediate care with the reasonable and adequate method, and two states paid for intermediate care with a mechanism classified as "other" (Table 8-1).

Table 8-1 Medicaid: Nursing Home Reimbursement Methods and Rates

	Skilled Care		Intermediate Care	
	Method (1984)	Average Per Diem Payment (1983)	Method (1984)	Average Per Diem Payment (1983)
Alabama	1	$32.34	1	$32.34
Alaska				
Arkansas	1	$28.13	1	$26.74
Arizona	No reimbursement for long-term care			
California	4	$37.06**	4	$28.14**
Colorado	3		3	
Connecticut	3	$49.60	3	$33.38
Delaware	3	$39.58	3	$39.58
Florida	4	$29.79	4	$28.05
Georgia	4	$29.59	4	$27.39
Hawaii	2	$86.29	2	$72.09
Idaho	3	$38.10	3	$38.10
Illinois	1	$35.58	1	$26.87
Indiana	1	$46.75	1	$36.52
Iowa	2	$76.59	1	$27.00
Kansas				
Kentucky	4	$48.09	4	$31.85
Louisiana	1	$34.80	1	I-$29.76 II-$23.87
Maine	1	$68.91	4	$43.04
Maryland	3	$45.84	3	$45.84
Massachusetts	1	$50.11	1	$37.21
Michigan	3	$40.58	3	$40.58
Minnesota	4	$52.29	4	I-$43.73 II-$28.26
Mississippi	4	$36.24	4	$27.85
Missouri	4	$46.05	4	$36.54
Montana	4	$40.26	4	$40.26
Nebraska	4	$38.59	4	$29.24
Nevada	3	$51.70	3	$44.05
New Hampshire	1	$64.33	1	$46.44

Table 8-1 continued

	Skilled Care		Intermediate Care	
	Method (1984)	Average Per Diem Payment (1983)	Method (1984)	Average Per Diem Payment (1983)
New Jersey	1	$58.16	1	$50.15
New Mexico	3	$71.41	3	$29.96
New York	1	$78.70	1	$49.21
North Carolina	3	$49.59	3	$35.64
North Dakota	1	$46.40	1	$32.31
Ohio	1	$44.73	1	$38.87
Oklahoma		Reimbursement system under revision		
Oregon	1	$46.79	1	$34.26
Pennsylvania	4	$39.97*	4	$32.97*
Rhode Island	5	$48.90	5	$44.60
South Carolina	3	$42.77	3	$32.69
South Dakota	4	$33.39	4	$29.66
Tennessee	3	$50.93	3	$32.28
Texas	4		4	
Utah	4	$44.96	4	$36.69
Vermont	4	$46.70	4	$46.70
Virginia	4	$53.18	4	$40.53
Washington	3	$37.22	3	$37.22
West Virginia	5		5	
Wisconsin	4	$49.00	4	$39.00
Wyoming	1	$40.85	1	$40.85

Notes:
1. Reasonable cost-related payments. Cost is determined according to methods developed by the state.
2. Reasonable cost-related payments. Cost is determined according to Medicare's definition.
3. Reasonable cost-related payments. Cost is determined according to Medicare's definition modified by the state.
4 Paid rates that are reasonable and adequate to meet costs incurred by efficiently and economically operated facilities to provide services in conformity with state and federal laws, regulations, and quality and safety standards.
5. Other.

*For private facilities only and excludes depreciation and interest payments.

**Skilled Care (60-299 beds): "all other counties" - $37.06; Los Angeles County—$36.85; San Francisco area—$40.66.

Intermediate Care (60-299 beds): "all other counties" - $28.14; Los Angeles County—$31.05; San Francisco area—$30.99.

Source: Data for Tables 8-1–8-4 were compiled from a survey of state Medicaid programs conducted by Robert J. Buchanan, Research Institute of Pharmaceutical Sciences, University of Mississippi, 1984.

The legislative history of the Boren Amendment makes clear that the states are to have the freedom to establish payments for long-term care "on a statewide or other geographic basis, or class basis, or an institution-by-institution basis."[71] Furthermore, the states are to have the option of including incentive allowances in their reimbursement systems to encourage cost containment through efficiency. It is also expected that the secretary of HHS will continue to apply current regulations in which Medicaid payments in excess of the amount that would be paid under Medicare reimbursement principles are prohibited.

Prospective vs. Retrospective Rate Setting

Advocates of prospective rate setting, in which the payment rate is established before the care is provided, believe that this system gives providers an incentive to contain the costs of health services. Those who endorse the retrospective mechanism, in which the payment rate is calculated after the care is provided, believe that this mechanism must be used in order to guarantee that Medicaid recipients have access to high-quality health services. The Social Security Amendments of 1967[72] authorize methods of paying for care that offer incentives for efficiency while protecting the quality of the health services provided. In addition, the Social Security Amendments of 1972[73] grant the secretary of HHS the power to authorize experiments and demonstration projects to determine the advantages and disadvantages of Medicaid prospective payment systems for nursing home care. Furthermore, federal regulations allow states the option of setting reimbursement rates prospectively.[74] An analysis of Medicaid reimbursement for long-term care revealed that the use of prospective rate setting produced lower per diem payment rates for nursing home care and did not affect the access of Medicaid recipients to care.[75]

State courts in Wisconsin and Washington have upheld the use of prospective reimbursement. The Wisconsin Court of Appeals ruled that the prospective reimbursement system used by that state's Medicaid program did not violate any federal or state laws or regulations.[76] The Washington Superior Court ruled that, although prospective rate setting is lawful, the state legislature did not intend for providers to bear the entire risk that miscalculations by the state in setting the prospective rates would result in Medicaid payments below the actual costs of care. Therefore, the Medicaid payment system in the state of Washington should have a method for "retroactively assuring payment of an efficiently and economically operated nursing home's audited cost."[77] This ruling was upheld by the Washington Court of Appeals.[78]

Thirty-nine state Medicaid programs reimbursed providers for intermediate care on a prospective basis, while six states calculated rates retrospectively. Nine states reimbursed skilled care on a retrospective basis, whereas thirty-six states established prospective rates (Table 8-2).

Table 8-2 Medicaid: Payment Limitations (1984)

	Prospective (P) or Retrospective (R) Rate	Final Cost Settlement	Facility (F) or Class-of-Care (C) Rate
Alabama	P	No	F
Alaska			
Arkansas	P	No	C
Arizona	No reimbursement for long-term care		
California			
Colorado	P	No	F
Connecticut	P	No*	F
Delaware	P	No*	F
Florida	P	Yes*	F
Georgia	P	No	F
Hawaii	R	Yes	F
Idaho	P	Yes	F
Illinois	P	No	F
Indiana	P	No	F
Iowa	P	SC:Yes IC:No	F
Kansas			
Kentucky	P	Yes**	F
Louisiana	P	No	C
Maine	SC:R IC:P	SC:Yes IC:No	F
Maryland	P***	Yes***	F,C
Massachusetts	R	Yes	F
Michigan	P	Yes	F
Minnesota	P	No	F
Mississippi	P	No	F
Missouri	P	No	F
Montana	P	No	F
Nebraska	P	No	F,C
Nevada	P***	Yes***	F***
New Hampshire	SC:R IC:P	SC:Yes IC:Yes*	F
New Jersey	P	Yes	F
New Mexico	R	Yes	F
New York	P	Yes*	F

Table 8-2 continued

	Prospective (P) or Retrospective (R) Rate	Final Cost Settlement	Facility (F) or Class-of-Care (C) Rate
North Carolina	P	Yes	F
North Dakota	P	No	F
Ohio	R	Yes	F
Oklahoma	Reimbursement system under revision		
Oregon	R	Yes	F
Pennsylvania	R	No	F
Rhode Island	P	No	F
South Carolina	P	Yes	F
South Dakota	P	No	F
Tennessee	SC:R	SC:Yes	F
	IC:P	IC:No	
Texas	P	No	C
Utah	P	No	C
Vermont	P	No	F
Virginia	P	No	F
Washington	P	Yes	F
West Virginia	P	No	F
Wisconsin	P	No**	F
Wyoming	P	No	F

Note: Unless otherwise noted, factors apply to both skilled and intermediate care.
*   Adjustments made only for audit findings or errors.
**   In some cases when rates are appealed.
*** On some cost centers.

Class-of-Care vs. Facility Reimbursement

Under a class-of-care system, a state Medicaid program establishes one payment rate for a specified class of care (e.g., intermediate care) and reimburses all facilities that provide that level of care within the state or specified subdivision of the state at that rate. As Table 8-2 indicates, thirty-nine states reimbursed nursing homes on an individual facility basis, four states reimbursed them on a class-of-care basis, and two states used both methods to set rates. Twenty states allowed a final cost settlement or adjustment to their Medicaid reimbursement rates for skilled care, twenty-five states did not. (Data were unavailable for five states.) The number of Medicaid programs allowing a final cost settlement for intermediate care dropped to seventeen states, while the number of programs not allowing a final adjustment increased to twenty-eight.

Ceiling

All state Medicaid programs reimburse providers for long-term care under the federal restriction that the amounts paid cannot exceed the amounts that would have been paid under Medicare. This requirement can be satisfied in either of two ways. The Medicaid payment is acceptable (1) if it is not more than the Medicare payment that would have been made to 90 percent of the providers in a random sample of all providers or (2) if the average Medicaid reimbursement payment to all providers in a class of care does not exceed the average payment that would have been made under Medicare. For providers that participate in Medicare, their Medicare payments, adjusted for services not covered by Medicaid, are used in calculating the Medicaid ceiling. For providers that do not participate in Medicare and those that provide intermediate care (not covered by Medicare), the state Medicaid programs must estimate Medicare payments by using Medicare reimbursement principles.[79]

Before 1976, federal regulations required state Medicaid programs to set their intermediate care payment rates at least 10 percent below the rate paid for skilled care.[80] Because of the requirements of reasonable cost-related payments mandated by the Social Security Amendments of 1972, however, this regulation was eliminated as of July 1, 1976.[81]

PROPERTY COST CONTAINMENT

According to one corporate leader in the provision of long-term care services, the average cost of a nursing home bed in 1983 ranged from $15,000 to $20,000, depending on the geographical location.[82] Since the number of beds in the typical facility ranges from 100 to 120, the average cost for a typical nursing home was $1.5 to $3 million in 1983. These long-term care facilities operate over an extended time period, which makes the depreciation or allocation of the costs of their fixed assets over the time that they are in use an important reimbursement issue. In the reimbursement of depreciation, state Medicaid programs have many factors to consider, such as the method of depreciation, the value of the nursing home, and the useful life of the facility.

Method of Depreciation

The state Medicaid programs may use straight-line depreciation or accelerated depreciation in calculating reimbursement rates. With straight-line depreciation, which is used by the vast majority of state programs (Table 8-3), the nursing home's fixed assets are depreciated in equal amounts each year over the useful life of the assets. With accelerated depreciation, the nursing home's fixed assets are depreciated in larger amounts in earlier years and in progressively smaller amounts in later years. Since depreciation is a reimbursable expense, the use of accelerated depreciation captures the expenses of using the nursing home's fixed assets more quickly than if the straight-line depreciation method were used.

Value of the Facility

Before the fixed assets of a long-term care facility can be depreciated, their value must be established. Various methods are used by the state Medicaid programs to place a value on the nursing home for purposes of depreciation (Table 8-3). Some state Medicaid programs, for example, Pennsylvania, calculate the value of the facility under the various options and use the lowest of these values for purposes of depreciation. The Alabama program places a value on the plant and equipment at $15,000 per bed, less accumulated depreciation. However, no change in value is allowed for seven years after a sale.

Table 8-3 Medicaid: Capital Related Costs (1984)

	Depreciation			Lease Payments
	Method: Straight Line (S) Accelerated (A)	Value of Facility	Useful Life: Buildings	
Alabama	S	7	B	Z
Alaska				
Arkansas	S	4	Wood: 20 years Masonry: 30 years	Arm's length: W Related party: X
Arizona		No reimbursement for long-term care		
California				
Colorado	S	4	B	Y
Connecticut	7	3	30 years	W

Table 8-3 continued

	Depreciation			Lease Payments
	Method: Straight Line (S) Accelerated (A)	Value of Facility	Useful Life: Buildings	
Delaware	S	C	C	C
Florida	S	6	C	X*
Georgia	S	1,3	40 years	Y
Hawaii	S,A	4	C	Arm's length: W Related party: X
Idaho	S	6		X
Illinois	S	3	30 years	Y
Indiana	7	3	20 years	X
Iowa	S	SC:2 IC:6	SC: 40 years IC: 30 years	SC:X IC:Y
Kansas				
Kentucky	S,A	4	35-40 years	X
Louisiana	S	4	30-50 years	Y
Maine	S	6		X
Maryland	7	1	Not applicable	Y
Massachusetts	S	3	33-40 years	X
Michigan	S	C	33⅓ years	X
Minnesota	S	4	35 years	Y (If related party)
Mississippi	S	4	7	Y
Missouri	7	7	7	Z
Montana	7	7	B	Z
Nebraska	S	6	A	X
Nevada	S	4	40 years from construction	X
New Hampshire	S	4	C	W
New Jersey	S	5	40 years	Y
New Mexico	S	2	30 years	Y
New York	S	3	40 years	Y
North Carolina	S	6	A	Y
North Dakota	S	6	40 years	W
Ohio	S	4	40 years	Y
Oklahoma		Reimbursement system under revision		
Oregon	S	3,4	B	Arm's length: W Related party: X
Pennsylvania	S	6	A	Y
Rhode Island	S	6	A	X
South Carolina	S	4	B	W; X (For new leases after 12/15/81)
South Dakota	S	3,4		Y
Tennessee	S	6	C	SC:Y IC:X
Texas	S	4	40 years	Related party: X
Utah	7	7	7	Z
Vermont	S	6	B	W

Table 8-3 continued

	Depreciation			Lease Payments
	Method: Straight Line (S) Accelerated (A)	Value of Facility	Useful Life: Buildings	
Virginia	S	6	40 years	X
Washington	S	4	30 years	Arm's length: W Related party: X
West Virginia	7	7	A	Z
Wisconsin	S	4	35 years	Y
Wyoming	S	4	40 years	Y

Note: Unless otherwise noted treatment of property cost factor applies to both skilled and intermediate care.

*Proposed as of 7/1/84.

1. Replacement costs
2. Market value
3. Historic cost (date of construction)
4. Historic cost (date of last sale)
5. Assessed value
6. Lowest of the listed options
7. Other

A. Varies
B. American Hospital Association Guidelines
C. Medicare Guidelines

W. Full lease payments reimbursed
X. Lease payments reimbursed not to exceed cost of ownership
Y. Lease payments reimbursed with other limit imposed
Z. Other

Source: Survey of state Medicaid programs compiled by Robert J. Buchanan, Research Institute of Pharmaceutical Sciences, University of Mississippi, 1984.

Useful Life

Because the value of the long-term care facility is depreciated over the useful life of the facility, the length of the useful life affects the amount of depreciation expenses for which the nursing home is reimbursed each year. With straight-line depreciation, for example, the amount of annual depreciation expenses reimbursed when the facility's useful life is defined as forty years is less than the annual depreciation expenses reimbursed when useful life is defined as thirty years. Various definitions of useful life are used by the state Medicaid programs (Table 8-3).

Lease Payments

Providers may lease nursing home facilities to deliver long-term care. Different state Medicaid programs reimburse providers for these lease expenses in different ways. Some states (e.g., Florida and Michigan) limit the amount of the lease payments reimbursed for each facility to the cost of ownership of that nursing home. Other states (e.g., Hawaii and Vermont) allow the full reimbursement of lease expenses.

Arm's Length Transactions vs. Related Organization Transactions

The reimbursement of lease, rental, or purchase expenses incurred by nursing homes in transactions with related business entities is subject to the related organization principle. The Maryland Medicaid program, for example, applies the related organization principle to lease agreements between organizations related by common ownership or control and limits the reimbursement of a lessee's lease expense to the ownership costs of the lessor under these circumstances. Accordingly, the Maryland State Department of Health and Mental Hygiene denied reimbursement to the Cuppett & Weeks Nursing Home for the rental charges of the Cuppett & Weeks Nursing Home Partnership.[83] The lessor was owned by Bessie Cuppett and two of her children; the lessee was owned by Bessie Cuppett, one of the children who also owned the lessor, and other relatives. The Maryland Court of Special Appeals reviewed this denial and upheld the decision, stating that the regulations were not applied arbitrarily or capriciously, that they relate to a "legitimate legislative goal," and that they are constitutional.

The attorney general for the state of Arkansas stated that the Arkansas Medicaid program's limits on reimbursable costs for services provided to a nursing home by a related organization were consistent with federal law.[84] In the opinion of the attorney general, federal regulations set as the upper limit on Medicaid reimbursable costs the actual costs incurred by the related party in providing the service. A still lower payment rate may be applied by the Arkansas Medicaid program if the actual costs to the related organization exceed the costs for a comparable service or facility provided by an independent third party.

New York Medicaid regulations limit the amount of reimbursement that a nursing home can receive for goods or services provided by a related organization to the lower of (1) the cost to the related organization of providing the goods or services or (2) the market price of comparable goods or services available in the nursing home's region of the state within the course of normal business operations.[85] In this regard, the New York Supreme Court was asked to resolve a dispute concerning Medicaid reimbursement for a real property lease and a movable equipment lease that the Haven Manor Health Related Facility had entered into with a partnership during 1974. The dispute involved the relationship between the operator of Haven Manor (Daniel Cantor) and this partnership.[86]

In 1969, Daniel Cantor purchased the land on which Haven Manor is located for $235,000; he then received approval to own and operate a health facility on the property. On March 16, 1971, Mr. Cantor assigned his contract for the purchase of the land to Arthur Simensky for $500,000. Also on March 16, Mr. Cantor and Mr. Simensky agreed to form a partnership based on the approval to own and operate a health facility that Mr. Cantor had received and Mr. Simensky's experience in construction. Under the terms of the partnership agreement, Mr. Cantor had to exercise one of two options when a certificate of occupancy was obtained for the facility or by January 15, 1974, whichever occurred first. Under one option, Mr. Cantor would withdraw as a partner and enter into a real property lease with the partnership; the lease would last twenty-one years, with an annual rental of $1,800 per bed. The lease would not include furniture or movable equipment. The other option required Mr. Cantor to contribute $100,000 to the partnership and sell a one-third interest in the operation of Haven Manor to another partner for $5,000. In December 1972, the partnership agreement was expanded, and Mr. Cantor agreed to contribute 16⅔ percent of the partnership capital.

In January 1974, Mr. Cantor exercised his option to withdraw from the partnership; in February 1974, he entered into a real property lease with the partnership as outlined in the March 16, 1971 memorandum. At the same time, the parties entered into a movable equipment lease at an annual rental of $200 per bed. The New York State Department of Health (Medicaid) initially considered these leases to be arm's length transactions for purposes of Medicaid reimbursement. Following an audit, however, Medicaid concluded that both these leases should be treated as transactions between related parties. After an administrative law judge upheld this decision, Mr. Cantor sought judicial review.

The New York Supreme Court ruled that the Commissioner of Health was wrong when he concluded that the real property lease was not at arm's length. Referring to *Hospital Affiliates Int. v. Schweiker*,[87] the court said that it relied "upon the consistent interpretation of the pertinent regulations which requires that a transaction be considered arm's length when the parties' relationship results from the transaction."[88] Citing *Northwest Community Hospital v. Califano*,[89] the court also stated that "the obvious purpose of the regulations is to prevent self-dealing and contrived relationships between related parties."[90]

The New York court ruled in the case at hand that there was no evidence that Mr. Cantor had ever dealt with Mr. Simensky or any of the other members of the partnership prior to March 16, 1971, when the terms were set for the real property lease. Hence, the court ruled that there was no valid basis to support Medicaid's conclusion that the real property lease should be treated as a transaction between related parties. With regard to the movable equipment lease, however, the court ruled that Mr. Cantor and the partnership had been related in business prior to the creation of this second lease. The court agreed with Medicaid that this second lease was not at arm's length.

In *Cliff House Nursing Home, Inc. v. Rate Setting Commission et al.*,[91] a Massachusetts case, the court resolved a dispute over Medicaid reimbursement for an arm's length lease. The Rate Setting Commission in Massachusetts disregarded the rent paid by Cliff House Nursing Home in 1972 under an arm's length lease (reported at $113,171) and allowed reimbursement of only $51,097, which was the sum of the lessor's expenses for real estate taxes, interest, and depreciation. After administrative review failed to reverse this decision by the commission, Cliff House petitioned for judicial review. The superior court affirmed the decision of the commission, and Cliff House appealed that ruling to the appellate court of Massachusetts.

To the appeals court, the "heart" of the proceedings was whether the Rate Setting Commission could disregard the rent paid by Cliff House and substitute the fixed property costs of the lessor in calculating Medicaid reimbursement. The court noted that Massachusetts law gave the commission the authority to establish regulations governing the rates to be paid by government units for health care services. The court also observed that the regulations allow the commission to disregard rental and lease expenses in computing the rate base for a provider if (1) the costs are not comparable to those of other properties in the area, (2) the lease expenses exceed what the provider would be allowed if the provider owned the facilities, (3) there is insufficient basis for comparison, or (4) the lessor and the provider are related.

The court noted that, by arguing that the Rate Setting Commission could not ignore the actual rent Cliff House was obliged to pay under the terms of an arm's length lease, Cliff House was actually challenging the validity of the regulation, "which expressly permits the RSC [Rate Setting Commission] to do just that. It is a challenge fated to fail."[92] The appeals court further noted that

Courts accord to regulations, including rate regulations, the same deference they extend to acts of the Legislature.... In consequence, a regulation is valid if it has reasonable relation to the goal advanced by the statute ... and regulations are entitled to particularly great weight where the statute itself... "vests broad powers in the agency to fill in the details of the legislative scheme."[93]

After concluding that the commission had the authority to disregard the actual rent paid by Cliff House ($113,171), the court examined the real estate cost component that the commission allowed Cliff House in its operating expenses ($51,097). This cost allowance differs greatly from the $107,236 Cliff House would have been allowed had it purchased the nursing home property in 1972 for the price that it paid when it did purchase the facility in 1973. The cost allowance also differs widely from the $90,659 rent expense the Governor Winthrop, a neighboring nursing home, was allowed by the Rate Setting Commission in 1972. The appeals court noted that, although this neighboring nursing home and Cliff House did not have comparable rental agreements (the Governor Winthrop had a rental arrangement that was not at arm's length), they were "otherwise comparable and surely the real estate expenses found by the RSC to be fair and reasonable for the Governor Winthrop should have furnished some useful guidance to what was fair and reasonable for Cliff House."[94]

The appeals court noted that, once the actual rental expense to Cliff House was disallowed, the commission had

> to determine the "reasonable and necessary expenses of both the provider and the lessor (including interest, depreciation, real estate taxes, insurance, and other reasonable and necessary expenses)." The RSC ... itemized only the costs of the lessor, Spector, and none of the provider, Cliff House.[95]

The court added that

> the RSC may have some expert knowledge, but from what appears in the record, neither profit nor other expenses for which the provider may have been responsible under the lease (e.g., insurance and repairs) were considered. There is no other way to explain the yawning gap between what the RSC allowed Cliff House and what it allowed the Governor Winthrop and appeared prepared to allow Cliff House as owner [Cliff House bought the facility in 1973] rather than lessee of the property.[96]

The appeals court therefore remanded the case to the Rate Setting Commission. In determining the appropriate property costs, the court stated that "the RSC may be guided in part by the real estate expenses allowed to owner occupied or affiliated nursing homes of similar size, age, and amenities, and operating in similar markets."[97]

REIMBURSEMENT FACTORS

Capital Interest Expenses

The provision of institutional long-term care is capital-intensive. The necessary capital can be obtained either through equity invested by the owners, through the issuance of debt, or a combination of the two. A study of thirteen corporations that were providing nursing home care from 1971 through 1980 revealed that these large nursing home chains were heavily dependent on long-term debt, raising $2 of debt for every $1 of equity.[98] Since the interest payments on this debt compose a significant cost center for the long-term care facilities, the way in which state Medicaid programs reimburse these expenses is an important issue (Table 8-4). The New York Medicaid program reimburses providers for capital interest expenses "at a rate which the Commissioner finds to be reasonable under circumstances prevailing at the time of placing the capital indebtedness."[99] Other states set more explicit ceilings on capital interest expenses. The Virginia Medicaid program, for example, limits the rate of reimbursable interest to the prevailing rates authorized by the Virginia Housing Development Authority at the date of closing of the permanent financing.[100]

Table 8-4 Medicaid: Reimbursement Factors (1984)

	Capital Interest Expenses	Profit	Inflation Factor	Cost Limiting Method
Alabama	6	C,E - (12.72%)	7%	U - (60th)
Alaska				
Arkansas	1	A	4%	U - (80th)
California	1			U - (50th)
Colorado	1	C	1.61785%	U - 100th-Health & Raw Food 90th-Admin., Property room and board
Connecticut	6	D	7.5%	X - (160%)
Delaware	3	Does not pay profit	5%	U - (75th)

Table 8-4 continued

	Capital Interest Expenses	Profit	Inflation Factor	Cost Limiting Method
Florida	1	E (⅔ Medicare rate)	Varies	X
Georgia	5	E (11%)	22.5% (1980 base year)	U - (75th)
Hawaii	4	D	N.A. - reasonable cost payment	Y
Idaho	1	C	Moving rate	X - plus 2 standard deviations
Illinois	5	F		U - (60th)
Indiana	5	F	5.7%	Z
Iowa	SC: 5 IC: 2	SC: C,E IC: A	SC: NA IC: 4.2%	SC: U (75th) IC: U (74th)
Kansas				
Kentucky	1	C	5.7%	X - (105%)
Louisiana	4	E - (5%)	5%	Z
Maine	1	SC: E (10%) IC: B,E (10%)	SC: NA IC:4.7%	Y
Maryland	6	E - profit-.0988 non-profit-.089	Varies	Z
Massachusetts	1 (with ceiling)	E - (15.98%)	9.9%	X - plus 1 standard deviation
Michigan	1	C	4.5%	U - (80th)
Minnesota	1 (with ceiling)	F - (11.3%)	6%	U - (60th)
Mississippi	5	A,D	5.5%	U - (60th)
Missouri	6	F	1.75%	X - (125%)
Montana	1	F	6%	
Nebraska	5	C	2.7%	X - (110%),Y
Nevada	5	D	None	Y
New Hampshire	1	SC: None IC: F	SC: None IC: 5%	SC: None IC: U (75th) on variable cost
New Jersey	N.A.	D (December 1976 rate)	Varies	Y
New Mexico	5	C	CPI	U - (80th)
New York	4	E - (19.172%)	SC: 5.8% IC: 5.7%	V
North Carolina	5	E - (14%)	4.5%	U - (75th direct care 60th indirect care)
North Dakota	1	E - (8.5%)	3.8% - variable costs 5.7% - salaries	NA
Ohio	5	D	NA - retrospective payments	Y
Oklahoma		Reimbursement system under revision		
Oregon	1,4	A - up to ceiling E - (10%)	4.0%	U - (75th)
Pennsylvania	5	C	4.7%	W

Table 8-4 continued

	Capital Interest Expenses	Profit	Inflation Factor	Cost Limiting Method
Rhode Island	5	A	6.4%	U - (percentile ranges from 70th to 90th for different cost centers)
South Carolina	5	C,D	Not determined	V,Y
South Dakota	1	E - (9%)	5%	X - (110%)
Tennessee	4	SC: D IC: D with max. of $1.50PPD	SC: 14.22% max. IC: 8.94% max.	U - (50th)
Texas	4	A	Varies with cost centers	X - (107%)
Utah	6	B	2.3%	Z
Vermont	1	D	4.4%	U - (90th)
Virginia	6	E - (10%)	4%	W
Washington	4	E - (12%)	3%	Z
West Virginia	6	F	CPI	Z
Wisconsin	1	E - (11%)	3%	
Wyoming	1	C	1.43% (Jan-June)	U - (84th)

Connecticut uses a Fair Rental Value System. Montana and Utah reimburse capital expenses on a flat formula rate, not cost related.

Note:

1. Actual expenses paid
2. Prevailing rates
3. Medicare rate of return
4. Actual expenses paid, but ceiling applies to related parties
5. Interest expenses limited by ceiling on capital reimbursement
6. Other

A. Fixed fee per patient day
B. Variable fee per patient day
C. Variable fee per patient day up to a ceiling
D. Return on net equity (Medicare rate)
E. Return on net equity (other rate)
F. Other
U. Percentile limit
V. Class mean
W. Class median
X. Percentage of mean/median
Y. Customary charges or Medicare rate
Z. Other

In December 1978, the Fishkill Health Related Facility, a nursing home, brought suit against the New York Medicaid program for its refusal to recognize as an allowable cost interest payments at the rate of 24 percent that the nursing home agreed to pay its landlord for a loan.[101] (The rate on the two-year loan was 8½ percent for the first three months and 24 percent thereafter.) The Commissioner of Health upheld this refusal, denying the nursing home's administrative appeal. The commissioner stated that the rate of interest was in excess of what a "prudent borrower" would have paid in the money market and that the interest was paid to a lender who was related to the borrower through "affiliation." The commissioner also concluded that reimbursing the nursing home for any portion of the interest payments would be a disincentive to improve services and initiate economies.

The provider appealed this ruling to the New York Supreme Court. The court ruled that, because money market rates were between 12 percent and 15 percent when the loan was made, the commissioner's decision not to allow the "substantially" higher rate could not be considered arbitrary and capricious. The court did not agree with the commissioner, however, that none of the nursing home's interest expense on this loan should be an allowable cost. The court decided that, because the relevant statute requires Medicaid reimbursement rates for nursing home care to be "reasonably related to the costs of efficient production of services," the commissioner "cannot contest the necessity of the loan in order to continue the facility's operation."[102] Therefore, the court reasoned, if the loan were valid, the provider must be reimbursed for some rate of interest.

The commissioner had also contended that the landlord-tenant relationship violated New York regulations requiring arm's length dealings between any borrower and lender. The court disagreed with the commissioner's conclusion, stating that courts have based decisions in these cases on the presence or absence of interrelated business structures and associations and that no business association beyond the landlord-tenant relationship has been alleged in this case. In addition, noting that the commissioner had accepted the lease between the landlord and the tenant as an arm's length transaction and had fully reimbursed the lease payments, the court stated, "It would certainly be inconsistent to hold that the lease was an arm's-length transaction and the loan between the same two parties was not."[103] The New York Supreme Court, therefore, ruled that the Fishkill Health Related Facility should be reimbursed, as an allowable Medicaid cost, interest payments on the loan in question at a rate of 15 percent.

The Pennsylvania Medicaid program disallowed the reimbursement of certain interest expenses incurred by Allied Services for the Handicapped, a provider of nursing home services.[104] The provider had borrowed money to pay interest expenses owed during construction and to establish a debt reserve fund. The Medicaid program determined that interest expenses on these loans were not reimbursable costs, and the provider appealed. The provider contended that these interest expenses were related to interest on capital indebtedness and were reimbursable. The Medicaid manual for Pennsylvania states that "necessary and proper interest on both current and capital indebtedness is an allowable cost" with capital indebtedness defined as "acquisition of facilities, equipment and capital improvements."[105] The state court ruled that an agency's interpretation of its own regulations cannot be reversed by a court of review unless the agency's interpretation is plainly erroneous or inconsistent with applicable statutes and regulations. The court ruled that the Medicaid agency's interpretation of the regulations was not inconsistent with the law because there was no specific authorization in the regulations concerning reimbursement of interest costs incurred to pay interest expenses or to establish a debt reserve fund.

In another case, the Quakertown Hospital Association, representing the owners and operators of skilled care and intermediate care facilities, contended that Medicaid reimbursement practices for interest and depreciation expenses in Pennsylvania violated the U.S. Constitution and the Medicaid Act.[106] The plaintiffs specifically challenged four regulations, policies, and practices used by the Pennsylvania Medicaid program to reimburse long-term care facilities for services:

1. the regulation limiting the reimbursement of depreciation expenses for existing, new, renovated, or purchased facilities to a maximum average statewide construction cost of $22,000 per bed
2. the regulation limiting the reimbursement of interest on capital indebtedness incurred to finance the cost of existing, new, renovated, or purchased facilities to a maximum cost of $22,000 per bed
3. the regulation establishing the cost basis for the depreciable assets of a nursing home purchased as an ongoing operation at the lower of the purchase price or the fair market value of these assets, less any depreciation taken by prior owners
4. the policy and practice, not set forth in a regulation, that denies the reimbursement of interest expenses incurred to finance that portion of the acquisition price of an operating long-term care facility equal to the amount of depreciation already deducted from the depreciation basis of the facility by the prior owner.

The providers contended that these state regulations and policies violate the Fifth and Fourteenth Amendments to the U.S. Constitution by taking property without just compensation. The plaintiffs argued that the regulations prevent the sale of nursing homes at their fair market value for two reasons. First, because of the regulations and practices, no purchaser would pay more than the net depreciated value of the facility or more than the $22,000 per bed limit. Second, no lender would finance an acquisition with a purchase price greater than those limits. Thus, the providers contended that these regulations and practices created an artificially low value for their facilities.

The court was not persuaded by these arguments and reasoned that "the 'taking' element of the just compensation clause has not been violated."[107] The court cited *Hempstead General Hospital v. Whalen*,[108] a case in which the plaintiffs had challenged federally approved state limitations on capital cost reimbursement to potential purchasers of health care facilities. The Medicaid regulations at issue in *Hempstead General Hospital* limited capital reimbursement for purchasers of a facility to the net depreciated value of the property rather than to either the purchase price or the fair market value. In other words, in the event that a health facility in New York state was sold, the capital cost component of the Medicaid payment paid to the new owner would remain the same as that paid to the previous owner. The plaintiffs argued that these capital reimbursement limitations constituted a "taking" because they eliminated potential buyers of health care facilities. The court in *Hempstead General Hospital* found that the elements of government invasion were lacking, however, because the plaintiffs had full right to use the medical center property; the regulations imposed no direct legal restraint on the property or its use; there was no physical entry by the state nor ouster of the owner; and there was no legal interference with the owner's power to dispose of the property. The *Hempstead Hospital* court concluded that there was no "taking," even though the regulations substantially decreased the market for hospital facilities and their potential sale price.

Using *Hempstead General Hospital* as a precedent, the court in *Quakertown Hospital Association* similarly concluded

> that the case at bar lacks the essential elements for a "taking." As the defendant pertinently points out, plaintiffs are free to do what they wish with their property. They can continue to operate as nursing homes in or out of the Medicaid program. They can discontinue operation as nursing homes and use or sell their property for other purposes. They suffer no fifth amendment "taking" as a result of the questioned regulations.[109]

The plaintiffs also asserted in *Quakertown Hospital Association* that the regulations, policies, and practices violated the Due Process Clause of the Constitution. Specifically, the plaintiffs argued that they had a property interest in receiving Medicaid payments at rates in compliance with federal law. The defendants countered that the Pennsylvania regulations and practices limiting capital cost reimbursement are clearly related to the state's legitimate interest in promoting efficient and economic use of its Medicaid funds consistent with the federal Medicaid statute. The court ruled on this issue that the defendants' motion for summary judgment was premature.

> The burden is on the party complaining of a due process violation to establish that the state has acted in an arbitrary or irrational manner, plaintiffs at this stage of the proceedings have not been afforded a sufficient opportunity to discover whether the state's regulations truly are arbitrary and unreasonable.[110]

Referring to *Hempstead General Hospital* the court concluded that

> once plaintiffs [Quakertown Hospital Association] have been afforded a sufficient opportunity, their burden of proof will certainly be heavy.... Furthermore, the Court notes that at this point it does not find compelling plaintiffs' arguments that the primary purpose of the regulations is to save money.[111]

The court also noted "the intent of Congress to limit the degree of federal scrutiny applied to the Medicaid regulation system"[112] for rate setting. The court declared on October 24, 1983 that it was premature to rule on the reasonableness of the regulations in question, as the plaintiffs needed more time to discover and present facts supporting their position. As of early April 1984 a final ruling in this case had not been issued.

Profits

Approximately three of every four long-term care beds are in profit-seeking facilities. If proprietary providers are to remain in the nursing home industry and if private investment is to be sufficient to meet future needs for long-term care beds, these providers must be able to earn a profit. Federal regulations allow each state the option of including a return on equity as a reimbursable cost to profit-seeking providers.[113] The state programs are allowed to set the rate of return on net equity at the level they calculate to be necessary to attract and maintain adequate investment of capital in the long-term care industry.[114] Federal regulations define equity capital as the provider's investment in plant, property, and equipment related to patient care, less depreciation, and funds deposited by a provider to lease plant, property, and equipment related to patient care. Also included in the definition of equity capital is net working capital maintained "for necessary and proper operation of patient care activities."[115]

The state Medicaid programs differ in the rate of return on equity that they allow. Many states, e.g., Ohio, Vermont, and Connecticut, use the Medicare rate of return in calculating this profit factor (see Table 8-4). As of July 1, 1984, the Florida Medicaid program reduced the return on equity it paid from the full Medicare rate to two-thirds of the Medicare rate for proprietary providers; nonprofit nursing homes are reimbursed at a rate equal to one-third the rate allowed to proprietary providers.

The Medicare rate of return on provider's equity capital investment in SNFs is a percentage equal to 1½ times the average rates of interest paid on special issues of public debt obligation issued to the Federal Hospital Insurance Trust Fund (FHITF). Congress intended this rate of return on equity to serve as a ceiling, not necessarily the mandated rate.[116] The HCFA has used this ceiling as the actual rate for Medicare reimbursement purposes, however. This rate of return on equity capital peaked at 22.875 percent during 1981, but declined by May 1984 to a rate approaching 18.9 percent.

The 1983 amendments to the Social Security Act required that, for purposes of reimbursing inpatient hospital services, the Medicare rate of return on equity capital be limited to 100 percent of prevailing interest rates. Although these amendments did not mandate such a reduction in the Medicare rate of return on equity for reimbursement of skilled care, the inspector general of HHS recommended in October 1983 that the HCFA also reduce the Medicare rate of return on equity for SNFs to 100 percent of the average FHITF investment rates.[117] If this recommendation becomes policy, state Medicaid programs using the Medicare rate of return on equity may also lower the rates at which they reimburse long-term care facilities.

Other state Medicaid programs have established their own rates of return on equity investments for long-term care facilities. During 1984, according to the survey of state programs conducted for this book, the Maine and Virginia Medicaid programs used a rate of return equal to 10 percent of average annual equity, and the Medicaid program in Louisiana used a rate of return on equity of 5 percent. The Minnesota Medicaid program reimburses profit by allowing an 11.3 percent "return on [the] historical cost of [the] building and attached fixtures," according to the survey, and the Wisconsin Medicaid program takes a similar approach, allowing an 11 percent return "on [the] net undepreciated owner's equity base equal to last sale price."

Other state Medicaid programs, through variations on prospective rate setting, use a variable fee per patient day to allow for a profit factor. Many of these methods contain efficiency incentives, linking profit to cost containment efforts. Federal regulations allow states this option in reimbursing both profit-seeking and nonprofit providers. For example, the Michigan Medicaid program allows proprietary providers to keep "up to 50¢ of the difference between [each facility's] allowable per patient day plant costs and the 80th percentile" of allowable per patient day plant costs for providers delivering that class of care. In addition, proprietary providers are permitted "to retain up to one dollar of the difference between [each facility's] allowable per patient day variable cost" and the 80th percentile of allowable per patient day variable costs for providers delivering that class of care.[118] The New Mexico Medicaid program also includes an incentive factor designed to encourage cost containment. The provider is paid 50 percent of the difference between the maximum Medicaid class allowable costs and the provider's current allowable cost, adjusted by a ratio of the provider's rate of cost increase to the Consumer Price Index. The New Mexico Medicaid program places a cap on this incentive factor at $2 per patient day.[119] The Medicaid program in South Carolina allows providers a profit factor through the use of both the Medicare rate of return on equity and a variable fee per patient day up to a ceiling according to the survey of state programs.

Cost Limiting Method

The state Medicaid programs have adopted a variety of reimbursement methods to limit the amounts they pay for long-term care (see Table 8-4). The most common method for containing payment rates is the basic percentile system, which involves ordering providers of similar classes of care in an ascending array of costs. The provider cost at the xth percentile, for example, the 80th percentile in Michigan or the 90th percentile in Vermont, becomes the target cost. This target cost can be either a prospective rate or a ceiling rate for the class of care.

Ceilings may also be established by limiting reimbursement payments to some variation of the median cost of similar types of care. For example, Medicaid reimbursement in Texas is limited to a ceiling of 107 percent of the median cost for similar types of care within the state. The Florida Medicaid program establishes separate payment ceilings for operating costs and for patient care costs in each of four classes of care. Reimbursement for operating costs is limited to the class median cost plus 1 standard deviation, and reimbursement for patient care costs is limited to the class median cost plus 2 standard deviations. The total Medicaid payment to the provider, however, cannot exceed the provider's average usual and customary per diem charges. In all states, the Medicaid rates cannot exceed the rate that would be paid under Medicare reimbursement principles.

FAMILY RESPONSIBILITY AND LONG-TERM CARE

The Reagan Administration, in a new interpretation of federal Medicaid law, has authorized state governments to require that the adult children of Medicaid recipients pay for part of the care provided to their parents by nursing homes. HHS released a special supplement to the state Medicaid manual in February 1983, declaring that "the law and regulations permit states to require adult family members to support adult relatives without violating the Medicaid statute.... Such contribution requirements are permissible as a state option.[120]

The Reagan Administration contends that two legally supportable interpretations of the Social Security Act form the basis for this family responsibility concept. First, the payments from family members must be required under a state statute of general applicability, not as part of the state Medicaid plan. A statute of general applicability, i.e., a law that applies to any citizen in the state, can be applied to health care or to other social services programs as well.[121] In this case, the statute would define the relationship between adult children and their parents. Such a statute is necessary in this instance, according to the Reagan Administration, in order not to violate the provision of the Social Security Act that prohibits a state Medicaid plan from considering the financial resources of relatives other than a spouse or parents in determining the eligibility of dependent, blind, or disabled children.

According to the Reagan Administration, the second interpretation of the Social Security Act that allows the family responsibility concept is that the state Medicaid plan cannot assume that the incomes of adult children, or payments from them, are available to the parent in the long-term care facility. Only the support actually received by the parent from the child as a result of a state support statute of general applicability can be counted for computation of Medicaid benefits. Furthermore, according to Daniel Bourque, deputy director of the HCFA, "no one would be denied access to a nursing home" because of the income rules of the family responsibility concept.[122]

Within these constraints, the states have the flexibility to define who is a relative responsible for financial support, the level of required support, and the administration of collection.

National Survey

The Research Institute of Pharmaceutical Sciences conducted a mail survey of state Medicaid programs in November and December 1983 to determine the status of the family responsibility concept in each state.[123] In the questionnaire, each program was given six options to describe the status of the family responsibility concept in its state (Table 8-5). The three-year experimental Medicaid program in Arizona does not cover long-term care services, but forty-eight of the remaining forty-nine states responded to the survey.

Table 8-5 Development of the Family Responsibility Concept in the States

	Adopted into Law	Under Consideration by Medicaid Program	Under Consideration by Governor	Under Consideration by the Legislature	Not under Consideration	Dropped or Debated	Other
Alabama					X		
Alaska					X		
Arizona							
Arkansas		X					
California					X		
Colorado		X	X	X			
Connecticut					X		
Delaware					X		
Florida					X		
Georgia					X		
Hawaii				X			
Idaho	X						
Illinois		X					
Indiana					X		
Iowa					X		
Kansas					X		
Kentucky							X
Louisiana	X						
Maine		X					
Maryland					X		
Massachusetts							X
Michigan					X		
Minnesota					X		
Mississippi							
Missouri		X	X				
Montana						X	
Nebraska		X					
Nevada					X		
New Hampshire						X	
New Jersey					X		
New Mexico					X		
New York					X	X	
North Carolina					X		
North Dakota				X			
Ohio							X
Oklahoma					X		
Oregon					X		

Table 8-5 continued

	Adopted into Law	Under Consideration by Medicaid Program	Under Consideration by Governor	Under Consideration by the Legislature	Not under Consideration	Dropped or Debated	Other
Pennsylvania		×	×	×			
Rhode Island					×		
South Carolina		×					
South Dakota					×		
Tennessee					×		
Texas		×					
Utah					×		
Vermont		×					
Virginia	×						
Washington					×		
West Virginia					×		
Wisconsin			×	×			
Wyoming					×		

Source: Reprinted from "Medicaid: Family Responsibility and Long Term Care" by Robert J. Buchanan *Journal of Long Term Care Administration* 12, No. 13 (Fall 1984). Used with permission.

The states of Idaho and Virginia have passed mandatory family responsibility laws, and the state of Louisiana has passed a voluntary family responsibility law with a tax credit provision for participating families. According to the survey, Medicaid programs in ten states were in various stages of considering the family responsibility concept. The Arkansas Medicaid program, one of those considering the concept, responded that it had only conducted some preliminary research on such legislation. In Pennsylvania, the family responsibility concept had been under consideration by the Medicaid program, the governor, and the legislature, but it had been "tabled indefinitely." Expanding on this further, a Medicaid administrator stated,

> The Commonwealth of Pennsylvania is currently [December 9, 1983] reviewing the "family responsibility" issue. Pennsylvania is leaning towards adopting a voluntary, rather than mandatory, contribution program for children with parents in nursing homes. However, a final decision has not been reached on this issue.[124]

In four states, the office of the governor was considering the family responsibility concept; five state legislatures were considering this issue.

Twenty-seven states responded in the survey that the family responsibility concept was not under consideration, and three states replied that it had been considered, but was dropped or defeated. The Medicaid program in New Jersey, checking "not under consideration" on the questionnaire, added that "the governor of New Jersey has decided to await results from other states who have enacted family supplementation laws."[125] The state of Connecticut responded, "The Department considers this to be a dramatic change in the Medicaid program. Hence, all aspects of the effects of this proposal must be addressed before timely supplementation can be considered."[126]

The Idaho Law

Idaho law authorizes the Idaho Department of Health and Welfare to recover from responsible relatives a portion of Medicaid payments for skilled care and intermediate care (including that for the mentally retarded) provided to Medicaid beneficiaries.[127] By definition, a responsible relative is a spouse, a natural or adoptive child or children, and the natural or adoptive parents of a Medicaid recipient who is under 18 years of age, blind, or disabled.[128] The gross income of a responsible relative is defined as the sum of

1. federal gross annual income
2. alimony
3. support money
4. income from inheritances
5. nontaxable strike benefits
6. the gross amount of any pension of annuity (including Social Security and Veterans Administration pensions)
7. nontaxable interest received from the federal government or any state governments
8. workmen's compensation
9. capital gains
10. all nontaxable investment income[129]

The level of income attributable to a responsible relative whose spouse is not a responsible relative is defined as one-half their combined income, as Idaho is a community property state.[130]

The gross income of responsible relatives is adjusted by deducting nonreimbursable medical expenses for themselves and their dependents, alimony and child support payments, tuition and fees for themselves and their dependents at elementary, secondary, higher education, or licensed trade or professional schools, any family responsibility payments made for other responsible relatives, and any payments made for the Medicaid patient above the $25 per month personal needs allowance.[131] This adjusted income is further reduced by deducting an amount equal to the federal annual poverty guideline, as calculated each July on the basis of family size. The annual family responsibility assessment for the responsible relative is calculated at 4 percent of the remaining adjusted, reduced income.[132]

The amount of the family responsibility assessment cannot exceed 25 percent of the Medicaid payments for skilled care or intermediate care (including that for the mentally retarded). If a relative is subject to family responsibility assessments for more than one Medicaid recipient (for example, if both parents are in a nursing home), the assessment cannot exceed 25 percent of the amount that the Idaho Medicaid program paid for the relative who receives the most expensive care.[133]

In order to preserve Medicaid eligibility for the patient, the Idaho law declares that, if the family responsibility assessment must be counted as income to the recipient under federal Medicaid regulations, the amount assessed to a responsible relative cannot exceed the amount that, when combined with the patient's own income, equals $1 less than the maximum income used to determine Medicaid eligibility.[134] If more than one relative is responsible, the financial responsibility of each is calculated as described, but the sum paid by all responsible relatives cannot exceed the Medicaid payment. The payment of each responsible relative is reduced, if necessary, on a pro rata basis so that their aggregate payments do not exceed the Medicaid rate.[135]

Under Idaho regulations, any responsible relatives are identified by the field office when a patient requests Medicaid assistance. Following the first Medicaid payment, responsible relatives are notified in writing of their responsibility to participate in the cost of this care.[136] Income and expense forms are included with the written notification. If the responsible relative does not respond within fifteen working days of the mailing date, a second notice is sent by certified mail. If there is no response to the second notice within ten working days of its mailing date, the assessment amount for that responsible relative is established at $250 per month or 25 percent of the Medicaid payment, whichever is less. A responsible relative who fails to provide the information necessary to calculate the assessment amount is also charged $250 per month or 25 percent of the Medicaid payment, whichever is less. Any responsible relative who fails to pay the calculated assessment is referred to the office of the state attorney general, who initiates collection proceedings and appropriate legal action (e.g., civil suit, garnishment, attachment) to obtain payment. No Medicaid patient is denied eligibility if a responsible relative fails to make the assessed payments, nor are Medicaid reimbursement rates to a nursing home reduced because of this failure, however.

The assessment of responsible relatives must be calculated annually and adjusted, if necessary.[137] A responsible relative whose income has decreased may request that the assessment be recalculated, but no more than four recalculations are permitted each calendar year. The payments of the assessment must be made to the Medicaid program on at least a quarterly basis. Identified responsible relatives who live outside Idaho are contacted and assessed family responsibility payments just as Idaho residents are. The Idaho Department of Health and Welfare is authorized to enter into reciprocal enforcement agreements with any other states that have enacted family responsibility programs.

In an ominous development for the future of the Relative Responsibility Act[138] in Idaho, however, the attorney general of Idaho has concluded that the act "is inconsistent with federal law regulating the use of Medicaid funds."[139] In an opinion issued on March 23, 1984, the attorney general stated that implementation of the law may result in federal sanctions and private court actions against Idaho that could bring about an invalidation of the statute.

The attorney general noted that "it has been suggested" that the family responsibility option allowed to states by the Reagan Administration "does not embody an appropriate interpretation of the relevant position of the Social Security Act." The legislative history of the Social Security Act specifically declares that "states may not include in their [Medicaid state] plans provisions for requiring contributions from relatives other than a spouse or a parent of a minor child."[140] The attorney general of Idaho further concluded that, even if the Reagan Administration's interpretation is correct, there is some doubt that the Idaho law is consistent with it. In the opinion of the Idaho attorney general, the Idaho law imposes financial obligations only on the relatives of Medicaid beneficiaries and, therefore, is not a statute of general applicability as the interpretation requires.

Because of this lack of compliance, the state attorney general suggested that federal sanctions could be imposed on the state of Idaho. For example, the federal government may seek the return of federal Medicaid funds from Idaho if it determines that Idaho's family responsibility statute and regulations distort eligibility requirements, extending Medicaid benefits to ineligible people or causing other improper expenditures. The attorney general found it "conceivable" that the federal government may even drop the state from the Medicaid program. He emphasized, however, that any consideration of federal sanctions as a result of Idaho's family responsibility law "is extremely speculative," but that implementation or enforcement of the law "would entail some risk." The attorney general thought it "far more likely" that the law would be challenged in court by a responsible relative after the state attempted to enforce collection of payment.

The attorney general concluded that the Idaho law itself is constitutional and does not violate equal protection provisions of the U.S. Constitution. Idaho has a legitimate state interest in protecting the public treasury, and the designation of parents and children as responsible parties "is rational in view of the special and, presumptively, perpetual nature of the relationship between parent and child."[141] In the opinion of the attorney general, however, equal protection suits may arise over alleged inequitable enforcement of Idaho's statute. If the state cannot obtain jurisdiction over responsible relatives who reside outside Idaho, charges of equal protection violations could be brought by Idaho residents forced to make family responsibility payments that their nonresident counterparts cannot be required to make. This opinion makes the future of the family responsibility concept uncertain not only in Idaho, but also in other states that are awaiting resolution of these legal uncertainties before they develop their own policies for family responsibility.

The Virginia Law

In Virginia, all persons eighteen years of age or over who have sufficient income available after "reasonably providing" for their "immediate" families are required to help support their mothers and fathers when the parents are "in necessitous circumstances."[142] If more than one person is "bound" to support a parent or parents, they "shall jointly and severally share equitably in the discharge of such duty."

The juvenile and domestic relations district court has original jurisdiction in all family responsibility cases in Virginia. This court has the power to order adult children to pay an amount for the support and maintenance of their parents that the court deems just. Any aggrieved person has the same right of appeal provided by law in other cases. The responsibility of financial support does not apply "if there is substantial evidence of desertion, neglect, abuse, or willful failure to support any such child by the father or mother" before the child reached adulthood.[143]

The state agency that is administering the program of assistance to the parent may initiate court proceedings to compel any adult child of that parent to reimburse the Commonwealth of Virginia for the portion of the costs incurred in providing services to the parent that the court considers reasonable. The child, however, is not responsible for these costs for more than sixty months of institutionalization. Any person who violates the provisions of the family responsibility concept in Virginia is guilty of a misdemeanor and, on conviction, is subject to a fine of up to $500, a jail term of up to twelve months, or both.

The Medicaid program must submit an amendment to the Medicaid state plan, outlining the procedures to be used in implementing the family responsibility concept in the Medicaid program.[144] As of September 1984, the Medicaid program in Virginia has not implemented the family responsibility concept.

The Louisiana Law

The state of Louisiana enacted a voluntary family responsibility program during 1983.[145] The program was implemented on February 28, 1984, for tax year 1983. Under the law, the Louisiana Department of Health and Human Resources is authorized to enter into written agreements with the responsible relatives of patients whose income and resources are inadequate to meet the costs of their care. In these agreements, the responsible relatives volunteer to contribute to the cost of the skilled or intermediate nursing home care that their needy relatives require. These voluntary funds are to be paid directly to the patient or to the health facility for the use and benefit of the patient. These funds go first to the personal needs of the patient, then to the medical needs. Any person entering into this written agreement is allowed to take a tax credit against taxes owed to Louisiana in an amount equal to one-third of the amount contributed under the family responsibility program. The amount of this credit cannot exceed $200 per year, however. The secretary of the Louisiana Department of Health and Human Resources has been authorized to promulgate the regulations necessary to implement this program.

OUTLOOK

The Reagan Administration granted states the family responsibility option, at least in part, because of the fiscal problems facing many state programs. The Medicaid costs of nursing home care have been rising, and federal contributions to the state Medicaid programs have been declining. The family responsibility concept could help offset these fiscal pressures in at least two ways. First, the payments from responsible relatives may generate revenue gains to the states. Second, perhaps most important, the program may discourage future placements of the elderly in long-term care facilities.

The future of the family responsibility concept is uncertain for both political and legal reasons, however. It is not clear, for example, whether a state can require the elderly to give the names of their children as a condition for Medicaid eligibility. An attorney for the National Senior Citizens Law Center stated, " 'The current Medicaid law prohibits that kind of disclosure requirement,' and she predicted that lawyers would challenge it in court."[146]

This attorney cited three legal arguments to support her contention that family responsibility laws are legally unenforceable:[147]

1. State Medicaid programs cannot force Medicaid applicants and recipients to name their adult children because the Medicaid statute prohibits state programs from taking the financial status of adult children into account.
2. Federal Medicaid regulations prevent state agencies from collecting family responsibility payments.[148]
3. State Medicaid agencies cannot give enforcement information about responsible family members to other state agencies that collect family responsibility payments.

The Social Security Act forbids the states to consider the financial status of any one else in determining an individual's eligibility for Medicaid assistance, unless the individual is blind, disabled, or under twenty-one years of age; in this case, the financial status of the applicant's spouse or parents may be considered. Did Congress intend to prevent policies like the family responsibility concept? Referring to the Reagan Administration's policy, Congressman Henry Waxman said,

> Nothing has changed since 1965 [the year Congress created the Medicaid program], when we prohibited exactly this kind of responsibility being placed upon the states to call for a contribution from the relatives of those in nursing homes. So we think the administration acted outside of the scope of the law that Congress passed.[149]

Supporting Congressman Waxman's position is the legislative history of the Social Security Amendments of 1965 that created the Medicaid program. In its report on these 1965 amendments, the Senate Finance Committee stated,

> The committee has heard of hardships on certain individuals by requiring them to provide support and to pay for medical care needed by relatives. The committee believes it is proper to expect spouses to support each other and parents to be held accountable for the support of their minor children and their blind or permanently and totally disabled children even though 21 years of age or older. Such requirements for support may reasonably include the payment by such relatives, if able, for medical care. Beyond such degree of relationship, however, requirements imposed are

often destructive and harmful to the relationships among members of the family group. Thus, states may not include in their plans provisions for requiring contributions from relatives other than a spouse or the parent of a minor child or children over 21 who are blind or permanently and totally disabled. Any contributions actually made by relatives or friends, or from other sources, will be taken into account by the state in determining whether the individual applying for medical assistance is, in fact, in need of such assistance.[150]

It remains to be resolved whether Medicaid family responsibility requirements enacted by state governments under laws of general applicability violate the intent of Congress when it prohibited Medicaid state plans from requiring family responsibility payments other than in the special circumstances that it mentioned.

In addition, according to Congressman Waxman, the Reagan Administration issued the family responsibility option as a directive to the states without following the established administrative process of allowing the public the opportunity to file comments on a proposed regulatory change. Did this violate federal regulatory procedural law?

In a study of Medicaid reimbursement practices for long-term care from 1975 to 1982, it was concluded that states using prospective reimbursement mechanisms always paid per diem rates for skilled and intermediate care lower than those paid by states making retrospective payments.[151] To contain rising Medicaid payments for nursing home care in the future, states may find it necessary to change their reimbursement method and rate, the scope of benefits, the eligibility standards, or a combination of these program factors.

NOTES

1. U.S. Department of Health and Human Services, Health Care Financing Administration, Office of Financial and Actuarial Analysis.

2. HOUSE COMM. ON INTERSTATE AND FOREIGN COMMERCE, BACKGROUND REPORT ON NURSING HOMES, 94th Cong., 1st Sess., p. 5 (1975).

3. MEDICARE AND MEDICAID GUIDE, 14,752.

4. 42 C.F.R. §440.150.

5. 42 C.F.R. §442.338.

6. 42 C.F.R. §442.339.

7. 42 C.F.R. §442.341.

8. 42 C.F.R. §442.342.

9. 42 C.F.R. §442.340.

10. 42 C.F.R. §442.346.

11. 42 C.F.R. §442.333.

12. 42 C.F.R. §442.334.
13. 42 C.F.R. §442.335.
14. 42 C.F.R. §442.336.
15. 42 C.F.R. §442.337.
16. 42 C.F.R. §442.343.
17. 42 C.F.R. §442.331.
18. 42 C.F.R. §442.332.
19. 42 C.F.R. §442.345.
20. 42 C.F.R. §442.321.
21. 42 C.F.R. §442.322.
22. 42 C.F.R. §442.323.
23. 42 C.F.R. §442.324.
24. 42 C.F.R. §442.325.
25. 42 C.F.R. §442.327.
26. 42 C.F.R. §442.326.
27. MEDICARE AND MEDICAID GUIDE, 31,527.
28. BUCHANAN, HEALTH CARE FINANCE Appendixes B and C (1981) [hereinafter cited as BUCHANAN]. These appendixes provide annual listings of the different nursing home reimbursement methods and per diem costs of the state Medicaid programs for 1973 through 1977.
29. *See* BUCHANAN, Chapter 5, for a discussion of the legislative history of P.L. 92-603, (§249) in the Congress.
30. P.L. 92-603, §249.
31. 41 Fed. Reg. 27,305-27,307 (July 1, 1976).
32. *Id.*
33. Alabama Nursing Home Ass'n et al. v. Joseph Califano, Secretary of Health, Education and Welfare et al., 433 F. Supp. 1325 (1977).
34. *Id.*, at 1331.
35. *Id.* at 1330.
36. *Id.*
37. 397 U.S. 397, 90 S.Ct. 1207, 25 L.Ed. 2d 442 (1970).
38. *See* note 33, *supra*, at 1330.
39. *See e.g.,* Nebraska Health Care Associates, Inc. v. Exon, No. CV77-L-41, U.S. District Court, District of Nebraska, December 8, 1977; Wisconsin Ass'n of Homes for the Aging v. Carballo, No. 76-C-78, U.S. District Court, Eastern District of Wisconsin, December 1, 1977; Illinois Health Care Ass'n v. Quern, No. 77-C-1109, U.S. District Court, Northern District of Illinois, Eastern Division, December 14, 1977.
40. Florida Dep't of Health and Rehabilitative Services v. Florida Nursing Home Ass'n, 101 S.Ct. 1032 (1981).
41. 442 F. Supp. 201 (1977).
42. *See* note 40, *supra*, at 1034.
43. *Id.*
44. 415 U.S. 651 (1974).
45. *See* note 40, *supra*, at 1034.
46. *Id.*

47. *Id.*

48. *Id.*, at 1036.

49. MEDICAL SERVICES ADMINISTRATION, DEP'T OF HEALTH, EDUCATION AND WELFARE, INFLATIONARY IMPACT STATEMENT: SECTION 249 OF P.L. 92-603 (1976).

50. P.L. 96-499, §962.

51. *Id.*

52. S. COMM. ON FINANCE, REPORT ON MEDICARE AND MEDICAID ADMINISTRATIVE AND REIMBURSEMENT REFORM ACT OF 1979, 96th Cong., 1st Sess. (1979).

53. *Id.*, at 28.

54. Nebraska Health Care Ass'n, Inc. v. Gina Dunning, U.S. District Court, District of Nebraska, No. CV82-C-472, November 16, 1983. In MEDICARE AND MEDICAID GUIDE, 33,535.

55. Coalition of Michigan Nursing Homes, Inc. v. Dempsey, 537 F. Supp. 451, 459 (E.D. Mich. 1982).

56. *See* note 54, *supra,* at pp. 9605-9606.

57. *Id.*, at p. 9606.

58. *Id,* at 9606.

59. *Id.*

60. Haven Home, Inc. v. Department of Public Welfare, Nebraska Supreme Court, No. 83-025, March 9, 1984. In MEDICARE AND MEDICAID GUIDE, 33,666.

61. *Id.*, at p. 10,153.

62. *Id.*

63. 701 F.2d 511 (5th Cir. 1983).

64. Minn. Stat. §256B.48.

65. U.S. District Court, District of Minnesota, Third Division, Civ. No. 3-77-467, April 26, 1983. In MEDICARE AND MEDICAID GUIDE, 32,873.

66. *Id.*, at p. 9377.

67. Minnesota Association of Health Care Facilities, et al., v. Minnesota Department of Public Welfare, No. 83-2446 and Minnesota Hospital Association, et al., v. Minnesota Department of Public Welfare, No. 83-2447. Consolidated before the U.S. Court of Appeals, Eighth Circuit, August 28, 1984.

68. *Id.*, at 15-16.

69. Highland Chateau, Inc. v. Minnesota Dep't of Public Welfare, Minnesota District Court, Second Judicial District, No. 463312, January 16, 1984. In MEDICARE AND MEDICAID GUIDE, 33,670.

70. *Id.*, at 10,176-10,179.

71. *See* note 52, *supra,* at pp. 28-29.

72. P.L. 90-248, §402.

73. P.L. 92-603, §222.

74. 43 Fed. Reg. 4,863 (February 6, 1978).

75. Buchanan, *Medicaid Cost Containment: Prospective Rate Determination*, INQUIRY XX, (1983), p. 334.

76. Milwaukee Jewish Home v. State of Wisconsin Nursing Home Appeals Board, Wisconsin Court of Appeals, Case No. 77-804, April 6, 1979. In MEDICARE AND MEDICAID GUIDE, 29,615.

77. United Nursing Homes, Inc. v. McNutt, Washington Superior Court in Thurston County, No. 59035, August 12, 1980. In MEDICARE AND MEDICAID GUIDE, 30,638.

78. United Nursing Homes, Inc. et al. v. McNutt, Washington Court of Appeals, 35 Wash. App. 632 (1983). In MEDICARE AND MEDICAID GUIDE, 33,501.

79. 42 C.F.R. §447.272.

80. 45 C.F.R. §250.30 (1975).

81. 41 Fed. Reg. 27,304 (July 1, 1976).

82. Telephone interview, Information Services Division, Beverly Enterprises, February 2, 1984.

83. Cuppett & Weeks Nursing Home, Inc. v. Department of Health and Mental Hygiene, Maryland District Court of Special Appeals, No. 1564, June 8, 1981. In MEDICARE AND MEDICAID GUIDE, 31,103.

84. Opinion of the Attorney General, Arkansas, No. 80-97, June 4, 1980. In MEDICARE AND MEDICAID GUIDE, 30,574.

85. State of New York, *State Plan under Title XIX of the Social Security Act*, Attachment 4.19-D, Subpart 86-2.26, April 1, 1980.

86. Daniel Cantor, doing business as Haven Manor Health Related Facility v. David Axelrod, 94 App. Div. 2d 595 (1983).

87. 543 F. Supp. 1380 (1982).

88. *See*, note 86, *supra*.

89. 442 F. Supp. 949 (1977).

90. *See*, note 86, *supra*.

91. 450 N.E. 2d 1135 (1983), WESTLAW computerized search.

92. *Id.*, at pp. 12-13.

93. *Id.*, at p. 13.

94. *Id.*, at pp. 16-17.

95. *Id.*, at p. 17.

96. *Id.*, at p. 18.

97. *Id.*, at pp. 18-19.

98. Buchanan, *The Financial Status of the New Medical Industrial Complex*, INQUIRY XIX (1982).

99. *See* note 85, *supra*, Section 86-2-21, p. 44.

100. State of Virginia, *State Plan under Title XIX of the Social Security Act*, Attachment 4.19-D, p. 5.

101. Fishkill Health Related Facility v. Robert P. Whalen, New York Supreme Court, Appellate Division, Third Department, No. 44867, June 30, 1983. In MEDICARE AND MEDICAID GUIDE, 32,972.

102. *Id.*, at p. 9825.

103. *Id.*, at p. 9826.

104. Allied Services for the Handicapped, Inc. v. Commonwealth of Pennsylvania, Pennsylvania Commonwealth Court, No. 12222 C.D. 1982, November 14, 1983. In MEDICARE AND MEDICAID GUIDE, 33,542.

105. *Id.*, at p. 9653

106. Quakertown Hosp. Ass'n et al. v. Helen O'Bannon, U.S. District Court, Eastern District of Pennsylvania, No. 82-0754, October 24, 1983. In MEDICARE AND MEDICAID GUIDE, 33,629.

107. *Id.*, at p. 10,012.

108. 474 F. Supp. 398 (1979), *affirmed without opinion,* 622 F.2d 573 (2d Cir. 1980).

109. *See,* note 106, *supra,* at p. 10,013.

110. *Id.*

111. *Id.*

112. *Id.*

113. 43 Fed. Reg. 4,863 (February 6, 1978).

114. *Id.*

115. 42 C.F.R. 405.429(b)(1)(ii).

116. Office of the Inspector General, Dep't of HHS, "Medicare Payment of Return on Equity to Proprietary Providers," Audit Control No. 09-32607, October 12, 1983, p. 1.

117. *Id.*

118. State of Michigan, *State Plan under Title XIX of the Social Security Act,* Attachment 4.19-D, pp. 7-9.

119. State of New Mexico, *State Plan under Title XIX of the Social Security Act,* Attachment 4.19-D, pp. 15-16.

120. HEALTH CARE FINANCING ADMINISTRATION, STATE MEDICAID MANUAL PART 3: ELIGIBILITY, HCFA-Pub. 45-3, Transmittal No. 2 (1983), §3812.

121. PBS, The MacNeil/Lehrer Report, April 19, 1983, *Paying for Parents,* Transcript No. 1972, Daniel Bourque, Deputy Director of HCFA.

122. *Id.*

123. Buchanan, *Medicaid: Family Responsibility and Long Term Care,* JOURNAL OF LONG TERM CARE ADMINISTRATION 12, No. 3 (Fall 1984).

124. Letter, Richard Lee, Director of Reimbursement Methods, Department of Public Welfare, Pennsylvania, December 9, 1983.

125. Survey response, January 1984.

126. Survey response, January 1984.

127. IDAHO CODE, §32-1002, 32-1008A, 56-203B, and 66-414.

128. Department of Health and Welfare, State of Idaho, *Rules Governing Medical Assistance,* MEDICAL ASSISTANCE MANUAL, Title 3, Ch. 9 §3-9031.02.

129. *Id.*, §3-9031.03.

130. *Id.*

131. *Id.*, §3-9031.04.

132. *Id.*, §3-9031.05.

133. *Id.*, §3-9031.06.

134. *Id.*

135. *Id.*, §3-9031.07.

136. *Id.*, §3-9031.08.

137. *Id.*, §3-9031.09.

138. IDAHO CODE, §32-1008A.

139. State of Idaho, Office of the Attorney General, Attorney General Opinion No. 84-7, March 23, 1984.

140. S. COMM. ON FINANCE, SOCIAL SECURITY AMENDMENTS OF 1965, S. REP. 404, Part I, 89th Cong., 1st Sess., p. 78 (1965).

141. *See* note 139, *supra.*
142. VA. CODE §20.88.
143. *Id.*
144. VA. CODE §32.1-74.
145. State of Louisiana, Senate Bill No. 665, Regular Session, 1983.
146. *U.S. Would Ask Children to Pay for Parent Care*, New York Times, March 30, 1984, at 1.
147. THE NURSING HOME LAW LETTER G (1983).
148. 42 C.F.R. §435.602.
149. *See* note 121, *supra.*
150. *See* note 140, *supra.*
151. *See* note 75, *supra.*

Chapter 9

Abortion and Family Planning Services

A woman's right to obtain an abortion under certain circumstances has been established since 1973. This right does not guarantee access to abortions for the indigent, however. Abortions have been denied to indigent women in some cases by limitations placed on Medicaid. Still, some abortions may be funded through Medicaid; the constitutions or laws of individual states may also allow or require funding for abortions for the indigent.

U.S. SUPREME COURT CASES

In 1973, the U.S. Supreme Court handed down its decision in *Roe v. Wade*.[1] In this decision, the Court recognized that a woman could obtain an abortion under certain circumstances and at certain periods during pregnancy.

The Court had decided earlier cases involving abortion on the basis of a right of privacy,[2] but the Court had acknowledged that some state regulation in areas protected by that right of privacy was appropriate. For example, the Court noted that a state may properly assert important interests in safeguarding health, in maintaining medical standards, and in protecting life. The interest of the state, at some point in pregnancy, becomes sufficiently compelling to sustain regulation of the abortion decision. Therefore, the court concluded that the right of personal privacy includes the abortion decision, but that this right must be considered against important state interests in regulation.

Under the Texas statute considered in *Roe v. Wade*, only those abortions procured or attempted on medical advice for the purpose of saving the life of the mother were legal. The Court concluded that this statute was too broad in that it did not make a distinction between abortions performed early in pregnancy and those performed at later stages. Furthermore, the statute did not recognize the other interests involved. For these reasons, the statute was found to violate the Due Process Clause of the Fourteenth Amendment.

Examining the stages of pregnancy, the Court said that the abortion decision and its effectuation must be left to the medical judgment of the pregnant woman's attending physician during the first trimester. In the second trimester, the state may, if it chooses, regulate the abortion procedure in ways that are reasonably related to maternal health. In the third trimester, the stage after viability, the state may, if it chooses, regulate and even proscribe abortions, except when an abortion is necessary to preserve the life or health of the mother.

In *Planned Parenthood of Central Missouri v. Danforth*,[3] a nonprofit Missouri corporation that maintained a facility for the performance of abortions challenged three portions of the Missouri law.[4] First, before an abortion could be performed during the first twelve weeks of pregnancy, the Missouri law required that the written consent of a woman's spouse be obtained, unless a licensed physician certified that the abortion was necessary to preserve the life of the mother. Second, the law required, during the same time period, written consent of one parent or person *in loco parentis* if the woman was unmarried and under the age of eighteen years. Again, abortions certified by a licensed physician as necessary to preserve the life of the mother were excepted. Third, the law imposed reporting and record-keeping requirements on health facilities and on physicians who perform abortions.

Assessing the spousal consent portion of the Missouri act, the Supreme Court stated that the wife could act unilaterally if spousal consent was not obtained. The court found the argument of the state against this point unconvincing since, if the husband and wife disagreed, the view of only one could prevail. The court observed that, inasmuch as "it is the woman who physically bears the child and who is more directly and immediately affected by the pregnancy, as between the two, the balance weighs in her favor."[5] Consequently, this part of the act was found to be inconsistent with *Roe v. Wade*.

The parental consent provision was also stricken. The Court observed that its opinion did not suggest that every minor, regardless of age or maturity, could give effective consent for termination of a pregnancy. In the Court's opinion, however, the Missouri law's special consent provision, requiring consent by a person other than the woman and her physician before a minor's pregnancy could be terminated, was a restriction without sufficient justification. The Court observed that minors, as well as adults, are protected by the Constitution and possess constitutional rights.

Missouri law required that certain records be kept for seven years, partly to increase the sum of medical knowledge through the compilation of relevant maternal health and life data. The Court concluded that the record-keeping requirements were not constitutionally offensive in themselves, although they approached impermissible limits. These requirements were seen as useful to the state's interest in protecting the health of its female citizens. The Court also noted that these records could be a resource that is relevant to decisions involving medical experience and judgment.

In *Belotti v. Baird*,[6] the Supreme Court considered, but did not outline, the type of consent that might be proper for an abortion on a woman under eighteen years old—the unemancipated minor. The Court in that case suggested that the district court should have asked the Massachusetts Supreme Judicial Court questions concerning the meaning of that state's statute. A majority of the Justices indicated that a state's interest in protecting the immature minor will sustain requirements of a consent substitute, either parental or judicial, but cautioned that the state must provide an alternative procedure whereby a pregnant minor woman may demonstrate that she is sufficiently mature to make the abortion decision herself or that, despite her immaturity, an abortion is in her best interest. This reasoning was reaffirmed in *Akron v. Akron Center for Reproductive Health*.[7] Also, a statute requiring judicial or parental consent was held to be constitutional in *Planned Parenthood Association v. Ashcraft*.[8] These Supreme Court cases are important, since they apply when state law regarding access to abortions is inconsistent with them.

In *Beal v. Doe*,[9] the Court held that Title XIX of the Social Security Act did not require the funding of nontherapeutic abortions as a condition of participation in the joint federal-state Medicaid program. In *Maher v. Roe*,[10] decided the same day, the Court was called upon to decide whether the Constitution requires a participating state that pays for childbirth to pay for nontherapeutic abortions. The Court stated that the Constitution imposes no obligation on the states to pay the pregnancy-related medical expenses of indigent women or to pay any of the medical expenses of indigents. When a state decides to alleviate some of the hardships of poverty by providing medical care, however, the manner in which it dispenses benefits is subject to constitutional limitations. The Court observed that the pregnant woman is not a member of a suspect class (a class of persons " ... saddled with such disabilities, or subjected to such a history of purposeful unequal treatment, or relegated to such a position of political powerlessness as to command extraordinary protection from the majoritarian political process."[11]) and that the Court has never held that financial need alone identifies a suspect class for purposes of equal protection analysis.

In substance, the Court held that the mere fact that an indigent woman has a right to an abortion does not mandate that the state provide funds for her abortion, even though the state would provide funds for delivery if she carries the child to term. The subsidization of childbirth by the state was seen by the

Court as a rational means of encouraging childbirth, a matter in which the state has an interest. The Court indicated in clear terms, however, that Congress could require states to provide medical benefits for abortions as a condition of their participation in the Medicaid program.

Harris v. McRae[12] raised two primary questions concerning the public funding of abortions under Title XIX of the Social Security Act (Medicaid). The first, a statutory question, was whether Title XIX requires a state that participates in the Medicaid program to fund the cost of certain medically necessary abortions for which the Hyde Amendment denies federal funding. The second question, a constitutional one, was whether the Hyde Amendment contravenes the liberty or equal protection guarantees of the Fifth Amendment Due Process Clause or the First Amendment Freedom of Religion Clause.

The Court found that Title XIX did not require a participating state to pay for those medically necessary abortions for which reimbursement was unavailable under the Hyde Amendment. In examining the constitutional question, the Court compared the facts in *Harris* with those in *Maher v. Roe*. It concluded that the Hyde Amendment, by encouraging childbirth except in the most urgent circumstances, is rationally related to the legitimate government objective of protecting potential life. The Court observed that this was a policy choice and that the appropriate forum for its resolution in a democracy is the legislature. The court reaffirmed this decision in *Williams v. Zbaraz*,[13] a case involving an Illinois statute that prohibited state medical assistance payments for all abortions except those necessary to preserve the life of the woman seeking treatment.

LEGISLATIVE RESTRICTIONS

The Hyde Amendment

The first Hyde Amendment, approved September 30, 1976, provided that "[n]one of the funds contained in this act shall be used to perform abortions except where the life of the mother would be in danger if the fetus were carried to term."[14] This amendment was effective for the fiscal year ending September 30, 1977.

The second Hyde Amendment, for Fiscal Year 1978, was approved December 9, 1977, and provided that

> none of the funds provided in this paragraph shall be used to perform abortions except where the life of the mother would be in danger if the fetus were carried to term; or except for such medical procedures necessary for the victims of rape or incest which has

been reported promptly to a law enforcement agency or public health service; or except in those instances where severe and long lasting physical health damage to the mother would result were the pregnancy carried to term when so determined by two physicians.[15]

The amendment approved October 18, 1978, for Fiscal Year 1979 was substantially the same.[16]

The 1980 Hyde Amendment, passed November 20, 1979, provided in part that

> none of the funds provided by this joint resolution shall be used to perform abortions except where the life of the mother would be in danger if the fetus were carried to term; or except for such medical procedures necessary for the victims of rape or incest, when such rape or incest has been reported promptly to a law enforcement agency or public health service.[17]

Congressional Resolutions

Subsequent to the Hyde Amendments, federal funding of abortions was restricted by means of congressional resolutions. Public Law 96-369, passed October 1, 1980, provided that

> none of the funds made available by this joint resolution shall be used to perform abortions except where the life of the mother would be endangered if the fetus were carried to term; or except for such medical procedures necessary for the victims of rape or incest, when such rape has within 72 hours been reported to a law enforcement agency or public health service; ...: provided however the several states are and shall remain free not to fund abortions to the extent that in their sole discretion, deemed appropriate.[18]

Public Law 96-536, passed December 16, 1980, effectively extended these provisions until June 5, 1981, apparently excluding the clause dealing with rape and incest, however. Public Law 97-12, effective June 5, 1981, was essentially the same as Public Law 96-369. Public Law 97-51, approved October 1, 1981, continued the provisions of the previous laws.

Public Law 97-92, approved December 15, 1981, covered funding activities from March 31, 1982, through September 30, 1982, providing in part that "none of the funds provided by this act shall be used to perform abortions except where the life of the mother would be endangered if the fetus were carried to term."[19] It also contained a clause freeing states to fund abortions with their own funds if they wished. Funding under the same terms was apparently anticipated by Public Law 97-276, approved October 2, 1982, and effective through December 17, 1982, as well as under Public Law 97-377, approved December 21, 1982, for the fiscal year ending September 30, 1983. These provisions are also apparently applicable to Public Law 98-139, approved October 31, 1983.

REGULATIONS

The use of federal funds for abortions is prohibited, except as provided for under the regulations. When the regulations conflict with statutes or public laws, the statutes or laws have ultimate control.

Federal funds are available for an abortion when a physician certifies in writing that, on the basis of his or her professional judgment, the life of the mother would be endangered if the fetus were carried to term. The certification by the physician must contain the name and address of the patient.[20] Federal funds may also be available for medical procedures performed on a victim of rape or incest if the medical agency has received from a law enforcement agency or public health service signed documentation indicating

1. that the patient on whom the medical procedure was performed was reported to have been the victim of an incident of rape or incest
2. the date of the incident
3. the date of the report, which must be within sixty days of the incident
4. the name and address of the victim
5. the name and address of the individual who reported the rape or incest if this person is not the victim
6. that the report included the signature of the individual who reported the incident

The state agency must receive the required documentation before making payments;[21] otherwise, federal funds are not available. If the life of the mother would be endangered by carrying the child to term, federal funds are available without regard to the listed factors.[22]

Federal funds may also be used to pay for drugs and devices to terminate ectopic pregnancies, including drugs or devices to prevent the implantation of the fertilized ovum, and to pay for medical procedures necessary to terminate ectopic pregnancy.[23] Specified records[24] must be kept for three years.[25]

LITIGATION

Disputes may reach the courts regarding reimbursements for abortions allowed under the Hyde Amendments. Disputes may also arise under state laws that may entitle Medicaid recipients to receive state-funded abortions.

Plan Conformity and Disallowance

All public assistance determinations under Medicaid are subject to administrative and judicial review.[26] When a state plan is submitted under Title XIX to the secretary of the Department of Health and Human Services (HHS), the secretary must determine whether the plan conforms to the requirements for approval within ninety days after the date the plan is submitted. The ninety-day period may be extended by written agreement.

A state dissatisfied with the secretary's decision on its plan may, within sixty days after it has been notified of the decision, file a petition with the secretary for a reconsideration of the plan's conformity to the requirements for approval. Within thirty days after receipt of the petition, the secretary notifies the state of the time and place of the hearing. The hearing is generally held between twenty and sixty days after the date on which the state is notified of the hearing, although the state and the secretary may agree in writing to hold the hearing at a different time. The original decision may be affirmed, modified, or reversed within sixty days.[27]

A state dissatisfied with the result of the reconsideration may, within sixty days after notification of the reconsidered decision, file a petition for review of the decision with the U.S. Court of Appeals for the circuit within which the state is located.[28] This procedure also applies when payments have been denied because the secretary finds that

1. the plan has been so changed that it no longer complies with the federal statute
2. in the administration of the plan there has been a failure to comply substantially with the statute[29]

The secretary has the burden of proof to show that his or her findings are supported by "substantial evidence."[30] If the decision is supported by such evidence, it is conclusive. If good cause can be shown, however, the court may remand the case to the secretary to take further evidence. If there are further proceedings and findings, the secretary provides the court with the transcript and record of them. Decisions resulting from these proceedings are also conclusive, if they are supported by substantial evidence. The court may affirm the action of the secretary or set it aside in whole or in part. The judgment of the circuit court is subject to review by the Supreme Court.

Within the bounds of the applicable statutes and regulations, the secretary may disallow federal funds for certain services. The state is entitled to request and receive a reconsideration of the disallowance. In *Illinois Department of Public Aid v. Schweiker*,[31] the state attempted to obtain reimbursement for abortions and payments to nursing homes. The case was submitted to the Seventh Circuit Court of Appeals as described earlier, but the secretary moved that the two petitions be dismissed for lack of jurisdiction.[32]

According to the court, *only* rejection of state plans receives initial review in the circuit court; disallowances are subject to initial review in the district courts. If the state plan is not in conformity, all funds to the state could be cut off, but disallowances apply only to items or classes of items for which federal funds are disallowed. It was difficult to determine in *Illinois Department of Public Aid* whether the denial was based on state plan nonconformity or a disallowance of payment because the regulations require a record to be made in disputes over disallowances.[33] If a full written record already exists, there is no clearly compelling reason to begin review of disallowances at the district court level.

The court in *Illinois Department of Public Aid* dismissed the petitions, but noted that initial review might be appropriate in the circuit court if the effect of a disallowance was to shut off all or most of the money the state was entitled to receive from the federal government. Disallowances for abortions under the Hyde Amendment obviously do not meet this test. The Eleventh Circuit Court of Appeals reached the same conclusion in a similar case, *Georgia Department of Public Assistance v. United States Department of Health and Human Services*.[34]

In *Commonwealth of Pennsylvania v. Department of Health and Human Services*,[35] the circuit court granted a petition for review and remanded the case for findings by the departmental grants appeal board. However, this case involved the narrow issue of payment for abortions and was decided between the time that the Hyde Amendment was adopted or became effective and the time that notice was provided to recipients. After the Supreme Court denied rehearing in *Harris v. McRae*,[36] the amendment became effective on September 19, 1980.

Pennsylvania had submitted reimbursement claims to the secretary for abortions that were performed between September 19 and November 10, 1980, and were medically necessary—but not in the categories for which the Hyde Amendment authorized reimbursement. Pennsylvania's argument was that the amendment could not become effective until notice was given to recipients. Notice to recipients was complete on November 10. The court was asked to determine whether the secretary's denial of funds to the state was based on a finding of noncompliance or a disallowance. The court concluded that the denial of funds to the state grew out of a finding of nonconformity with federal requirements and could be reviewed by the circuit court.

In *Georgia Department of Medical Assistance v. Heckler*,[37] the question was who should bear the cost of Medicaid payments made for abortions because of a district court order that was vacated after the U.S. Supreme Court reached the opposite conclusion.[38] The state argued that, since federal regulations mandate reimbursement for payments made in accordance with a court order,[39] the federal government must pay for abortions performed while the injunction was in effect. The federal government argued that these payments were not within the scope of federally aided public assistance programs because the payments were forbidden by the Hyde Amendment. The court determined that the payments were within the scope of federally aided public assistance programs made in accordance with a court order. Consequently, the state of Georgia was entitled to reimbursement from the federal government under the regulation.

Illinois Department of Public Aid and *Commonwealth of Pennsylvania* seem to be at the extremes in determining whether the district court or the circuit courts should hear most disputes. The expansive reading (liberal construction) of the Third Circuit would seem to include virtually all cases.[40] The more restrictive reading of the Seventh Circuit would include fewer cases. In either case, it is clear that all the cases are procedural, only addressing which court will hear a petition from the states regarding denial of reimbursement. *Georgia Department of Medical Assistance* merely permits states and provider to rely on valid court orders, even though the orders may be vacated or overruled later.

State Court Cases

Citizens of the United States have come to rely on the federal constitution for the protection of their individual rights. State constitutions may be separate sources of individual rights, however.[41] Indigent pregnant women who wish to have abortions may, in some states, receive state funds for abortions in spite of the Hyde Amendment and its progeny.

In 1982, the New Jersey Supreme Court was asked to determine the validity under the New Jersey Constitution of a statute that prohibits Medicaid funding for abortions except where it is medically necessary to preserve the woman's life.[42] Medicaid paid for abortions to save the life of the mother, but not for therapeutic abortions to protect the health of the mother or for elective, nontherapeutic abortions. Although the court found in *Right to Choose v. Byrne*[43] that nontherapeutic abortions need not be funded, the court concluded that the state may not fund only those abortions to preserve a woman's life, but must fund abortions to protect her health as well. The court also found that the statute violates the right of pregnant women to equal protection of the law under the state constitution.[44] Of course, federal funds are not available for such abortions because of the Hyde Amendment.

The state of New Jersey sought to justify its policy by asserting a compelling interest in the protection of life. In the court's opinion, however, the state must proceed in a neutral manner. It was not neutral, according to the court, to fund services medically necessary for childbirth while refusing to fund services medically necessary for abortion. The state's action was seen as an attempt to use its treasury to persuade an indigent woman to sacrifice her health by remaining pregnant.

In a California case, *Committee to Defend Reproductive Rights v. Meyers*,[45] the Supreme Court of California considered statutes that afforded full funding of medical expenses incurred by indigent women who decided to bear a child, but except in a few limited circumstances, denied funding to those indigent women who chose to have an abortion.[46] The plaintiffs in the lawsuit claimed that this selective or discriminatory public funding scheme violated a number of distinct constitutional guarantees under state law.

The court considered the issue in this case to be whether the state, having enacted a general program to provide medical services to the poor, may selectively withhold benefits from otherwise qualified persons solely because they seek to exercise a constitutional right of procreative choice in a manner that the state does not favor and does not wish to support. Although federal courts apparently require no special justification for disparate treatment so long as the program places no new obstacles in the path of the woman seeking to exercise her constitutional right, California courts, in decisions based on state law, have long held that a discriminatory or restricted public benefit program demands special scrutiny even if it does not erect some new or additional obstacle to the exercise of constitutional rights.

In order to show that a statutory scheme is constitutional under California law, the state must demonstrate three things:

1. The imposed conditions relate to the purpose of the legislation that confers the benefit or privilege.
2. The advantage to be gained by imposing the condition manifestly outweighs any resulting impairment of constitutional rights.
3. There is no less offensive alternative available for achieving the state's objective.[47]

First, the court found that the restrictions were contrary to the purpose of the Medi-Cal (Medicaid) program, i.e., to provide indigents with access to medical services comparable to that enjoyed by more affluent persons.

Second, the court found that the benefits of the funding restrictions did not manifestly outweigh the impairment of constitutional rights. Finally, the court felt that the restrictions clearly did not aid indigent women who chose to bear children in a manner least offensive to the rights of those who chose abortion.

In conclusion, the California court observed that there is no greater power than the power of the purse. If the government can use this power to nullify a constitutional right by conditioning benefits only on the sacrifice of such rights, the Bill of Rights could eventually become a yellowing scrap of paper, according to this California court. Therefore, attempts by the California legislature to limit funding by budget restrictions have failed thus far.[48]

In *Planned Parenthood Association, Inc. v. Department of Human Resources for the State of Oregon*,[49] the court examined an administrative rule promulgated by the Oregon Department of Human Resources.[50] The rule permitted funding for abortion if the life of a woman was in danger and allowed funding for up to two other elective abortions, depending on the age of the woman. The petitioners challenged the refusal to fund an abortion for a woman who had expended her one or two elective abortions, but whose life was not threatened by the pregnancy. Among the claims was the assertion that the rule violated the Oregon Constitution's equal privileges and immunities section.[51]

Since the rule allowed up to two elective abortions and, thus, did not undertake to protect all potential human life, the Oregon appeals court found that the rule was too broad and inconsistent to be justified by the state's interest in protecting potential life as against the woman's interest in her health. The court did not discuss the state's interest in restricting abortions from the purely financial perspective of repetitive abortion, a consideration that may explain the reason that one elective abortion was allowed for all women and two elective abortions were allowed for women 17 years of age or under. Although the Oregon court's decision is subject to modification or reversal on appeal, it demonstrates a slightly different rationale for funding abortions under a fairly unique state approach to the problem.

STERILIZATION

State Medicaid plans must reimburse providers for sterilization procedures in certain circumstances.[52]

In order to be sterilized, a person generally must (1) be over twenty-one years of age, (2) be mentally competent, (3) have given informed consent, and (4) submit to the procedure between thirty and eighty days after giving consent. Exceptions to the time limit are made in cases of premature delivery and emergency abdominal surgery, when the minimum periods are thirty days and seventy-two hours, respectively. Federal funding is not available for the sterilization of mentally incompetent or institutionalized persons.

Federal funding is not available for hysterectomies if the sole or dominant reason for the hysterectomy is sterilization. In other instances, hysterectomies may be funded if they comply with conditions listed in the federal regulations.[53] Before making payments for sterilizations or hysterectomies, the Medicaid agency must obtain documentation demonstrating compliance with federal requirements, including a signed consent form and acknowledgment that hysterectomy information has been received or a physician's certification as applicable.[54]

The patient's consent must be an informed consent. The persons obtaining the consent not only must answer questions, but also must indicate that the patient may withdraw consent at any time without a penalty. The individual must be advised of several considerations, including other family planning methods, the irreversibility of the procedure, and the individual's right to have a witness of his or her choice present when the consent is signed.[55] Consent may not be obtained when the individual is (1) in labor or childbirth, (2) seeking to obtain an abortion, or (3) under the influence of a substance that affects the individual's state of awareness.

The consent form must be that designated by the regulations or another form approved by the secretary. The form must be signed and dated by four individuals:

1. the individual to be sterilized
2. the interpreter, if one was provided
3. the person who obtained the consent
4. the physician who performed the sterilization procedure[56]

In signing the form, the person certifies that federal requirements have been met.

Hospitals and clinics must be careful to follow the regulations controlling sterilization precisely, as shown by *Sewichley Valley Hospital v. Commonwealth of Pennsylvania Department of Public Welfare,* in which the hospital sued because claims for reimbursement had been denied.[57]

The Pennsylvania Department of Public Welfare had issued a memorandum explaining the federal restriction on reimbursement for nontherapeutic sterilization. Included with the memorandum was Form MA-71, "Consent Document for Sterilization Procedure," which was to accompany each claim. The department's consent form consisted of two parts. Part 1 consisted of a numerical list of the elements of informed consent consistent with federal regulations; Part 2 involved a summary of the oral presentation of the basic elements of informed consent. The first part of the form was properly completed; the second part was not. The Pennsylvania Department of Public Welfare had a policy of refusing supplementation of the consent documents after their initial submission. The court overruled the department's policy, reasoning that completion of the form in no way determined informed consent. The informed consent under the procedure was obtained prior to preparation of the summary.

OUTLOOK

The prospects for Medicaid funding of all lawful abortions for eligible persons are bleak. Even though the Senate defeated a resolution calling for a constitutional amendment to outlaw abortions, the mere serious consideration of such a resolution indicates the difficulty of expanding the availability of abortions under Medicaid. For the moment at least, the best prospects for reimbursement for abortions that do not fall within the Hyde Amendment exceptions come from rights based on state law. The outlook for funding of abortions from state sources also seems questionable, however, in view of the cost cutting propensity of legislative bodies.

In summary, it is apparent that the federally protected right granted to women to obtain abortions is a negative right. Although the government must allow a woman to have an abortion, it is not required to provide her with the means to obtain the abortion.

NOTES

1. 410 U.S. 113 (1973).
2. *See, e.g.*, Griswold v. Connecticut, 381 U.S. 479 (1965).
3. 428 U.S. 52 (1976).
4. House Committee Substitute House Bill No. 1211 (1974).
5. 428 U.S. at 71.
6. 443 U.S. 622 (1979).
7. City of Akron v. Akron Center for Reproductive Health, Inc., 103 S.Ct. 2401 (1983).
8. Planned Parenthood of Kansas City, Missouri v. Ashcraft, 103 S.Ct. 2517 (1983).
9. 432 U.S. 438 (1977).
10. 432 U.S. 464 (1977).
11. San Antonio School District v. Rodriquez, 411 U.S. 1, 28 (1973).
12. 448 U.S. 297 (1980).
13. 448 U.S. 358 (1980).
14. P.L. 94-439, §209.
15. P.L. 95-205, §101.
16. P.L. 95-480, §210.
17. P.L. 96-123, §109.

18. P.L. 96-369, §101(c).
19. P.L. 97-92.
20. 42 C.F.R. §441.203.
21. 42 C.F.R. §441.205.
22. *Id.*
23. 42 C.F.R. §441.207.
24. 42 C.F.R. §§441.203-441.205.
25. 45 C.F.R. §74.20 (42 C.F.R. §441.208).
26. 42 U.S.C. §1316.
27. 42 U.S.C. §1316(a)(2).
28. 42 U.S.C. §1316(a)(3).
29. 42 U.S.C. §1396c.
30. 42 U.S.C. §1316(4).
31. 707 F.2d 273 (7th Cir. 1983).
32. The state agreed, but the court issued an opinion because the question was one of jurisdiction.
33. 45 C.F.R. §201.14(d).
34. 708 F.2d 627 (11th Cir. 1983).
35. 723 F.2d 1114 (3d Cir. 1983).
36. *See* note 12, *supra.*
37. Civ. Action No. C83-594, April 6, 1984, State of Georgia by Department of Medical Assistance v. Heckler, 583 F. Supp. 1377 (N.D. Ga. 1984).
38. Harris v. McRae, note 11, *supra*; Williams v. Zbaraz, note 13, *supra.*
39. 45 C.F.R. §205.10(b)(3).
40. *See* New Jersey v. HHS, 670 F.2d 1300 (3d Cir. 1982), in which it was held that a denial of reimbursement to an improperly certified nursing home could not be heard in circuit court.
41. Brennan, *State Constitutions and the Protection of Individual Rights*, 90 HARV. L. REV. 489 (1977).
42. N.J. STAT. ANN. §30.4D-6.1.
43. 91 N.J. 287, 450 A.2d 925 (1982).
44. New Jersey Constitution, Article 1, 1.
45. 625 P.2d 779 (1981).
46. Statutes 1978 Chapter 359, section 2, item 248, Statutes 1979, Chapter 259, section 2, item 261.5 and Statutes 1980, Chapter 510, section 2, item 287.5.
47. Bagley v. Washington Township Hosp. District, 65 Cal.2d 499, 55 Cal. Rptr. 40, 421 P.2d (1966).
48. *See also* Committee to Defend Reproductive Rights v. Cory, 132 Cal. App. 3d 862, 183 Cal. Rptr. 475 (1982); Committee to Defend Reproductive Rights v. Rank, 151 Cal. App. 83, 198 Cal. Rptr. 630 (1984).
49. 63 Ore. App. 41, 663 P.2d 1247 (1983), *review allowed*, 668 P.2d 384 (1984).
50. Administrative Rule, OAR 461-052.
51. "No law shall be passed granting to any citizen or class of citizen privileges, or immunities which, upon the same terms, shall not equally belong to all citizens." Oregon Constitution, Article 1, §20.
52. 42 C.F.R. §441, Subpart F.

53. 42 C.F.R. §441.255.
54. 42 C.F.R. §441.255(d)(2).
55. 42 C.F.R. §441.257.
56. 42 C.F.R. §441.258.
57. 409 A.2d 496 (Pa. 1979).

Chapter 10

Fraud and Abuse in Medicaid

Medicaid claims, like Medicare claims, have a great potential for fraud and abuse—in Fiscal Year 1983, the Medicaid budget was $19 billion.[1] As mentioned in Chapter 6, the provisions of the Medicaid and Medicare Offenses and Penalties sections are very similar. Therefore, the cases construing these provisions are generally applicable to both Medicare and Medicaid.

STATUTES

Illegal Patient Admittance and Retention Practices

Persons or providers who knowingly and willfully charge for any patient services paid for wholly or partially under the state Medicaid plan at a rate in excess of the rates established by the state are guilty of a criminal offense.[2] Those who knowingly and willfully charge or solicit, accept or receive a gift, money, donation, or other consideration, in addition to an amount lawfully received under the state plan, may incur criminal liability under certain circumstances. Criminal liability may be incurred when the charging or soliciting, accepting or receiving the gift, money, donation, or other consideration is (1) a precondition of admitting a patient to a hospital, skilled nursing facility, or intermediate care facility or (2) a requirement for the patient's continued stay in such a facility.

Persons violating this statute are guilty of a felony. Upon conviction, they are fined not more than $25,000, imprisoned for not more than five years, or both.

Fraud Control

In order to assist the states in implementing Medicaid fraud control, Congress provided for the establishment of state fraud control units. These units are separate entities that investigate and assist in the prosecution of fraud.

In 1977, Congress authorized federal funding of 90 percent of the costs that the states would incur in their fraud control programs for three years.[3] After September of 1980, this percentage was to drop to 50 percent, with maximum payments to be limited further.[4] The amount of funds that the secretary was otherwise obligated to pay a state during a quarter could not exceed the higher of $125,000 or one quarter of 1 percent of sums expended by the federal, state, and local governments during the previous quarter in carrying out the state's plan.[5]

In 1980, these provisions were amended to allow 90 percent payment to a state for the first twelve quarters. Additional federal funding will decrease to 75 percent rather than the original 50 percent; however, the maximum payment remains $125,000 or one quarter of 1 percent of the funds expended in carrying out the state's plan.

The state Medicaid fraud control unit may be a part of the state attorney general's office or another department of state government that possesses statewide authority to prosecute criminal violators.[6] In a state that has no such statewide authority, the unit must have formal procedures approved by the secretary of the Department of Health and Human Services (HHS) to ensure that (1) suspected criminal violations related to Medicaid will be referred to the appropriate authority or authorities in the state for prosecution and (2) the unit will provide assistance and coordinate its activities with such authority or authorities. Lastly, the unit may be one that has a formal working relationship with the office of the state attorney general. Formal procedures for referral of suspected criminal violations to this office must be approved by the secretary and must also provide effective coordination of activities with respect to the detection, investigation, and prosecution of those who are suspected of criminal violations.

The fraud control unit must also

1. be a distinct entity from the single state agency
2. conduct a statewide program of investigation and prosecution
3. have procedures for receiving complaints of the abuse and neglect of patients
4. provide for the collection, or referral for collection to a single state agency, of overpayments that it discovers

5. employ auditors, attorneys, investigators, and other necessary persons and be organized in a manner as is necessary to provide the effective and efficient conduct of the entity's activities
6. submit to the secretary an application and annual reports containing such information as the secretary determines by regulation to be necessary to determine whether the entity must meet other requirements of the law

REGULATIONS

Fraud Detection and Investigation Program

The methods and criteria used by state Medicaid agencies to identify and investigate suspected fraud cases must meet certain federal requirements.[7] The methods of investigation must not infringe on the legal rights of the person involved and must also afford due process of law. In addition, procedures for referring suspected fraud cases to law enforcement officials must be developed in cooperation with state legal authorities.[8]

Investigations

When a state agency receives a complaint of fraud or abuse from any source or discovers any questionable practice, it must conduct a preliminary investigation to determine whether a thorough investigation is warranted.[9] The procedure to be followed in a full investigation varies. If a provider is suspected of fraud or abuse, the agency must—in states with a state Medicaid fraud unit under the regulations—refer the case to the unit if it has entered into an agreement with that unit.[10] When a state has no certified Medicaid fraud control unit or when no referral to the state Medicaid fraud control unit is required by the regulations, the agency must conduct a full investigation or refer the case to the appropriate law enforcement agency. When an investigation indicates that a recipient has defrauded the Medicaid program, the agency must refer the case to an appropriate law enforcement agency. The agency must conduct a full investigation if there is reason to believe that a recipient has abused the Medicaid program.[11]

Agencies must cooperate with certified state Medicaid fraud control units where they exist, referring all cases of suspected provider fraud to these units.[12] The unit is to have access to the information and computerized data stored by the agency or its contractors. When the unit determines that such action is necessary, the agency must initiate any available administrative or judicial action to recover improper payments. The agency need not duplicate responsibilities that are placed on the fraud control unit in other areas of the regulations.

A full investigation continues until appropriate legal action is initiated, until the case is closed or dropped because of insufficient evidence to support the allegations of fraud or abuse, or until the matter is resolved between the agency and the provider. Resolving the matter may include

- sending a warning letter to the provider (or recipient), giving notice that continuation of the activity in question will result in further action
- suspending the provider from participation in the Medicaid program
- seeking recovery of payment made to the provider
- imposing other sanctions provided under the state plan[13]

Reporting Requirements

The state agency must report certain fraud and abuse information to the appropriate HHS officials at intervals prescribed in instructions. Such information includes the number of complaints of fraud and abuse that have been made to the agency. For each case of suspected fraud and abuse that warranted a full investigation, the state agency must provide

1. the provider's name and number
2. the source of the complaint
3. the type of provider
4. the nature of the complaint
5. the approximate range of dollars involved
6. the legal and administrative disposition of the case, including action taken by law enforcement officials to whom the case has been referred[14]

Provider Statements

Provider claim forms for reimbursement should include the following or alternate wording approved by the regional administrator of the Health Care Financing Administration (HCFA) unless alternate wording is included on checks to providers:

1. This is to certify that the foregoing information is true, accurate and complete [;]
2. I understand that payment of this claim will be from federal and state funds, and that any falsification or concealment of a material fact, may be prosecuted under federal and state laws.[15]

The adopted statement is printed above the claimant's signature; or a reference to the statement appears above the signature, and the statement appears on the reverse of the form. The language specified for inclusion on checks is

> I understand in endorsing or depositing this check that payment will be from federal and state funds and that any falsification, or concealment of a material fact, may be prosecuted under federal and state laws.[16]

The agency must have a method to verify with recipients whether services billed by providers were actually received. In states that receive federal matching funds for a mechanized claims processing and information retrieval system under the regulations, the agency must provide written notice to recipients to verify that services billed by providers were received.[17]

Disclosure of Information by Providers and Fiscal Agents

Providers and fiscal agents must disclose certain information on ownership and control, including the name and address of each person who has an ownership interest of 5 percent or more in the provider or subcontractor.[18] Federal funds are not available for payments to a provider that fails to disclose this ownership or control information.[19] Providers must also disclose certain information regarding business transactions. For example, the ownership of any subcontractor with whom the provider has had business transactions totaling more than $25,000 during the previous twelve months must be disclosed. Significant business transactions between the provider and any wholly owned supplier or subcontractor for the five years previous to the date of a request for reimbursement should be disclosed. Federal funds may be denied for failure to disclose this information.[20]

If a person who owns or has controlling interest in the provider has been convicted of a federal offense related to that person's involvement in any program under Medicare, Medicaid, or the Title XX services program, the Medicaid agency must be informed of this before it enters into or renews a provider agreement. The Medicaid agency then notifies the inspector general. If there has been a conviction or a failure to meet the full disclosure requirements, the agency may refuse to enter into a provider agreement or may terminate an existing agreement.

Exclusion of Providers

Medicaid providers may be excluded from program participation because of fraud and abuse. The state agency must have administrative procedures that enable it to exclude providers when it has been determined that these providers have done certain prohibited things, such as

- knowingly and willfully making or causing to be made false statements or misrepresentations of material fact in claims used in determining the right to payment under Medicaid
- furnishing or ordering services under Medicaid that are substantially in excess of the recipient's needs or that fail to meet professionally recognized standards for health care
- submitting or causing the submission to Medicaid of bills or requests for payment containing charges or costs that are substantially in excess of customary charges or cost, unless they are justified by unusual circumstances or medical complications

The agency may base its determination that services were excessive or of unacceptable quality on reports, including sanction reports from

1. the PSRO for the area served by the provider
2. state or local licensing or certification authorities
3. peer review committees, fiscal agents, or contractors
4. state or local professional societies
5. other sources deemed appropriate by the Medicaid agency or the HCFA[21]

Before a provider is excluded, the agency must send a written notice that states the reason for the proposed exclusion and the right to review.[22] After notification, the provider must be given the opportunity to submit documents and written argument against the exclusion. The provider must also be given any additional rights to appeal under procedures established by the state.[23]

If the agency makes a final decision to exclude the provider, it must send written notice fifteen days before the exclusion becomes effective. The notice must include

1. the reason for the decision
2. the effective date
3. the effect of the exclusion on the party's participation in the Medicaid program

4. the earliest date on which the agency will accept a request for reinstatement
5. the requirement and procedures for reinstatement[24]

The agency must also give notice of the exclusion and the effective date to the HCFA, the public, and, as appropriate, to the following:

1. recipients
2. PSROs
3. other providers
4. medical societies and other professional organizations
5. state licensing boards and affected state and local agencies and organizations
6. Medicare carriers and intermediaries[25]

The agency must not make Medicaid payments for services furnished by a provider that has been excluded from Medicaid participation. Likewise, federal funds are not available for payments to a provider that has been excluded under any state plan. Federal funds are also not available to pay for services rendered by a Medicaid provider while that provider is excluded from participation or otherwise sanctioned because of fraud and abuse under the Medicare program.[26] The denial of federal funds applies to services furnished on or after the effective date of the exclusion from Medicare, with specific exceptions. The exceptions include inpatient services furnished in a hospital, skilled nursing facility, or intermediate care facility to a patient who was admitted before the effective date of Medicare exclusion; federal funds are available to pay for these services through the end of the calendar year in which the exclusion became effective. Federal funds are available to pay for services furnished by the provider after reinstatement in the Medicare program.[27]

Suspension of Practitioners

The state agency must suspend from the Medicaid program any party who has been suspended from participation in Medicare for conviction of a program-related crime.[28] In addition, the agency must suspend any convicted party who is not eligible to participate in Medicare whenever the HCFA directs such action.[29] The suspension from Medicaid must be effective on the date established by the HCFA for suspension under Medicare and must be for the same period or longer. Under its own authority, the state agency may impose a sanction that may be effective before or may extend beyond the mandatory period designated by the HCFA.[30]

Whenever an individual who is receiving reimbursement under Medicaid is convicted in a state or local court of a criminal offense related to participation in delivery of medical care or services under the Medicaid program, the agency must notify the HCFA. If the agency was involved in the investigation or prosecution of the case, it must send notice within fifteen days after the conviction. If the agency was not involved, it must give notice within fifteen days after it learns of the conviction.[31]

The effect of the suspension may be denial of payment. With certain exceptions, the agency must not make any payment under the plan for services furnished directly by, or under the supervision of, a suspended party during the period of suspension. Under certain circumstances, however, payment may be made after suspension. First, payment may be made to a suspended party who provides care in a hospital or skilled nursing facility to a recipient who was admitted to the hospital or skilled nursing facility before the effective date of suspension. Furthermore, federal funds are available for this purpose up to thirty days after the date of suspension. Second, suspended practitioners may be paid for health services furnished under a plan established before the effective date of the suspension. In this case, federal funds are available for services furnished through the end of the year in which the suspension became effective.[32]

Parties may request waiver of suspension. The agency involved may ask the HCFA to waive suspension if it concludes that, because of a shortage of providers or other health care personnel in the area, individuals eligible to receive Medicaid benefits will be denied adequate access to medical care.[33] The HCFA notifies the agency if and when it waives suspension in response to the agency's request.[34]

Reinstatement Procedures

If a party has been suspended from Medicaid participation as a result of a suspension from Medicare or at the direction of the HCFA, that party may not be reinstated in the Medicaid program until the HCFA notifies the agency that the party may be reinstated. If the HCFA notifies the agency that it has reinstated a party under Medicare, the agency must automatically reinstate the party under Medicaid. This reinstatement is effective on the date of reinstatement under Medicare, unless a longer period of suspension was established in accordance with the state's own authorities and procedures.[35]

If a state provides suspended parties with an opportunity for reinstatement, it must follow certain procedures. A party who has been excluded from Medicaid may be reinstated only by the Medicaid agency that imposed the exclusion. The excluded party may submit to the agency a request for reinstatement at any time after the date specified in the notice of exclusion as the earliest date on which the agency will consider a request for reinstatement. In considering a request for reinstatement, the agency examines

1. the number and nature of the program violations and other related offenses
2. the nature and extent of any adverse impact the violations have had on recipients
3. the amount of damages
4. any mitigating circumstances
5. other facts bearing on the nature and seriousness of program violations or related offenses[36]

There are guidelines or restrictions on approving reinstatement requests.[37] The agency may grant reinstatement only if it is reasonably certain that the violations that led to the exclusion will not be repeated. In order to make this determination, the agency considers two factors: (1) whether the party has been convicted in a federal, state, or local court for other offenses related to participation in Medicare or Medicaid programs that were not considered in the original decision to exclude the party and (2) whether the state or local licensing authorities have taken any adverse action against the party for offenses related to participation in the Medicare or Medicaid program that were not considered in the original decision.

If the agency approves the request for reinstatement, it must give written notice to the excluded party and to all others who had been informed of the exclusion, specifying the date on which Medicaid program participation may resume. When the agency does not approve the request for reinstatement, it must notify the party of its decision not to reinstate.[38]

Fraud Control Units

The fraud control unit must be separate and distinct from the Medicaid agency. No official of the Medicaid agency may have authority to review the activities of the unit or to review or overrule the referral of a suspected criminal violation to an appropriate prosecuting authority. In addition, the unit may not receive funds either from or through the Medicaid agency.[39] Finally, the unit must enter into an agreement with the Medicaid agency under which the Medicaid agency agrees to comply with all regulatory requirements dealing with the unit's access to information under the control of the agency.[40]

Duties

State fraud control units are to conduct statewide programs for investigating and prosecuting, or referring for prosecution, violations of all applicable state laws pertaining to fraud in the administration of the Medicaid program, the provision of medical assistance under the Medicaid program, or the activities of providers of medical assistance under the Medicaid plan. In addition, the unit reviews complaints alleging abuse or neglect of patients in health care facilities that receive payments under the state Medicaid plan. It may also review complaints of the misappropriation of patients' property in such facilities. These complaints are to be referred to the appropriate criminal investigating or prosecuting authority if there is substantial potential for prosecution, or to an appropriate state agency if there is no substantial potential for criminal prosecution.

If, in performing its duties and responsibilities, a fraud control unit discovers that overpayments have been made to health care facilities or other providers of medical assistance under the state Medicaid plan, the unit attempts to collect the overpayment or refers the matter to an appropriate state agency. If a person who has allegedly committed a criminal violation is to be prosecuted by another authority, the unit must ensure that this authority has the fullest possible opportunity to participate in the investigation. The unit must also make all information available to federal investigators and cooperate with them in federal and state investigations. The unit must, however, safeguard the privacy rights of all individuals and shall provide safeguards to prevent the misuse of information under the unit's control.

Staff

The staff of a fraud control unit must include persons with varying professional backgrounds:

- one or more attorneys experienced in the investigation or prosecution of civil fraud or criminal cases, knowledgeable about the applicable laws and procedures, and capable of being an effective liaison with other prosecutors
- one or more experienced auditors capable of supervising the review of financial records and advising or assisting in the investigation of alleged fraud
- a senior investigator with substantial experience in commercial or financial investigations who is capable of supervising and directing the investigative activities of the unit

In addition, the unit must employ or have available to it professional staff who are knowledgeable about the provisions of the Medicaid statutes and the operations of health care providers.

CASES

Impact of Fraud and Abuse on Medicaid

According to a report of the inspector general for January to September 1982, audits in eight states revealed $78 million in unallowable cost claims.[41] Among the fraudulent or unallowable costs were $34.6 million provided to intermediate care facilities for the mentally retarded that either were not certified or failed to meet minimum certification standards. In addition, $21.6 million pertained to per diem rates that were not computed correctly for intermediate care facilities, including those for the mentally retarded, in four states.

The House Select Committee on Aging concluded that "state enforcement of the Medicaid program has been an unmitigated disaster."[42] A review of the record suggests that the states may not be able to police Medicaid. Twenty states did not convict a single Medicaid provider suspected of fraud or abuse.[43] According to an article in *The New York Times*, New York's Medicaid prosecutor was the best in the United States, since this "prosecutor had obtained 406 indictments and 297 convictions and received $19.1 million in improper payments discovered through audits and investigations."[44]

One of the larger crackdowns in New York was on pharmacies that substituted generic drugs for more expensive brand name drugs. According to a state deputy attorney general, the illegal substitutions represented a potential annual loss of at least $4 million in Medicaid funds.[45] The total funds expended in New York City were approximately $85 million. In an earlier crackdown, there had been ninety convictions and $370,000 in fines; however, cheating remained widespread.

Fraud under Medicaid programs may result not only in administrative sanctions, but also in criminal prosecution on either the federal or state level. The federal regulations define fraud as an intentional deception or misrepresentation made by a person with the knowledge that the deception could result in some unauthorized benefit to himself or herself or to some other person or entity.[46] It includes any act that constitutes fraud under applicable state law.

Illegal Patient Retention Practices

The regulations in effect when the following cases were decided have been changed. The case of *Lapin v. Mathews*[47] involved the father of a 27-year-old severely mentally retarded man who had filed an application on behalf of his son with the Social Security Administration for Supplemental Security Income (SSI) benefits. Benefits were denied, however, because the monthly $450 payments that the father made to the school attended by the son were considered income to the son; therefore, the son's yearly income exceeded the maximum level set by statute on supplemental benefits. The school specialized in the care of mentally disabled individuals. The $450 paid by the father covered the son's room, board, and 24-hour supervision, but it did not cover clothing and other necessities. It also did not cover the cost of medical care and medications necessary to treat the foot and eye ailments from which the son suffered.

At the time of the lawsuit, a person whose income was over $1,752 for a calendar year was ineligible for SSI benefits.[48] Income was composed of both earned and unearned income and included payments for room, board, and other incidentals necessary for an individual's normal sustenance.[49] Income as then defined did not include the value of third party payments for medical payments or medical services furnished to a beneficiary. Room and board paid for by the third party during medically necessary confinement was also excluded from income.[50]

The court upheld the denial of payments in *Lapin* because the care provided to the son was custodial or nonmedical in character. Hence, payments were not denied because the school was receiving an illegal supplementation, but because the patient in question did not qualify on the basis of the type of care that he was receiving.

The court in *Slavin v. Secretary of the Department of Health, Education and Welfare*[51] supported the *Lapin* opinion. The plaintiff was a severely mentally handicapped man who functioned at a profoundly retarded level. His father had also applied for SSI benefits on behalf of his son. The son was a citizen of New York, but resided at a school in New Jersey. The administrative law judge concluded that the son was entitled to benefits, but that the basic SSI benefit payment should be reduced to take into account payments being made to the school by the father.

When the father appealed, the court observed that federal payments are reduced by the amount of any income received by the eligible individual.[52] Support and maintenance received in kind were, at that time, presumed to have a value of one-third of the federal payment level. Payment by a third party for support and maintenance of an eligible individual in a nonmedical institution, either proprietary or private nonprofit, were treated as in kind support and thus presumed to have a value of one-third of the standard payment level. This requirement was in accordance with the regulation at that time.[53] Third party payments for medical services furnished to a beneficiary were excluded from the definition of income and, hence, would not result in a reduction in payments under the regulations applicable at that time.[54]

In *Slavin,* the district court concluded that the care received by the plaintiff was custodial and not medical. The personnel were not medically trained, and only about $200 of the $8,100 annual cost of Slavin's care went for medicines. The court observed that the SSI program was instituted to provide the basic needs of eligible persons—food, clothing, and shelter—and that medical care was provided under Medicaid. The two programs had different purposes and criteria for eligibility, as noted by the court. The court concluded that the reduction in SSI payments equal to the beneficiary's other income, including support and maintenance by others, was intended to avoid government payment for need already met. The court added that allowing payments from other sources for medical care to be disregarded for SSI purposes was in accord with the statutory scheme of separate SSI and Medicaid programs.

In *Resident v. Noot,*[55] the plaintiff was a 96-year-old woman who lived in a nursing home, but did not require skilled nursing care and a private room. Her daughter, although not financially responsible for her under Minnesota law, offered to pay the nursing home the difference between the daily charge for a private room ($40) and the medical assistance reimbursement rate for a double room ($19.95). The nursing home refused the offer because of a Department of Public Welfare policy that precluded a provider's request or receipt of any third party payments.

Observing that the Minnesota medical assistance program was a part of the federal Medicaid program, the court in *Resident v. Noot* recalled briefly the history of the mandatory phase out of supplementation, which had previously been the practice.[56] The court examined the regulation presently in effect,[57] which required a state Medicaid agency to limit participation in the Medicaid program to providers who accept as payment in full the amount paid by the agency. The Minnesota court concluded, based on regulations similar to those mentioned in *Lapin* and *Slavin,* that the money to be paid by the daughter in *Noot* was not income, but rather was a third party payment for medical care or medical services furnished to a beneficiary.[58] This case differs from previous cases because the confinement was for medical reasons.

Deciding in favor of the plaintiff, the court held that the rules of the Minnesota welfare department did not prohibit a nursing home from receiving payments for noncovered items, which were not income to the patient because they were third party payments for medical care or services.

A New York appellate court has decided a case similar to *Noot*, although the New York court distinguished its case from the Minnesota case. In *Glengariff Corporation v. Snook*,[59] the nursing home brought suit in an attempt to enforce an earlier contract with the defendant to care for his mother. The son had contracted to pay the current rate for a private room, but later applied to Medicaid on behalf of his mother. This application was granted after an initial denial. The question facing the New York court was whether the son was obligated under the initial contract for the difference between what Medicaid paid and what he initially contracted to pay or whether he would pay the nursing home the amount of the contract for its full term, eighteen months, with the nursing home then reimbursing Medicaid. Like the pertinent Minnesota law in *Noot*, the New York law required the Medicaid payment to constitute full payment.[60]

The New York case differed from the Minnesota case in that the son was not volunteering to pay money that he was not legally required to pay. Instead, the nursing home was trying to force him to supplement Medicaid payments pursuant to his contract. The court observed that individual rights may be waived, but that rights based on public policy considerations, as in this case, cannot be waived. Consequently, the nursing home lawsuit was dismissed, and the son was not required to supplement Medicaid payments.

Although the foregoing cases were not criminal cases, they suggest that third parties may be allowed to make voluntary contributions in some instances without running afoul of the law. *Noot* demonstrates that, even though federal regulations require providers to accept the Medicaid payment as payment in full for services rendered,[61] other services may be rendered and paid for voluntarily by third persons.

Investigations

Hospitals, nursing homes, and other practitioners who receive reimbursement from Medicaid may have certain privileged communications with their patients, just as physicians do. This privilege may conflict with the work of state fraud control units and other law enforcement personnel.

A case from Hawaii, *Psychiatric Society District Branch v. Ariyoshi*,[62] involved this issue in relation to a state Medicaid fraud control unit that was part of the department of the attorney general. Each provider was required by law to maintain for three years "records as are necessary to disclose fully the type and extent of health care, service or supplies provided to Medicaid recipients."[63] Failure to provide that information to the attorney general on request constituted a misdemeanor. The statute authorized the issuance of warrants to inspect, copy, and maintain the records, although it also provided for confidentiality of the records obtained.

In December 1978, an administrative inspection warrant was issued for the search and seizure of a psychologist's records on Medicaid beneficiaries, including therapeutic notes, patient history forms, medical records, and reports. The individual plaintiff and his association of psychiatrists filed a lawsuit to challenge the constitutionality of the Hawaii statute. The issue raised was the right of privacy inherent in the psychotherapist-patient relationship and the reasonableness of administrative searches of psychiatrists' offices. The plaintiffs were granted an injunction.

A certain right of privacy has been recognized by the U.S. Supreme Court.[64] Given compelling interests, however, the government may curtail certain rights. Privacy rights inherent in the psychiatrist-patient relationship are extremely significant, and the intrusion on those interests by the searches, based merely on a valid public interest, was considered by the court to be substantial. The court concluded, however, that the reading and copying of confidential medical files were not necessary to achieve the purpose that the state offered as justification for its actions, and that public interest did not outweigh the right of privacy.

The court had previously concluded that administrative searches of psychiatrists' confidential files may not be justified as regulation of a "pervasively regulated business" (i.e., a business that, if not properly regulated, would pose a serious threat to the public). The court concluded that some showing of an "individualized, articulable suspicion"[65] should be required before a warrant can be issued to search or seize the confidential medical records of a psychiatrist.

Few, if any, criminal cases arising as a result of Medicaid fraud or abuse require copying and reading patient files. Generally, evidence of fraud may be lawfully obtained without reading files. In a Michigan case, *People v. American Medical Centers of Michigan, Ltd.*,[66] the defendants were convicted for medical fraud on evidence obtained through interrogation of former patients. The complaint alleged that the defendants had submitted claims for direct diagnostic laryngoscopies (visual examinations of the exterior of the larynx) that had never been performed. Since the procedure for direct laryngoscopy differs from that for indirect laryngoscopy, evidence that such operations had not been performed was obtainable from former patients.

In some instances, records have been lawfully obtained by fraud control units as aids to prosecution. In a Louisiana case, *In re Rocas Gipson Pharmacy of Eunice, Inc.*,[67] the Medicaid fraud control unit of the attorney general of Louisiana issued subpoenas to the owners and president of the pharmacy to produce certain computer logs and forms. It was alleged that the pharmacy had billed the state for brand name drugs, although it had provided the nursing home patients with generic drugs. The Louisiana court noted that, as a condition to participation in the state Medicaid program, representatives of the pharmacy had signed a Medicaid provider agreement that obligated the corporation to keep records of services provided to Medicaid patients and to disclose those records to the state. The form signed by the provider contained the following statement:

> I hereby agree to keep such records as are necessary to disclose fully the extent of services provided to individuals under the state's title XIX plan and to furnish information regarding any payment of claim for providing such service as the state agency may request for three years from date of service.[68]

The court upheld the imposition of this record-keeping requirement.

The Medicaid reimbursement request necessarily destroys some degree of confidentiality in that privileges are waived with regard to billing and administrative records. Such a rationale explains why a psychiatrist's files cannot be seized, but the kind of drug provided (brand name or generic) can be discovered from records.

In another case, *In re Pebsworth*,[69] a subpoena was issued to an employee of Blue Cross/Blue Shield of Illinois to produce a psychotherapist's records, including physician service records, claims submission records, checks, bank drafts, and other records of payment. The physician was under investigation for fraudulently obtaining reimbursement from medical insurance companies by submitting false psychiatric patient care records. The requested records included the names of some patients, a listing of their visits, and, in some cases, their diagnoses. In determining whether the patient's authorization of disclosure to the insurance carriers effected a waiver of confidentiality regarding the investigation for fraud, the court concluded that the confidentiality had been waived. The court indicated, however, that it might have decided the case differently had the information sought involved detailed psychological profiles of patients or substantive accounts of their sessions.

State Fraud Cases

Most of the reported medical fraud cases have been prosecuted under state law. In a representative case, *People v. Rucker*,[70] the court overruled the dismissal of an indictment by the lower court that arose from the applicability of the Michigan Medicaid False Claims Act. Nurses at the defendant-physician's clinic performed routine tests on new Medicaid patients before a physician met with these patients. These tests were not routinely performed on cash-paying clients, however. Furthermore, the tests were not part of a diagnostic process, nor was it determined that the patients needed them. The Michigan court noted that, under the Medicaid statute, only those tests necessary for a diagnosis may be billed to Medicaid.[71] Rucker had submitted bills to Medicaid for payments, representing these tests as services performed pursuant to diagnosis. The performance of the tests was defended on the theory that, although some of the tests may have been unnecessary, it is not a crime to render unnecessary medical service. Rucker also argued that necessity was a subjective determination for the physician.

The position of the prosecutor, which was adopted by the court, was to admit that the performance of the unnecessary service was not a crime. Instead, the prosecutor argued that the physician was guilty of fraud because he billed Medicaid for services that he knew did not meet the requisite determination of eligibility (necessity). In adopting such an argument, the prosecutor was not questioning the ethical practice of medicine, but rather the responsibility for payment for the services. The court concluded that claims for noncompensable services are fraudulent claims.

OUTLOOK

The outlook for fraud and abuse enforcement in the Medicaid program is similar to that in the Medicare program. With the very real possibility of reduced federal funding, the only way to maintain current eligibility requirements is to root out waste and corruption. States are likely to follow the lead of New York and become much more aggressive in prosecuting all classes of providers for abuses of the Medicaid program.

NOTES

1. DEP'T OF HEALTH AND HUMAN SERVICES, REPORT OF THE INSPECTOR GENERAL, January 1982-September 30, 1982, cited in MEDICARE AND MEDICAID GUIDE, 32,891.
2. 42 U.S.C. §1396h(d).
3. 42 U.S.C. §1396b(a)(6).
4. 42 U.S.C. §1396b(b)(3).
5. 42 U.S.C. §1396b(a)(6).
6. 42 U.S.C. §1396b(q). For a summary of the organization of state Medicaid programs and the location of the fraud control unit, see MEDICARE AND MEDICAID GUIDE, 15,501-15,660.
7. 42 C.F.R. §§455.13-455.21.
8. 42 C.F.R. §455.13.
9. 42 C.F.R. §455.14.
10. 42 C.F.R. §455.21.
11. 42 C.F.R. §455.15.
12. 42 C.F.R. §455.21.
13. 42 C.F.R. §455.16.
14. 42 C.F.R. §455.17.

15. 42 C.F.R. §455.18.
16. 42 C.F.R. §455.19.
17. 42 C.F.R. §433.113(e) and (f).
18. 42 C.F.R. §§455.100 and 455.102.
19. 42 C.F.R. §455.104.
20. 42 C.F.R. §455.105.
21. 42 C.F.R. §455.203.
22. 42 C.F.R. §455.204.
23. 42 C.F.R. §455.205.
24. 42 C.F.R. §§455.206.
25. *Id.*
26. 42 C.F.R. §§420.101 and 474.10.
27. 42 C.F.R. §455.208.
28. 42 C.F.R. §420.122.
29. 42 C.F.R. §455.210.
30. 42 C.F.R. §455.211.
31. 42 C.F.R. §455.212.
32. 42 C.F.R. §455.213.
33. 42 C.F.R. §455.210.
34. 42 C.F.R. §455.214.
35. 42 C.F.R. §455.230.
36. 42 C.F.R. §455.232.
37. 42 C.F.R. §455.234.
38. *Id.*
39. 42 C.F.R. §455.300.
40. 42 C.F.R. §455.21(a)(2).
41. DEP'T OF HEALTH AND HUMAN SERVICES, ABBREVIATED ANNUAL REPORT BY THE INSPECTOR GENERAL, January 1, 1982-September 30, 1982, *citing* MEDICARE AND MEDICAID GUIDE, 32,891.
42. Robert Pear, Panel Says Most States Fail on Policing Medicaid Fraud, *The New York Times* (March 27, 1982), Sec. 1, p.9.
43. *Id.*
44. *Id.*
45. Ronald Sullivan, 53, Are Charged with Fraud over Medicaid Prescriptions, *The New York Times* (May 7, 1982), Sec. B, p. 4.
46. 42 C.F.R. §433.203.
47. 422 F. Supp. 1089 (D.C. 1976).
48. 42 U.S.C. §1382(a)(1), 1975.
49. 20 C.F.R. §416.1125(a).
50. 20 C.F.R. §416.1109(a).
51. 486 F. Supp. 204 (S.D. N.Y. 1980).
52. 42 U.S.C. §1382(b).
53. 20 C.F.R. §416.1125.

54. 20 C.F.R. §416.1109(a).
55. 305 N.W.2d 311 (Minn. 1981).
56. 45 C.F.R. §250.30(d)(6) (1972).
57. 42 C.F.R. §447.15.
58. 20 C.F.R. §§416.1101-416.1190.
59. N.Y. Supreme Court, Nassau County Special Term, Part I, No. 2143/83, January 4, 1984.
60. N.Y. PUB. LAW §280sf.
61. 42 C.F.R. §447.15.
62. 481 F. Supp. 1028 (D. Hawaii 1979).
63. State of Hawaii SESSION LAWS Section 6, Act 105, 1978.
64. Roe v. Wade, 410 U.S. 113 (1973).
65. 481 F. Supp. at 1050, *citing* Delaware v. Prouse, 440 U.S. 648, 662 (1979).
66. 118 Mich. App. 135, 324 N.W.2d 782 (1982).
67. 382 So.2d 929 (La. 1980).
68. *Id.*, at 932.
69. 705 F.2d 261 (7th Cir. 1983).
70. 329 N.W.2d 510 (Mich. App. 1982).
71. 42 U.S.C. §1320c(9)(a)(1).

Epilogue

Medicare and Medicaid program expenditures will have grown from $1,135 million and $734 million, respectively, in 1966 to an estimated $74,463 million and $40,762 million, respectively, in 1985. Federal Medicare and Medicaid outlays have grown from 1 percent of the gross national product (GNP) in 1970 to an estimated 2.4 percent of the GNP during 1985. The rate of growth in expenditures for these health care programs will be twice that of the GNP between 1980 and 1985. Spending for the Medicaid and Medicare programs equals 10 percent of the total federal budget. These rapidly escalating costs threaten the fiscal solvency of both programs.

THE MEDICARE PROGRAM

The Medicare program is threatened with bankruptcy. According to one estimate, the Medicare Trust Fund will be exhausted in 1990 and will have accumulated a projected deficit of $155 billion by 1995.[1] By the year 2005, the deficit of the Medicare Trust Fund will exceed an estimated $1 trillion. In its budget requests for Fiscal Year 1985, the Reagan Administration proposed a number of legislative initiatives to reduce Medicare expenditures and raise Medicare revenues by a total amount projected at more than $1.4 billion in 1985. Among the Medicare proposals are

- a one-year freeze on payments to physicians (savings of $600 million in 1985)
- a limit on tax-free, employer-paid health benefits (total revenues to the federal government equal to an estimated 3.9 billion in 1985, with $207 million accruing to the Medicare Trust Fund)
- a gradual increase of 1.66 percent per year in the Part B Medicare premiums until 1990 (an increase in income of $269 million during 1985)

- a one-month delay in eligibility of new Medicare beneficiaries (savings of $265 million in 1985)
- indexing increases in the Part B deductible of $75 per year to increases in the Medicare Economic Index (savings of $40 million in 1985)
- other proposals saving $34 million during 1985[2]

These proposals are basically the same initiatives the Reagan Administration introduced the previous year without gaining congressional approval.

On July 18, 1984 President Reagan signed the "Deficit Reduction Act of 1984" which included changes in Medicare law.[3] The new law placed a 15-month freeze on Medicare customary and prevailing fees for physician services, similar to the proposal by the Reagan Administration. The new law, however, did not provide for a one-month delay in Medicare eligibility or for indexing the Part B deductible to increases in the Medicare Economic Index as proposed by President Reagan. In addition, the current policy under which the Part B premium equals 25 percent of Part B program costs was retained in the new law. The new law also provided that the capital related costs of a hospital or skilled nursing facility are to be based on the lesser of the acquisition cost to the first owner on or after the date of enactment of this statute or the acquisition cost to the new owner of the facility. Expenses related to acquisitions and mergers, such as lawyers' fees and feasibility studies, are no longer allowable costs after the new law was enacted.

Senator Edward Kennedy and Representative Richard Gephardt introduced legislation in February 1984, titled the Medicare Reform Act of 1984.[4] One cost containment policy that it includes is a proposal to incorporate everyone who pays for hospital care, not just the Medicare beneficiaries, into the Medicare diagnosis-related group (DRG) payment system. Senator Kennedy and Representative Gephardt concluded that, when some purchasers of hospital care do not pay the DRG rates, hospitals do not contain costs through efficiency, but merely pass along the costs that Medicare does not pay to these other purchasers. The Kennedy-Gephardt bill would also modify this all-payer DRG system to include the costs of physician services. The sponsors of this proposal theorize that including physician fees in a prospective rate, which the current Medicare DRG system does not do, will give hospitals and physicians incentives to work together to provide care efficiently. The proposed legislation also would establish lower payment rates for excessive increases in hospital admissions to decrease the number of unnecessary admissions and would extend to all purchasers of health care the rate-of-increase limits Congress has already approved for Medicare.

The authors of these legislative initiatives propose a two-part phase-in of the program if passed into law. In Phase I, lasting two years, the Medicare DRG system would be extended to private payors, and the incentives to reduce excessive admissions and the inclusion of physician payments in the Medicare payment rates would be implemented. In Phase II, physician payments would be included in the DRG rate paid by private purchasers of care, and the system would be unified for all purchasers of hospital care. Rather than a deficit of over $1 trillion by the year 2005, Senator Kennedy and Representative Gephardt project a Medicare surplus of $166 billion and total private sector savings of $74 billion by 1989 if their proposals are adopted into law.

While there are no assurances that these proposals by the Reagan Administration or by Senator Kennedy and Representative Gephardt will be enacted into law, nor any guarantees that their estimates of cost savings are accurate, these proposals should generate considerable debate in Congress.

THE MEDICAID PROGRAM

To moderate Medicaid spending increases, the Reagan Administration's budget for Fiscal Year 1985 includes a number of legislative initiatives for the Medicaid program.[5] One proposal is to require copayments for both inpatient and outpatient hospital services. A $1 per visit copayment would be required from the categorically needy, and a $1.50 per visit copayment would be required from the medically needy for physician, clinic, and hospital outpatient services. A copayment of $1 per day would be required from the categorically needy, and a copayment of $2 per day would be required from the medically needy for inpatient hospital services. These copayments would generate savings estimated at $270 million in 1985. The Reagan Administration also proposes to continue to reduce the federal share of Medicaid payments to the states by 3 percent per year, saving $567 million in 1985. The Administration's suggested changes in the Aid to Families with Dependent Children (AFDC) and Medicare programs affecting Medicaid and innovations to increase third party collections (such as child support), would generate savings estimated at $330 million during 1985.

The "Deficit Reduction Act of 1984" also included changes in Medicaid law.[6] This legislation, however, did not require copayments from Medicaid beneficiaries for the health services proposed by the Reagan Administration. (Existing federal regulations already allow state Medicaid programs the option of imposing copayments, deductibles, and coinsurance, within limits.)[7] This new legislation also did not include a provision to extend the 3 percent reduction in the federal share of Medicaid payments to the states as requested by the Reagan Administration. It did require state Medicaid programs to provide Medicaid coverage to first time pregnant women, to pregnant women in two-parent families if the principal wage earner is unemployed, and to children up to the age of five (born after October 1, 1983) if these pregnant women and children also meet the AFDC income and resources requirements. Effective October 1, 1984 the new Medicaid law limits the amount state Medicaid programs can reimburse for the costs associated with the sale or change of ownership of hospitals and nursing homes to the rate of payment reasonably expected when calculated using Medicare principles. State Medicaid programs must also require that Medicaid patients be recertified at regular intervals as needing nursing home care under the new law.

A national study group of nine present or former directors of state Medicaid programs has developed proposals involving a restructure of the Medicaid program.[8] The group concluded that the present Medicaid system is inefficient because its traditional fee-for-service and cost-based payment systems lack incentives for cost containment. Contributing to this inefficiency, according to the national study group, is the administrative confusion caused by overlapping responsibilities between the Health Care Financing Administration (HCFA) and the state programs. The group also found an inequity in the current system in the denial of Medicaid benefits to the poor who cannot be linked to AFDC, Supplemental Security Income (SSI), or the pre-SSI adult welfare categories under the Social Security Act.

In order to correct these inefficiencies and inequities, the national study group has recommended replacing the current Medicaid system with two basic programs. The proposed National Primary Care Program, which would be federally funded and administered, would provide basic health care benefits through a prepaid, capitated financing and delivery system. The proposed Continuing Care Program, which would be state-administered and funded by both the federal and state governments, would provide a full range of medical and social long-term care services to individuals with functional impairments. Federal financial contributions to this program would be on a capitation basis, adjusted each year for inflation. The emphasis of these proposed programs would be on prepaid health care delivery systems, similar to health maintenance organizations (HMOs). Anyone with income and resources below a certain level, for example, 55 percent of the poverty level, would be eligible for these programs; eligibility would not be linked to the other welfare programs.

CONCLUSION

Out of fiscal necessity, the federal and state governments will continue to develop policies to contain the rising costs of the health care services for which the Medicare and Medicaid programs reimburse providers. The focus should not be just on developing restrictive payment rates, which can result in lower quality care for Medicare and Medicaid beneficiaries, but on developing mechanisms that give incentives to health care providers to decrease costs by increasing their efficiency. Given the increasing for-profit orientation of the major segments of the health care industry, proprietary providers should be particularly responsive to new efficiency incentives. There is a limit to the cost cutting that even the most efficient provider can do without affecting the quality of care, however. If payment rates are too restrictive, the range and quality of services provided to Medicare and Medicaid patients will decline. The future challenge to Medicare and Medicaid policymakers is to develop reimbursement methods that will encourage providers to become more efficient—that is, to reduce costs without reducing the quality of care.

NOTES

1. U.S. Congress, Senate, Statement of Senator Edward M. Kennedy on the Kennedy-Gephardt Medicare Solvency and Health Care Financing Reform Act of 1984, February 13, 1984.
2. Report Letter No. 416, February 9, 1984, MEDICARE AND MEDICAID GUIDE.
3. P.L. 98-369.
4. *See* note 1, *supra*.
5. *See* note 2, *supra*.
6. P.L. 98-369.
7. 42 C.F.R. 447.53-447.55.
8. Report Letter No. 417, February 16, 1984, MEDICARE AND MEDICAID GUIDE.

Table of Cases

A

Akron v. Akron Center for Reproductive Health, 239
Alabama Hospital Association case, 153-55
Alabama Nursing Home Association v. Califano, 10
Alabama Nursing Home Association v. Harris, 61, 175
American Hospital Management Corporation v. Harris, 78
American Medical International, Inc. v. Secretary of HEW, 117
American Medicorp, Inc. v. Schweiker, 39, 41

B

Baylor University Medical Center case, 46
Beal v. Doe, 239
Belotti v. Baird, 239
Beth Israel Hospital v. Heckler, 46, 49

C

California Hospital Association case, 157, 175
Cambridge Nursing Home v. Blue Cross Association/Blue Cross/Blue Shield of Minnesota, 73
Catholic Medical Center v. New Hampshire-Vermont Hospitalization Services, Inc., 53
Central DuPage Hospital et al. v. Schweiker, 49
Charleston Memorial Hospital (South Carolina) case, 159-60
Children's Memorial Hospital v. Illinois Department of Public Aid, 176
Cliff House Nursing Home, Inc. v. Rate Setting Commission et al., 210-11
Committee to Defend Reproductive Rights v. Meyers, 246
Commonwealth of Pennsylvania v. Department of Health and Human Services, 244, 245
Concourse Nursing Home v. Travellers Insurance Company, 68-69

Cook v. Ochsner Foundation Hospital, 50

D

Dialysis Centers, Ltd. v. Schweiker, 104-106

E

Edelman v. Jordan, 192-93
Employment Retirement Income Security Act (ERISA) case, 168-69
Estaugh Corporation v. Califano, 75

F

Fairfax Hospital Association, Inc. v. Califano, 78
Fallston General Hospital v. Harris, 82
Fishkill Health Related Facility (New York nursing home) case, 215
Forest Hills Nursing Home, Inc. v. HHS, 72-73

G

Georgia Department of Medical Assistance v. Heckler, 245
Georgia Department of Public Assistance v. United States Department of Health and Human Services, 244
Glengariff Corporation v. Snook, 266
Golden Isle Convalescent Center, Inc. v. Califano, 192
Goleta Valley Community Hospital v. Schweiker, 81

H

Harper-Grace Hospitals case, 52, 53
Harris Hospital case, 46
Harris v. McRae, 140, 240, 244

Hempstead General Hospital v. Whalen, 217
Homan & Crimen, Inc. v. Harris, 41-42
Hospital Affiliates Int. v. Schweiker, 209

I

Illinois Central Community Hospital v. Blue Cross Association/Health Care Service Corporation, 75
Illinois Department of Public Aid v. Schweiker, 244, 245
Illinois Hospital Association v. Illinois Department of Public Aid, 172-76, 177
Iredell Memorial Hospital, Inc. v. Schweiker, 52, 54

J

John Muir Memorial Hospital, Inc. and Mt. Diablo Hospital District v. Davis, 54
Johnson County Memorial Hospital et al. v. Heckler, 48-49
Johnson County Memorial Hospital et al. v. Schweiker, 52, 53, 54

L

Lapin v. Mathews, 264

M

Magee-Womens Hospital (Pennsylvania) case, 158-59
Maher v. Roe, 239, 240
Marbury v. Madison, 2
Metropolitan Medical Center and Extended Care Facility v. Harris, 52, 54
Minnesota Association of Health Care Facilities, Inc. v. Minnesota Department of Public Welfare, 197

Mississippi Hospital Association case, 164-66
Mississippi Hospital Association, Inc. v. Heckler, 196
Mount Zion Hospital and Medical Center v. Schweiker, 47

N

Nebraska Health Care Association case, 194-95
Northwest Community Hospital v. Califano, 209

P

Pacific Coast Medical Enterprises v. Harris,, 40-41
Pebsworth case, 268
People v. American Medical Centers of Michigan, Ltd., 267
People v. Rucker, 268-69
Planned Parenthood Association v. Ashcraft, 239
Planned Parenthood Association, Inc. v. Department of Human Resources for the State of Oregon, 247
Planned Parenthood of Central Missouri v. Danforth, 238
Presbyterian Hospital of Dallas case, 50, 52, 53
Psychiatric Society District Branch v. Ariyoshi, 266

Q

Quakertown Hospital Association case, 216-17

R

Rapids General Hospital v. Mathews, 51, 52
Resident v. Noot, 265-66
Right to Choose v. Byrne, 245

Rocas Gipon Pharmacy of Eunice, Inc. case, 267-68
Roe v. Wade, 237, 238
Rosado v. Wyman, 191

S

Saine v. Hospital Authority of Hall County, 51
St. James Hospital v. Harris, 52, 54
Saint Mary of Nazareth Hospital Center et al. v. Schweiker, 46, 47, 48-49, 53, 54
Schupak d/b/a Queens Artificial Kidney Center v. Califano, 109
Schupak v. Mathews, 109-110
Sewichley Valley Hospital v. Commonwealth of Pennsylvania Department of Public Welfare, 248
Shaw v. Delta Airlines, 168
Slavin v. Secretary of the Department of Health, Education, and Welfare, 264-65
South Carolina Hospital Association case, 159-60
Sun Towers, Inc. v. Heckler, 43

T

Tarrant County Hospital District v. Schweiker, 47
Trustees of Indiana University v. Harris, 76-77

U

United Hospital Association (California) case, 157
United Optical Workers Insurance Fund case, 168-69
United States v. Adler, 131
United States v. Edgewood Health Care Center, 132
United States v. Hancock and Palombi, 133
United States v. Huckaby, 131, 132

United States v. Porter, 132
United States v. Radetsky, 131-32
United States v. Ruttenberg, 133
United States v. Zacker, 132-33

V

Virginia Hospital Association v. Kenley, 161

W

Washington Township Hospital District v. Schweiker, 47
Williams v. Zbaraz, 240
Wisconsin Hospital Association case, 155-57
Wisconsin Hospital Association v. Reivitz, 175

Index

A

Abortion. *See* Family planning services, abortion
Abuse. *See* Fraud and abuse
Administrative judicial review (DRGs), 35-36
Administrative Procedure Act (APA), 105
Administrative regulation, 2
Administrators, 24, 25, 74
 ESRD program, 106-107
 hospice care participation and, 88-89
Admissions
 illegal, 253
 long-term care and, 64
Aid to Families with Dependent Children (AFDC), 137-38, 275-76
Alabama, 35, 153-55, 160
Alabama Nursing Home Association (ANHA), 190-91
Anesthesiology, 27
Appeals
 fraud, 129
 Medicaid, 13-14
 Medicare, 11-13
Appeals courts, 4, 6
Arkansas, 208
Arm's length transactions v. related organization transactions, 208-212
Assets
 depreciation and, 71-74
 revaluation and acquisition and, 39-43
Assignment terms violations, 125-26

B

Blood banks, 27
Blue Cross/Blue Shield of Illinois, 268
Blue Cross (New York), 166
Blue Shield (New York), 166
Boren Amendment, 194, 195, 201
Bourque, Daniel, 221
Bownes, Judge, 49
Bribes. *See* Fraud and abuse
Buildings, 28-29
Bylaws (hospital), 24

C

California, 157-58, 178-79, 246-47
Cancer treatment, 35

Cantor, Daniel, 209, 210
Case law, 2-3
Ceilings, 204, 220
Certificate-of-need (CON), ESRD and, 114
Charity care, 50
Class-of-care vs. facility reimbursement, 203-204
Code of Federal Regulations, 8-9, 29, 68
Committees, 24
Common law, 2
Community hospital, 34
Congressional Budget Office, 91
Congressional resolutions, family planning, 241-42
Consent, sterilization and, 247, 248
Constitution, 1
Consumer price index (CPI), 90-91
Contract actions, 3
Control (organizational principles), 78-80
Cost containment. *See also* Reasonable costs
 DRGs and, 29, 30
 hospices and, 97
 Medicare inpatient reimbursement and, 29-30, 58
 property, 204-207
Cost limiting method, 220
Costs. *See also* Reasonable costs
 capital-related
  asset revaluation and acquisition and, 39-43
  depreciation and, 37-39, 71-74
  forecasting and, 55
  interest and, 75-77
  return on equity and, 36-37, 77-78
  for nonprofits, 43-44
 hospice, 93-95
 responsible concept and, 194, 198-201
Cost sharing, 141-42
Counseling service, 89, 107
Court systems, 4-6
Criminal laws, 3

Criminal provisions, 123. *See also* Fraud and abuse
Cuppett, Bessie, 208

D

Delivery room days, 45-49
Dentistry, 27
Department of Health, Education, and Welfare, 29, 148, 190, 193, 264
Department of Health and Human Services (HHS), 64, 68, 77, 88, 96, 112, 148, 149, 190, 201
 abortion and, 243, 244
 Alabama and, 153-55
 California and, 157
 capital costs and, 36
 cost containment and, 29-30, 31
 DRG and, 31, 34
 family responsibility and, 228
 fraud and, 126, 254
 Hill-Burton and, 50
 Mississippi case and, 164
 NAPHT and, 113-20
 Nebraska and, 194-95
 overpayments and, 140
 renal disease and, 103
 statutory authority and, 11
 utilization review and, 28
Depreciation
 allowable, 74, 216
 cost containment (property) and, 204-207
 inpatient reimbursement analysis and, 37-39
Diagnosis-related groups (DRGs), 147, 176
 capital-related costs and, 36-44
 cost containment and, 29, 30
 HHS and, 29-30, 31
 Medicaid inpatient care and, 147, 152, 153, 162, 163
 payment system (FY 1955) and, 57-58
 reform act and, 274-75
 reimbursement based on, 31-36

Diagnostic services, 30-31, 65
Dialysis. *See* End-stage renal disease (ESRD) program
Dietary department, 26, 66, 89. *See also* Food
  ESRD program and, 107
Disability, 18
Disallowance, family planning, 243-45
District court, 4, 5
Drugs. *See* Medication; Pharmacy

E

Elderly, 63
Emergency department, 27
Employment Retirement Income Security Act of 1974 (ERISA), 168-69
End-stage renal disease (ESRD) program
  defined, 101, 102-103
  eligibility and, 101
  objectives of, 101-102
  participation conditions, 103-107
  program analysis and, 102-103
  reimbursement
    legislation, 107-108
    regulation, 108-113
    NAPHT and, 113-20
Equalization statute (Minnesota), 196-98
Equipment depreciation, 71
Equity
  defining, 218
  return on, 36-37, 43-44, 117
Exclusions, 126-28
Executive committee, 24
Exemptions
  DRG and, 34-35
  organizational principles and, 80
Expenditures (health care)
  ESRD program, 111
  long-term care, 63
  Medicaid, 142-44, 147
  Medicare, 20, 23

F

Facilities, 28-29
  depreciation and, 71-74
  ESRD program, 102-103, 104, 107
  purchase of, 80-82
  reimbursement formula and, 203-204
Facility vs. class-of-care reimbursement, 203-204
False statements, 123-24, 131-32
Family planning services
  abortion
    forecasting and, 249
    legislative restrictions and, 240-42
    litigation and, 243-47
    regulation and, 242
    Supreme Court cases and, 237-40
    sterilization and, 247-49
Family responsibility concept
  Idaho law and, 224-27
  Louisiana law and, 228
  national survey on, 221-24
  Virginia law and, 227-28
Federal court system, 4-5
Federal Hospital Insurance Trust Fund (FHITF), 77-78, 83, 219
Federal medical assistance percentage (FMAP), 139
Federal Register, 7, 11, 165
Federal Reporter, 9, 69
Finley Hospital, 39
Florida, 220
Florida Nursing Home Association (FNHA), 191-92, 193
Flushing Hospital and Medical Center, 45
Food, 26, 66, 89, 187-88, 107
Forecasting
  costs and, 55, 58
  ESRD program and, 113-20
  family planning and, 249
  fraud and abuse, 133-34, 269
  future trends, 276-77
  hospice care and, 96-97

inpatient care and, 55, 58, 179-80
long-term care, 83
Medicaid and, 228-30
Fraud and abuse
  Medicaid
    cases
      illegal patient retention, 264-66
      impact of, 263
      investigations and, 266-68
      state, 268-69
    control and, 254-55
    forecasting and, 269
    regulations and, 255-63
    statutes and, 253-54
  Medicare
    cases
      false statements, 131-32
      illegal remunerations, 132-33
    forecasting and, 133-34
    regulations and, 126-30
    statutes, 123-26

G

General Accounting Office (GAO), 55-57, 90, 92, 123
Gephardt, Richard, 274-75
Ghantous, Walid, 104
Governing body, 23-25
  ESRD program, 106

H

Handicapped, 67
Haven Home (Nebraska), 195
Haven Manor (New York), 209-210
Hawaii, 35
HCA, 55, 56
Health care expenditures. *See* Expenditures, health care
Health Care Financing Administration (HCFA), 43, 45, 74, 83, 189, 276
  costs and, 95-96
  DRG and, 32, 57
  fraud and, 126, 127-28, 129-30, 256, 258, 259-60
  interest and income and, 76
  labor/delivery and, 45
  lease arrangement and, 81
  overpayments and, 140
  physical environment and, 29
  prospective payment and, 91-92
  reasonable costs and, 69
  reimbursement legislation and, 108, 110, 111, 112, 113, 116
  review and appeal and, 11-13
Health services, 64, 186-88
Hearings, 11-13
Heckler, Margaret, 195
HHS. *See* Department of Health and Human Services (HHS)
Highland Chateau (nursing home, Minnesota), 198
High Point Memorial Hospital, 37-38
Hill-Burton Act, 160
  background on, 49
  reimbursement
    allowed, 50-52
    not allowed, 52-54
Home care
  continuous, 94
  routine, 93-94
Hospice care
  coverage, 87-88
  defined, 87
  forecast and, 96-97
  participation conditions and, 88-90, 97
  reimbursement
    legislation and, 90-91
    regulation and, 91-96
Hospital Affiliates International (HAI), 55, 56
Hospital insurance. *See* Insurance
Hyde Amendment, 240-41, 245
Hysterectomies, 248

I

Idaho, 162
  family responsibility and, 224-27
Illegal remunerations, 124-25, 132-33

Illinois, 172-78
Income, family responsibility and, 224, 227
Individual Hospital Limitation on Expenditures (IHLE, Michigan), 171-72
Individual Hospital Operating Cost Limitations (IHOCL, Michigan), 171-72
Infection committee, 29
Information disclosure, 257
Inpatient care
  Medicaid
    federal and state regulations and, 148-52
      DRGs and, 147, 152, 162, 163
      prospective rate and, 166-71
    forecasting and, 179-80
    legislative history and, 147-48
    limits to, 159-62
    reasonable and adequate litigation and, 153-59
    state reimbursement and, 162-79
  Medicare
    capital costs and, 36-44
    cost containment and, 29-30, 58
    DRGs and, 29, 30, 31-36, 57-58
    federal regulations covering acute care and, 23-29
    forecasting and, 55, 58
    Hill-Burton and, 49-54
    hospices and, 94-96
    labor/delivery room days and, 45-49
    TEFRA and, 29-30, 32, 34, 54-55
Insurance
  Medicare and, 17-18
  supplementary program for, 18-19
Interdisciplinary team, 87, 89
Interest, 75-77
Intermediaries
  fiscal, 11-12
  labor/delivery and, 45
Intermediate care facilities, 186-88
Investigations, Medicaid fraud, 255-56, 266-68

J

Judicial review, 2
  administrative, 35-36
Jurisdiction courts, 4, 5

K

Kennedy, Edward, 274-75
Kickbacks. *See* Fraud and abuse
Kidney disease. *See* End-stage renal disease (ESRD) program
Kidney transplants, 101, 102, 104, 109

L

Laboratory department, 27, 65-66
Labor (hospice), 96
Labor/delivery room days, 45-49
Law. *See* Legal concepts
Lease payments, 208
Legal concepts
  court systems and, 4-6
  ESRD program and, 107-108
  family planning and, 240-41, 243-47
    U.S. Supreme Court cases and, 237-40
  hospice care and, 90-91
  major areas of, 3-4
  Medicare fraud and abuse, 123-26
  Medicare and Medicaid reimbursement and, 6-14, 67-70, 153-59, 194-98
  sources of law and, 1-3
Legislature, 2
Library, 29
Licensure, 23
Life Safety Code, 29, 66, 188-89
Loans, 75-77
Long, Russell, 110
Long-term care
  Medicaid and
    intermediate care, 186-89
    property cost containment, 204-208

reimbursement
  law, 189-98
  policies, 198-204
 SNFs, 185-86
Medicare and
 forecasting, 83
 reimbursement law, 67-78
 related organizational principles, 78-82
Loose-leaf services, 10-11
Louisiana, 228

M

McGowan, Judge, 49
Maryland, 208
Massachusetts, 140-41, 210-11
Medicaid
 analysis of program, 275-76
 cost limiting method and, 220
 costs and, 56
 cost sharing and, 141-42
 coverage and, 137-39
 DRGs and, 147, 152, 153, 162, 163
 expenditures, 142-44, 147
 family responsibility concept and, 221-28
 financing of, 139-41
 forecasting and, 228-30
 inpatient reimbursement
  DRGs and, 147, 152, 162, 163
  federal regulations and, 148-52
  forecasting and, 179-80
  legislative history and, 147-48
  limits to, 159-62
  litigation and, 153-59
  state policies and, 162-79
 legal system and, 6-14
 long-term care reimbursement
  ICF and, 186-89
  property cost containment and, 204-208
  reimbursement
   law and, 189-98
   policy and, 198-204

 SNFs, 185-86
 profits and, 218-20
 reviews and appeals under, 13-14
 utilization review and, 28
Medical director (long-term care), 64
Medical education expenses, 35
Medical library, 29
Medical records department, 28, 106-107
Medical staff, 24, 25
 ESRD program, 107
Medicare
 analysis of program, 273-75
 defining, 17
 ESRD program
  analysis of, 101-107
  forecasting and, 113-20
  reimbursement and, 107-113
 expenditures of, 20
 fiscal intermediaries and, 11-12
 fraud and abuse
  cases
   false statements, 131-32
   illegal remuneration, 132-33
  forecasting and, 133-34
  regulation and, 126-30
  statutes and, 123-26
 hospice care
  coverage, 87-88
  defined, 87
  forecast and, 96-97
  participation conditions and, 88-90, 97
  reimbursement
   legislation, 90-91
   regulation, 91-96
 inpatient reimbursement
  acute care hospital
   facilities and, 28-29
   governing body and, 23-25
   staff and departments and, 25-28
  capital-related costs and, 36-44
  cost containment and, 29-30, 58
  forecasting and, 55, 58
  Hill-Burton and, 49-54
  labor/delivery room days and, 45-49

prospective payment and, 23, 31, 57
TEFRA and, 29-30, 32, 34, 54-55
insurance and, 17-18
supplementary program and, 18-19
legal system and, 6-14
long-term care reimbursement forecasting and, 83
reimbursement law and, 67-78
related organizational principles and, 78-82
SNFs and, 63-67
reviews and appeals under, 11-13
services of, 18-19
Medicare and Medicaid Guide, 11
Medication, 26, 65, 80, 187
Michigan, 171-72, 267
Minnesota, 169-70, 196-98, 266
Mississippi, 163-66

N

National Association for Home Care, 97
National Association of Patients on Hemodialysis and Transplantation (NAPHT), 113-20
National Fire Protection Association, 29, 66, 188-89
National Medical Care (NMC), 120
National Primary Care Program, 276
National Reporter System, 10
National Senior Citizens Law Center, 228
Nebraska, 194-96
Needy, 137-38
Network areas (ESRD program), 103
New Jersey, 163, 245
New Mexico, 220
New York, 166-69, 208-209, 215
New York Times, 263
Nursing department, 25-26
ESRD program and, 107
Nursing facilities, 18, 77, 80, 83, 95, 219
capital costs and, 69-70

hospice care and, 89-90
legal concepts and, 13-14
long-term care and, 63-67, 185-86
Nursing home care, 63, 185

O

Office of Hearings and Appeals, 13
Oklahoma, 159
Omnibus Reconciliation Act, 194
Oregon, 247
Outpatient department, 27
therapeutic services and, 30
Ownership (common), 78-80

P

Pacific Coast Medical Enterprises (PCME), 40-41
Parents. *See* Family responsibility concept
Partnership, 79, 81
Patient activity, 66, 188
Patient retention, 253, 264-66
Patient rooms, 67
Payment freeze, 273
Payment systems, DRG and, 32-34, 57-58. *See also* Prospective payment
Pediatric care, 34
Pennsylvania, 158-59, 215-18, 248-49
Pharmacy, 26, 65, 80
fraud (New York) and, 263
Physical environment, 28-29, 66-67
Physically handicapped, 67
Physicians, 26, 64, 273
ESRD program, 107, 118-19
fraud definition and, 126, 259-60
Private law, 3-4
Private Pay Law (Equalization statute, Minnesota), 196-98
Procedural law, 3
Profits, 218-20
Professional standards review organizations (PSROs), 126, 127, 129, 258

Property actions, 3
Property costs, 204-207
Prospective payment, 23, 31, 57, 91-92.
  See also Payment systems
  ESRD program, 111-13
  Medicaid and, 152, 166-71
Prospective vs. retrospective rate
  setting, 201-202
Provider Reimbursement Manual, 31,
  38, 45, 68, 69, 73, 78-79
Provider Reimbursement Review Board
  (PRRB), 68, 69, 72, 73
  charity care and, 50
  depreciation and, 37-38
  equity and, 43
  Homan & Crimen and, 41
  interest expense and, 75, 76
  judicial review and, 35-36
  labor/delivery and, 45-46
  partnership and, 79, 81
  PCME and, 40
  reimbursement allowed, 50, 51
  review and appeal and, 11-13
Provider statements (fraud), 256-57
Psychiatric care, 34
Public Health Service Hospitals, 111
Public abortion laws, 241-42
Public law, 3

R

Radiology department, 27, 65-66
Railroad retirement program, 18
Rate setting, prospective vs.
  retrospective, 201-202
Reagan administration, 97, 221, 226,
  229, 230, 273-74, 275
Reasonable cost, 154. *See also* Costs
  ESRD program, 108-111
  limitations to, 68-70
  Medicaid and, 148-49, 150-52,
    190-94, 198-201
Rebaldo, Sebastian, 168
Rebates. *See* Fraud and abuse
Referral centers, 35

Regional adjustment (DRG), 31
Regulation
  administrative, 2
  Medicaid
    DRGs and, 147, 152, 162, 163
    family planning, 242
    federal and state, 148-49
    fraud, 255-63
    prospective rates and, 152, 166-71
    state, 149-52
  Medicare
    acute care hospital, 23-29
    capital-related costs and, 70-71
    ESRD program, 108-113
    fraud and abuse and, 126-30
    hospice care, 91-96
Rehabilitation, 27, 65, 187
Reinstatement (fraud), 129-30, 260-61
Reimbursement. *See also* Medicaid,
  inpatient reimbursement; Medicaid,
  long-term care reimbursement;
  Medicare, inpatient reimbursement;
  Medicare, long-term care
  reimbursement
  ESRD program and, 107-113
  hospice care legislation and
    regulation and, 90-96
  legal concepts and, 6-14, 67-70
  limits (Medicaid) to, 159-62
Related organization transaction vs.
  arm's length transactions, 208-212
Renal disease. *See* End-stage renal
  disease (ESRD) program
Rental expenses, 82
Reporters (records of actual cases), 9-10
Reporting requirements (fraud), 256
Research Institute of Pharmaceutical
  Sciences, 221-24
Respite (hospice) care, 94-95
Retrospective vs. prospective rate
  setting, 201-202
Reviews
  Medicaid, 13-14
  Medicare, 11-13
  nurse evaluation, 26
Room sizes, 67

Rural areas, 35
  hospices and, 97

S

Safety standards, 188-89
Services
  ESRD program, 107
  hospice care, 89-90
  medical program, 18-19
Simensky, Mr., 209, 210
Skilled nursing facility (SNF), 18, 77, 80, 83, 95, 219
  capital costs and, 69-70
  hospice care and, 89-90
  legal concepts and, 13-14
  long-term care and, 63-67
Skilled nursing services, 25
Social services, 66, 188
South Carolina, 159-61
Standard metropolitan statistical area (SMSA), 32, 69-70, 104, 165
Stare decisis rule, 2-3
State
  family planning and, 245-47
  Medicaid policies
    DRGs and, 147, 152, 162, 163
    fraud and, 268-69
    prospective rates and, 152, 166-71
    reasonable litigation concept and, 153-59
    reimbursement methodologies and, 162-79
State court system, 5-6
Statements (fraud), 256
Statutes
  defined, 1-2
  reference sources for, 6-11
Sterilization, 247-49
Subcontracting, 97
Substantive law, 3
Supreme Court, 4-5
  family planning cases in, 237-40
Supreme Court Reporter, 9

Surgery, 27
Suspensions, 128, 259-60

T

Target Rate Reimbursement Agreement, 110
Tax Equity and Fiscal Responsibility Act of 1982 (TEFRA), 29-30, 32, 34, 54-55, 83, 87, 90-91, 141-42
Team (interdisciplinary) work, 87, 89
Terminal illness. *See* Hospice care
Tort cases, 3
Transplants (kidney), 101, 102, 104, 109

U

United States Code (U.S.C.), 6
United States Law Week, 9
United States Supreme Court Reports, 9
U.S. Reports, 9
Utilization rate (ESRD program), 103-104
Utilization review, 28

V

Veterans Administration, 11
Virginia, 170-71, 212
  family responsibility and, 227-28

W

Wage adjustments (hospice labor), 96
Waxman, Henry, 229-30
Winthrop, Governor, 211
Wisconsin, 155-57

Y

Yale University, 31

About the Authors

Robert J. Buchanan, Ph.D., is a Research Assistant Professor with the Health Services Research Division of the Research Institute of Pharmaceutical Sciences at the University of Mississippi. He has published numerous articles on health care cost containment, with special focus on state Medicaid programs and long-term care. Mr. Buchanan received his Ph.D. in Government (Public Affairs) and his M.A. in Public Administration from the University of Virginia and an A.B. in Political Science from Grinnell College. Future research will focus on public policy, the law, and politics relating to health care cost containment.

James D. Minor, J.D., is an Assistant Professor and an Assistant Dean at the University of Mississippi Law School. Courses taught by Professor Minor include Legal Problems of the Elderly, Juvenile Courts and Criminal Law. Dr. Minor received his B.A. from the University of Mississippi in 1969 and his J.D. from the University of Mississippi in 1972. Since that time he has been in private practice in Gulfport, Mississippi, a staff attorney with a legal service program, and the director of a criminal research service. He will end his employment with the University of Mississippi during the 1984-85 academic year and will devote full time to the general practice of law including health care and juvenile matters.

WIDENER UNIVERSITY-WOLFRAM LIBRARY
CIR   KF3605.B82 1985
Legal aspects of health care reimburseme

3 3182 00296 0299